SOCIAL CHANGE

SOCIAL CHANGE

*Josiah Mason Lectures
delivered at the
University of Birmingham*

IAN HOGBIN

MELBOURNE UNIVERSITY PRESS

First published 1958 by C. A. Watts & Co. Ltd, London
Second impression 1970
Printed in Singapore by
Times Printers SDN. BHD. for
Melbourne University Press, Carlton, Victoria 3053
Great Britain and Europe: ISBS Inc., Harlington, Middlesex
USA and Canada: ISBS Inc., Zion, Illinois 60099

ISBN 0 522 83986 X
Dewey Decimal Classification Number 301.2

CONTENTS

PREFACE TO SECOND IMPRESSION

DURING the past twelve years, since the first publication of this book, a very great many further changes have taken place in the Melanesian societies described. New Guinea, indeed, is probably on the threshold of independence. Yet the principles outlined for the study of the processes of change remain as valid now as they were in 1958. I have therefore left the text as it was.

IAN HOGBIN

February, 1970

PREFACE

THE argument of this book is in essentials that put forward in my Josiah Mason lectures, but I have rewritten the original MS. to meet the needs of a different form of presentation and in the process considerably expanded the illustrative examples.

When preparing the lectures I profited greatly from discussions with the late Camilla H. Wedgwood. I regret that this acknowledgment is now the only means of repayment open to me. My thanks are also due to Professor J. A. Barnes, Mr M. J. Meggitt, Miss R. Atkins, and Mrs W. M. Balding for their constructive criticism of the revised MS.

I have to express my gratitude to the British Council for a travel grant and to Professor P. Sargant Florence, Professor Charles Madge, and Professor and Mrs Leonard Russell for their many kindnesses while I was in Birmingham.

IAN HOGBIN

Department of Anthropology
University of Sydney
September 1, 1957

CHAPTER I

Introduction

KAMEHAMEHA, king of the Hawaiian Islands, died in the pagan faith of his fathers in May 1819. The natives had already been visited by several of the great Pacific navigators, including Captain James Cook, whom they had killed, had welcomed two or three European adventurers as residents, and had begun giving traders their valuable sandalwood timber in exchange for goods from the outside world; but as yet no missionaries had landed, and the people were unacquainted with Christianity.

Kamehameha had appointed his son Liholiho as successor but given the post of official advisor, which carried equal powers, to his favourite wife Kaahumanu. He had also acknowledged the high status of his nephew Kekuaokalani by making him the custodian of the image of the most important deity, Ku, the god of war. Other powerful members of the court were Liholiho's mother, a woman named Keopuolani, and the chief priest Hewahewa.

A system of religious taboos, which placed severe restrictions both on the lower orders and on all females, served to buttress the power and privileges of the Hawaiian king, aristocracy, and priesthood. The commoners were forced on pain of supernatural penalties to show great deference to their social superiors and to pay tribute to them with quantities of valuables and foodstuffs; and the women, regardless of their rank, were prohibited from eating with the men or from partaking of any of the more esteemed delicacies. Kamehameha had in his lifetime greatly strengthened the monarchy, and the taboos were increasingly burdensome and unpopular. Kaahumanu, now that the old king was dead, determined that they must be abolished. She first won over her co-wife Keopuolani, then the priest Hewahewa, and at length a number of the lesser chiefs. The two queens dowager, as high-ranking women, had obviously much to gain, but Hewahewa's part in the conspiracy is puzzling, since he apparently had everything to lose. Presumably personal motives influenced his decision. Liholiho had sworn to his father to stay faithful to the gods and needed some persuasion before he would yield. He spent several days at sea in a drunken debauch but in the end agreed to co-operate. The queens prepared a great public feast, and after they had each consumed some of the forbidden foods he walked over and ate with them. The commoners were at first appalled at such impiety, but, when there was no divine intervention, they raised a joyful shout, 'The taboos are at an end, and the gods are a lie'. Hewahewa, who was waiting nearby, now took a torch and set fire to one of the temples. The effect was like that of displacing the keystone of an arch: the structure of Hawaiian religion at once fell in ruins.

Liholiho's cousin Kekuaokalani fled with the image of Ku to a remote village and organized a revolt. He hoped to kill the king and then usurp the throne. But Kaahumanu was prepared. She had persuaded Liholiho to purchase guns and ammunition from an American sandalwood trader, and the loyal forces quickly defeated the rival party, which was armed only with spears.

'Hawaii', in the words of a later writer, 'presented to the world the strange spectacle of a nation without a religion.' The first missionaries, who arrived in April 1820, found the population ready to receive them, and, although many relics of the old beliefs persisted, their work proved to be easier here than in the other Pacific-island groups.[1]

The collapse of the Hawaiian religious system is an example

---

[1] W. D. Alexander, *History of the Hawaiian People*, American Book Company, 1899, Chap. XXII.

of spontaneous social change brought about by causes operating inside the community. Some of the younger men may have been influenced by their contacts with Europeans, but the prime reason for the upheaval was undoubtedly general dissatisfaction with the restrictions inherent in the existing social order. The fact that the leaders belonged to the respected royal family was largely responsible for their success. Had the initial impetus come from below there might have been a long civil war.

Other causes of social change include alterations in the density of population, either upwards or downwards; modification of the natural environment, as by soil erosion or volcanic eruption; the migration of the group to a new country; and invasion by foreigners possessing superior tools.

If the population increases, the power of the chief may in some cases be narrowed and in others broadened. Where he depends for his position on wealth contributed by his subjects he suffers if extra cultivable land is not available. They no longer make him such large offerings, and in the end he cannot afford to finance tribal undertakings. This was the situation in tiny Tikopia, a Polynesian outlier in the western Pacific, when a recent series of disastrous hurricanes destroyed the orchards and gardens. Here the loss of chiefly prestige may be only temporary, it is true, though the island is rapidly approaching a state of over-population.[1] Where the chief's influence is bound up not with storehouses and granaries, however, but with the body of warriors at his command, his strength grows as they become more numerous. He then organizes wars to ravage his neighbours and perhaps make them slaves.

For an example of change following on a decrease in population we can turn to Ontong Java, another isolated Polynesian community in the western Pacific. These people occupy a coral atoll so remote from the nearest centre of government in the Solomon Islands that adequate medical supervision has proved

[1] J. Spillius, 'Natural Disaster and Political Crisis in a Polynesian Society', *Human Relations*, Vol. X, pp. 3-28, 113-26.

impossible. Europeans introduced malaria and other diseases, and in fifty years numbers have fallen from over 5,000 to a few hundreds. The natives are divided into patrilineages, the bulk of which own one of the smaller islands of the atoll. In earlier days the members spent most of their time on this property, taking with them their wives, who usually came from other patrilineages. There is a central settlement, however, and here all congregated for the religious festivities, which lasted for a month of every year. While these were in progress the husbands always went to live with their spouses in dwellings owned jointly by groups of sisters and their non-resident brothers. Today the individual patrilineages have become so depleted that the members cannot by themselves carry out the various tasks that demand general collaboration. They accordingly live mostly in the main village and restrict their visits to the outlying islands to a few days' duration. The pattern of residence after marriage has thus been altered—the men now reside with their wives instead of the women residing with their husbands. In addition, new working groups, a union of related patrilineages, have had to be built up.

The effect of a variation in the environment may be illustrated by reference to Ireland. Here the diminishing fertility of the soil was directly responsible for a revision of inheritance and marriage practices. Until the middle of the nineteenth century the peasant farmers were in the habit of dividing their land more or less evenly among the sons. The young men could then marry early, and the population grew. Cultivation was so intensive, however, that the ground became impoverished, and families found it harder and harder to make a living from a small holding. At length, after the great famine, it was apparent that the property would have to be reserved for one son only. He was obliged, too, to wait until after he had inherited it before he took a wife. No provision could be made for the younger sons, and, as there were few industries to absorb them as labourers, more and more emigrated. Those who stayed were too poor to set up independent households, and the majority continued to live as bachelors till their death. By 1926 the proportion of single persons of both sexes was larger in Ireland than in any other country where records were kept. Eighty per cent of the males in the age group 25–30 were still unwed, 62 per cent in the group 30–35, 50 per cent in the group 35–40, and 26 per cent in the group 55–60 (the corresponding figures for the U.S.A. were 39 per cent in the 25–30 group, 10 per cent in the 55–60 group). The illegitimacy rate was low, and the population steadily declined.[1]

The mass movement of a community to a new country inevitably produces social changes. A familiar instance is that of the Pilgrim Fathers. They brought their English institutions with them but were soon obliged to modify some of these in the face of pioneering conditions in America. The Polynesians who in the fourteenth century left Raiatea in the Society Islands to found the Maori colony in New Zealand are an even better illustration for they worked out their destiny in an isolation lasting over four hundred years. The Raiatea culture had been developed in the tropics and in some of its aspects required complete remodelling to meet the needs of the temperate zone.

The voyagers probably took with them such Raiatea food plants as the yam, taro, breadfruit, coconut, and sweet potato, but of these only the last flourished, and even this produced not a continuous harvest, as in the Society Islands, but a seasonal crop. Local need led to the development of an accurate calendar so that work could be planned ahead and to the construction of storage pits and sunken sheds with an earth-covered roof, both of which were unknown in central Polynesia. Further, a god to promote the growth of the sweet potato was added to the Pantheon and represented in images of stone. The paper-mulberry, which elsewhere supplies the material for garments, also made the journey; but, although the cuttings took root in the warmer parts of the north island, growth stopped when the plant was a

[1] K. H. Connell, *The Population of Ireland 1750–1845*, Oxford, 1950; and C. M. Arensberg and S. T. Kimball, *Family and Community in Ireland*, Harvard, 1940.

couple of feet high. Even if it had reached normal size, however, thin cloth made from paper-mulberry bark would hardly have provided adequate protection in chilly New Zealand. The people experimented with fibres from the leaves of the flax plant, using the same techniques as they employed in weaving fish-traps, and soon evolved a variety of suitable clothing, including capes with an outer thatch of overlapping fringes to shed the rain. The dogs survived the voyage, but the pigs and fowls must have died on the way. Fortunately the forests teemed with birds to make up the deficiency in the diet, and processes were invented for catching and preserving them.

The greatest wonder of all must have been the trees, which are far larger than those of the small tropical islands. Plenty of stone was available for shaping into tools, and the natives, using larger and heavier adzes, felled the timber and carved it into canoes. These were so wide that they floated like a boat, and the provision of an outrigger prop at the side, hitherto essential, was unnecessary.

The settlers had also to give thought to a new kind of dwelling. The simple structure of tropical Polynesia was unsatisfactory for the colder climate, and they now sank the floor below ground-level and thatched the walls to keep the warmth inside. To provide for public meetings, which in winter could not be held out of doors, they also erected roomy community buildings and ornamented them with painted scroll-work, designs in cord, and wooden carvings.

In course of time the population grew, and a tribal organization came into being. Warfare was of regular occurrence, and these New Zealand Maori, alone of the Polynesians, took to living permanently in villages fortified with terrace, ditch, and palisade. This led to certain changes in religious practices. Temples were no longer built in the settlement, and the priest retreated to a secluded grove, where he could take counsel with the gods away from the multitude.[1]

Association with foreigners, especially if they are politically

[1] P. H. Buck, *Vikings of the Sunrise*, New York, 1938, Chap. XIX.

dominant and possess superior technical equipment, is a further stimulus to change. The results of such contacts are to-day visible all over the world. I quote the case of Hanuabada in southern New Guinea.

The great-grandfathers of the present inhabitants of Hanua-bada were near-naked savages. They fashioned their tools from wood and stone and lived in simple houses of adzed timber and palm-leaf thatch. The waters nearby were full of fish, but the rainfall was low and seasonal, and the yam gardens did not pro-duce as much as in other parts of New Guinea. Extra supplies of food had therefore to be obtained from outside. A deposit of clay suitable for pot-making was located in the vicinity, and from this the Hanuabada moulded cooking-vessels, which they then exchanged for packages of sago from the natives on the far side of the Gulf of Papua. Status depended not on birth but on generosity in providing lavish feasts. Those who gave the biggest and most frequent entertainments were ultimately ac-cepted as headmen. These persons preserved law and order within the village, but the only means of securing redress for an offence committed by the residents of other settlements was for the wronged man to persuade his fellows to join him in a raid. Such action often led to war. The religious system, the details of which were peculiar to these folk, was centred on the worship of ancestors and spirits represented by the sun and the moon.

The Hanuabada of today is located on the same spot but is very different in appearance. It now forms 'the native quarter' of Port Moresby, the capital of the colony. The houses are of European construction, made from sawn timber and corru-gated iron, and the people enjoy the advantages of the town electricity, water, and garbage disposal services. Everybody has received some schooling, and one of the young men re-cently represented the dependency at a conference of the South Pacific Commission, where the deliberations were carried on in English and French. The economy is based on money, and the villagers earn their living as white-collar workers, skilled

B

mechanics, or contractors. The bulk of the food comes from shops, a few of which are co-operatively owned, and meals are cooked and served in European style. Much of the clothing worn is indistinguishable in material, cut, and finish from that of the white townspeople, and such appliances of the civilized world as the telephone, radio, and internal-combustion engine are now taken for granted.[1] Inter-village disputes, of course, are no longer settled by force of arms. Offenders now come before an Australian magistrate or judge. Village affairs are conducted by a native council, the members of which are formally elected by secret ballot. A year or two ago the councillors requested the government to make provision for the aged and unfit, who earlier would have been the responsibility of their kinsmen, by a scheme for old-age and invalid pensions. New religious movements have occasionally flourished, but at the present time the people are all Christians, members of either the Congregational or Roman Catholic Churches.[2]

The elements in the present culture of Hanuabada, as of other places subjected to similar influences, can be separated into three categories. First there are those, like the language, that stem from the past. Then there are those that have come from Western society. Some in this second group have been imposed by force. Thus the people were prohibited from carrying out raids and compelled to deal with offenders through the processes of the Australian legal system. But some European elements, such as Christianity, have come in not by compulsion but by persuasion, whereas others the natives have taken over of their own volition without either coercion or exhortation. Nobody has given them orders or advice on how to eat, yet

---

[1] During the past few years some of the younger men have initiated a movement for a return to the loincloth, now regarded as traditional, though it also was a European introduction. They choose stout woollen material for preference, and the garment is then tailored to measure.

[2] Primitive Hanuabada is described by C. G. Seligman, *Melanesians of British New Guinea*, Cambridge, 1910, pp. 41–193; modern Hanuabada by C. S. Belshaw, *The Great Village*, London, 1957. Neither author mentions the new religious movements, but various Hanuabada natives have given me an account of them. Such manifestations will be dealt with in a later chapter.

they have chosen to adopt table linen, cutlery, and china. The third set of elements cannot be referred back either to the primitive culture or to civilization. The strange religious movements, for example, are a response to contact.

The same division may also be applied to the culture of the white colonists of New Guinea and elsewhere. They have brought most of their civilized habits with them, but here and there changes have occurred. A number of words from the native languages have been incorporated into the vocabulary— *kai* for 'food' and *bung* for 'market'—and some of the native vegetables form part of the regular diet. The third series of elements arises directly from the colonial situation. The form of government is different from that of any metropolitan country, cheap labour has made it easier to run a house, and isolation has meant that the men have had to acquire a variety of skills that in the homeland could safely be left to specialists. The planter on an out-station must know something about not only agriculture but also animal husbandry, carpentry, civil engineering, and navigation, and he should be able to repair a broken-down engine, whether of a pump, refrigerator, car, or schooner.

My purpose at present is not so much to emphasize these distinctions in the type of social change as to draw attention to the variety of influences that may operate to bring about the change itself. The Hawaiians abandoned their religion on account of forces inherent in the traditional culture, the Ontong Javanese adopted a different form of residence as their numbers declined, the Irish modified their inheritance rules when the soil became impoverished and the population outran the food supply, the Maori of New Zealand adjusted themselves to unfamiliar surroundings, and the Hanuabada villagers are acquiring the new ways of living that have become familiar through recent contacts with the world at large.

Community, Society, and Culture

Before proceeding further it will be advisable to have a clear
definition of the terms 'community', 'society', and 'culture',
which will recur constantly in the discussion.

By 'a community' or 'a society' I mean a political unit within
which the employment of force is either forbidden or else restricted by well-defined rules. Such a group is generally associated
with a particular territory which the members are prepared to
defend and from which they sally forth to attack other groups.[1]
The two expressions thus refer to an autonomous local body
such as a national State in the civilized world, or, among primitives, a tribe, as in Polynesia or Africa, an independent settlement,
as in Melanesia, or a horde, the persons who habitually camp together, as among the nomadic hunting aborigines of Australia.

The word 'society' alone, without an article, and the word
'culture' give rise to greater difficulty. 'Culture', indeed, has
been defined in dozens of different ways.[2] 'Society', in the sense
in which I shall use it, refers to the totality of social relations
between the members of a community, 'culture' to the totality
of standardized behaviour patterns. Each is thus a facet of the
same thing.

I am here following Firth and Nadel. Firth's view is that
'society' emphasizes the human side, the collection of persons
and the links between them, 'culture' the behaviour that has
been socially acquired. If 'society' is the aggregate of social
relations, then 'culture' is their content; or if 'society' is an
organized set of human beings with a given way of life, then
'culture' is that way of life.[3]

Nadel gives a more detailed account. Social reality, he maintains, is perceived in two aspects, one resting on the criterion of
the aim of the action patterns, the other on the criterion of the

---

[1] This definition has been criticized but will serve our present purpose (see E. R.
Leach, *The Political Systems of Highland Burma*, London, 1954, pp. 5–6).

[2] See A. L. Kroeber and C. Kluckhohn, *Culture*, Peabody Museum Papers, Harvard
University, Vol. XLVII, No. 1.

[3] R. Firth, *Elements of Social Organization*, London, 1951, p. 27.

relationships between individual persons. The order of standardized action patterns contains the social entities we know as institutions, the order of relationships the social entities we know as groups. Every social fact belongs to both orders at once, and there can be no group that does not imply some definite action pattern through which it is mobilized and alone visible and no action pattern that does not imply some form of group through which it operates. Further, we can make no statement about the one without referring at least implicitly to the other. A group built on particular relationships, say the family, will be visible, however, in a series of action patterns—care of children, productive co-operation, religious observances, and so on—and, conversely, a particular action pattern with certain aim contents, perhaps protection of infants, may activate more than one group—the family and the State. Social facts, it is clear, are two-dimensional and can therefore be projected on to one or other of a pair of co-ordinates and viewed in one or other aspect. 'Society' means the totality of social facts projected on the dimension of relationships and groupings, 'culture' the totality projected on the dimension of action. At the same time, Nadel warns that considerable linguistic difficulty is entailed in preserving the consistency of this distinction and that the adjective 'social', in particular, often has a double connotation.[1]

Behaviour alone is open to observation, and relationships must of necessity be inferred. Conclusions on the nature of the ties between husbands and wives, or between parents and children, can only be reached when information has been collected about what the members of the family in the particular community under review actually say and do. Correspondingly, class groupings, age groupings, sex groupings, and the rest only become apparent after conduct has been analysed. Again, if the aim is the investigation of change, then it is the alteration in the customary modes of acting that provides the clue to any modification of the bonds uniting persons.

[1] S. F. Nadel, *Foundations of Anthropology*, London, 1951, pp. 78–80.

The fact that new behaviour patterns may have reper-
cussions in the social field is brought out forcibly in the well-
known passage in the *Anatomy of Abuses* in which Stubbes
laments the new Elizabethan fashion of everyone wearing similar clothing regardless of his rank. The disappearance of the
visible differences between the gentry and the commoners, he
complained, was likely to cause chaos.

'Now there is such confuse mingle mangle of apparel . . . and
such excesse thereof [Stubbes wrote] as everyone is permitted
to flaunt it out in what apparel he lust himself, or can get by
any kind of meanes. So that it is very hard to know who is
noble, who is worshipfull, who is a gentleman, who is not: for
you shall have those that are neither of the nobylitie, gentility,
nor yeomanry: no nor yet anie magistrate, or officer of the
common wealth, go daylie in silkes, velvets, satens, damasks,
taffeties, and such like, notwithstanding that they be base by
byrthe, meane by estate, and servyle by calling. This is great
confusion, and a general disorder.' [1]

Social Change and Social Continuity

Much has remained constant in English society despite the
overwhelming changes since the end of the eighteenth century.
The Prince Regent, were he to be reincarnated today, would
not be entirely at home, but we still speak his mother tongue,
respect the sovereign as head of the State, and retain among the
statutes many of the bills to which he gave his royal assent.
Some features have persisted despite the fact that everyone
agrees that they might with advantage be modified. English
spelling at once comes to mind. We all deplore its lack of logic
and long for a revised alphabet. Yet the inconvenience would
be so great that no movement for wholesale reform is likely to
be successful. Adults would have to go back to school, our
books would require transliteration, and for some years newspapers and other publications would have to be issued in two

[1] *Phillip Stubbes's Anatomy of Abuses in England in Shakespere's Youth, A.D. 1583*
(ed. F. J. Furnivall), London, 1877-9, Pt. I, p. 34.

different editions. The Russians faced the same problem, but even in the days of the revolution stopped short after liquidating three redundant letters. The conservatism of the professions is also common knowledge. The medical fraternity at first opposed vaccination, chloroform, and even elementary cleanliness. Lister's communication on antisepsis in the *Lancet* of September 21, 1867, appeared not in the place of honour but in the middle pages. Many of our laws, too, conflict with the findings of psychologists. Probably only the misinformed would now defend the McNaghten Rules, yet they continue to be generally applied. Again, when we rebuilt our bombed cities, instead of following the new plans drawn up for the purpose, we too often reproduced the same crooked narrow streets and consequently find ourselves still delayed by the old traffic blocks. Such examples as these are an indication that social change must always be considered in relation to social continuity.

Human personality, at first so pliable that it can be bent into almost any cultural pattern, soon hardens. Culture provides a set of answers, all apparently effective, to most of the problems with which individuals living in organized groups are likely to be faced, and once they have mastered the language, customs, and beliefs current among their fellows there is seldom much need for major reconstruction. The number of innovations deliberately adopted in any one generation is therefore as a rule small.

Yet every culture has its limitations. The tools are never as efficient as they might be, properties of the physical environment await further exploitation, and the institutions do not fit together as neatly as the cogs in a machine—nobody, that is to say, fulfils all his social responsibilities willingly and carries out all his obligations to the complete satisfaction of his companions. The inadequacies of the technical apparatus are especially likely to be revealed if the community comes into contact with foreigners possessing a better type of equipment. Primitive natives everywhere have at once recognized the superiority of steel to stone and of rifles to spears and arrows. It follows that change in particular aspects of the culture is at any moment possible and is almost a foregone conclusion if persons who are technologically more advanced visit or settle in the country. Peoples may invent appliances for themselves, or, if the opportunity offers, they may take them over from outside. (The process of invention, even if it occurs inside the community, is always the work of gifted individuals or teams, and for the majority the problem of acceptance is the same whether the device comes from one of their fellows or from outside.) This is true also of skills, crafts, modes of conduct, and vocabulary. Ideas, too, or the perception of new relationships between familiar facts, may produce results that are ultimately as far-reaching as those brought about by a new implement. Even abstract notions can become symbols or rallying cries and so affect action. We have only to think of the effects of the adoption of such concepts as the dignity of man, freedom of conscience, and the equality of all before the law. It would be impossible to write history without reference to ideas. In the seventeenth and eighteenth centuries the divine right of kings and the sovereignty of the people were important, in the nineteenth the theory of organic evolution, and those who in the future write about us will certainly have to consider the impact of the writings of Marx and Freud, misinterpreted as these have often been.

Analysis of Change

The dynamics of social change have only recently become the subject of anthropological study. Many of the workers of the nineteenth and early twentieth centuries were interested in change, but from other points of view. They assumed that any society selected for examination was at that particular moment stable, and devoted their attention to discovering what had happened to it in the remote past before the present state was reached and what was likely to occur in the equally remote future.

The social sciences, no less than the biological sciences, were for a long period dominated by the theory of evolution. Early anthropologists accepted the hypothesis that all societies were progressing upwards along the same line towards some final objective. The civilized peoples had made the greatest headway, they supposed, and the various primitive societies were placed at different points along the route, some near the bottom, others closer to ourselves. Students of this era referred to natives as 'our contemporary ancestors' and argued that the development of institutions could be worked out by a survey of present-day customs, starting with the 'lowest' societies and climbing step by step to the groups 'higher' on the scale. Sollas, in a book dealing ostensibly with the prehistory of Europe, wrote that 'The Tasmanians, though recent, were at the same time a Palæolithic, or even . . . Eolithic, race, and they thus afford us an opportunity of interpreting the past by the present'. He followed his account of Eolithic remains in Europe with a description of the habits of the Tasmanians and inferred that this is how the ape-men who made the tools must have lived. Similarly, he concluded that because some of the implements of the mid-Palæolithic cultures resembled those of the Australian aborigines tribal life in Australia would provide information about the social organization and beliefs of Neanderthal man.[1] Morgan and McLennan, using methods of this kind, worked out an evolutionary sequence for the family. They suggested that the first stage was complete promiscuity and that then came group marriage, polygamy, and, finally, monogamy. Maine, Hartland, and Vinogradoff propounded corresponding sequences for law; and Tylor, Marett, and Frazer others for religion. All these writers were attracted by customs that differ markedly from our own. They regarded them as evidence for the prior existence of a less evolved type of society no longer visible in its pure form. So current examples of matrilineal descent and matrilineal inheritance were of interest as relics of promiscuity and group marriage. Paternity, so it was

[1] W. J. Sollas, *Ancient Hunters*, London, 1911.

maintained, could never have been established until the stage of polygamy was reached, and patrilineal descent and patrilineal inheritance must necessarily belong solely to the higher forms of society. Except for Morgan, who had had first-hand experience of American Indians, these evolutionists relied for their material on travellers' tales and missionary accounts that were mostly prejudiced and always inadequate. Had they visited the colonial territories they might even at that date have observed cases of matriliny gradually giving way before patriliny. But it was not till this decade that books and papers began to appear citing instances of such a change-over, with details of the causes and effects.

Anthropologists still believe in social evolution, but this crude unilinear theory has long since been abandoned.[1] As a dominant theme it was replaced for a time by diffusion, the attempt to trace the spread of cultural items, mainly techniques and material objects, through past migrations. The diffusionists were equally indifferent to what was actually going on while they were spinning their theories. Perry, in *The Children of the Sun*, for instance, tried to prove that wherever such practices as mummifying the dead, building pyramids, and wearing gold and pearls as ornaments were carried on they had been introduced by the ancient Egyptians or by peoples in contact with them. The Maya culture of Mexico, the Inca culture of Peru, and the island culture of the Torres Straits were all supposed to be derived from a civilization which, after its creation on the Nile, travelled around the world. At each point reached the status of the simple food-gatherers was raised. Perry, and the members of the several other diffusionist schools, assumed that each present-day culture was a sort of rubbish-heap of custom, the careful picking over of which would reveal a series of strata.

[1] Evolutionary problems are treated from the modern point of view by S. F. Nadel, *Foundations of Anthropology*, pp. 104–6; R. Redfield, *The Primitive World and its Transformations*, New York, 1953; and M. Ginsberg, 'On the Diversity of Morals', *Journal of the Royal Anthropological Institute*, Vol. LXXXIII, pp. 113–35. See also J. H. Steward, 'Evolution and Process', *Anthropology Today* (ed. A. L. Kroeber), Chicago, 1953.

Thus Rivers in his *History of Melanesian Society* said that he had reached the conclusion that Melanesian culture had come into existence as a result of a fusion of a number of peoples possessing different institutions. He maintained that waves of voyagers had blended with the original population and that the culture we now regard as typical of the area was a hotch-potch. He sorted out the betel-chewers from the kava-drinkers, the groups that cremated their dead from those that preserved them, and discussed the wanderings of each among the islands. His most spectacular triumphs were in convincing himself that the peculiar privileges of uterine nephews in relation to their maternal uncles, a feature of many societies following the principles of patrilineal descent, were derived from a state of affairs in which the elders were able to monopolize all the young women and that cross-cousin marriage became an established custom when the older men began giving their superfluous wives to their sisters' sons.[1]

In England the reaction set in just before 1920, when the younger anthropologists at length realized that the method of reconstructing history by conjecture was unscientific because the conclusions, even those that appeared to be reasonable, were incapable of proof. Simultaneously it came to be accepted as normal procedure for students not only to visit the colonial areas themselves—this, indeed, Rivers had done—but also to learn the vernacular and participate to some extent in native life. For another decade, however, field workers continued to be attracted by the unfamiliar. They did their best to select remote societies out of reach of traders and missionaries, and if this proved for some reason impossible, and they were obliged to go to a place where the old culture had, as they put it, 'broken down', they concentrated on the tribal elders and tried through them to recapture the more romantic past. Malinowski's volumes on the Trobrianders provide a striking illustration of the way in which the present was ignored, the more so

[1] W. H. R. Rivers, *History of Melanesian Society*, Cambridge, 1914, Vol. II, pp. 59–61.

as we owe so much of the modern technique of research to him. Europeans, including Methodist missionaries, had been living permanently in the islands for a full twenty years when he first reached there in 1915, yet he makes only casual references, generally in regretful or derisive terms, to the modification of custom. 'I was still able with but little effort', he wrote, 'to re-live and reconstruct a type of human life moulded by the im-plements of the stone age.' [1]

The workers of this period analysed the interrelationships of the various institutions and their reactions on one another. They studied single cultures with the object of discovering how the different aspects interlock. It is significant that this was the era of depopulation theories. Tampering with any part of a culture led to the collapse of the whole, various writers in-sisted—Malinowski, again, among them—and the natives were then doomed to extinction through boredom. A vague psycho-logical malaise overcame them, and they lost the will to live.[2] We now know that a more probable explanation for the high death-rate during the initial years of contact is to be sought in imported firearms, introduced diseases to which the people had no immunity, and poor diet. In point of fact, the only native groups that did die out were those killed off by gunfire and poison, as in south-east Australia and parts of North America, and those located in isolated areas—Ontong Java is an example —too far away for regular patrolling. Elsewhere, now that adequate medical services are available, numbers are starting to increase.

At last, a little before 1930, it became obvious that social change could no longer be overlooked. Western influences had spread so far that the only untouched primitive peoples left

[1] B. Malinowski, 'The Rationalization of Anthropology and Administration', *Africa*, Vol. III, p. 406.

[2] See *Essays on the Depopulation of Melanesia* (ed. W. H. R. Rivers), Cambridge, 1922; S. H. Roberts, *Population Problems of the Pacific*, London, 1927; G. H. L-F. Pitt-Rivers, *The Clash of Culture and Contact of Races*, London, 1927; and B. Malinow-ski, 'Ethnology and the Study of Society', *Economica*, Vol. II, pp. 208-19. The theory is criticized by H. I. Hogbin, *Experiments in Civilization*, London, 1939, Chap. V.

were those from a few inaccessible islands in the Pacific or from the further regions in the interior of New Guinea and South America. The 'savages' elsewhere were being baptized, learning to read and write, entering European employment, and buying the products of Sheffield, Birmingham, and Manchester.

Malinowski altered his approach and in 1929 wrote that 'a new branch of anthropology must sooner or later be started, an anthropology of the changing native. Nowadays, when we are intensely interested, through some new anthropological theories, in problems of contact and diffusion, it seems incredible that hardly any exhaustive studies have been undertaken on the question of how European influence is being diffused into native communities.' [1]

A further reason for re-orientation was the fact that many workers wished to offer advice, from purely humanitarian motives, about the problems confronting colonial administrators and missionaries.[2] Malinowski, for example, never conceived of a study of change divorced from what he called 'practical anthropology'.[3] I am not suggesting that the anthropologists wished to abandon science for welfare work; rather that they began to feel that, in addition to being scientists, they were also citizens and under a moral obligation to show how their knowledge could be applied. They shared the daily routine of primitive peoples, and had they not developed a regard for them their job would have been intolerable. Personal experience of the maladjustments resulting from European contact impelled them to believe that they were sometimes in a position to help their native friends by indicating to those in authority

[1] B. Malinowski, 'Practical Anthropology', *Africa*, Vol. II, p. 22.

[2] Cf. A. R. Radcliffe-Brown, 'Practical Anthropology', *Australian and New Zealand Association for the Advancement of Science*, Brisbane Meeting, 1930, p. 276: 'In the past anthropology has too often concerned itself only with academic questions that have no bearing on practical problems such as the administrator of a native people has to face. It has been more concerned with trying to discover the unrecorded past than with understanding the present and anticipating the future.'

[3] See L. P. Mair, 'Malinowski and the Study of Social Change', *Man and Culture* (ed. R. Firth), London, 1957.

how the impact might best be cushioned. Such counsel was only of value, they realized, if backed up by a record of day-to-day events—in other words, by an analysis of recent changes. Many of the governments and missionary organizations appreciated the value of this information and furnished assistance for further research.

The first books written from the new point of view within the British Commonwealth were F. M. Keesing's *Changing Maori* (New Plymouth, New Zealand, 1928), L. P. Mair's *African People in the Twentieth Century* (London, 1934), and the volume with the title *Western Civilization and the Natives of South Africa*, edited by I. Schapera (London, 1934).[1]

A shift of focus also occurred in the United States, in part, according to one authority, as a reaction against the reconstruction of the Indian cultures from the memories of the old men, in part as a result of concern with social issues raised by the depression of the nineteen-thirties.[2] The earliest major publication in America devoted to the effects of Western civilization on a native people was Margaret Mead's *Changing Culture of an Indian Tribe* (New York, 1932).

In this introduction I have listed some of the factors responsible for social changes taking place, given a few preliminary definitions, and briefly glanced at the varying interests of anthropologists over the years. The next task will be to consider recent theories relevant to the discussion of change.

[1] F. E. Williams's *Vailala Madness*, Anthropological Report of Papua No. 4, Port Moresby, 1924, deserves recognition as a pioneer study but is in a slightly different category. The work deals solely with a new religious cult that was causing the Papuan Administration concern.

[2] R. Beales, 'Acculturation', *Anthropology Today* (ed. A. L. Kroeber), Chicago, 1952, pp. 621-41.

CHAPTER II

The Approach to the Study of Change

ANTHROPOLOGISTS must be concerned with culture: the question is, are they to stop there, or go further and deal with society? Should they be content with describing miscellaneous ways of behaving or sort them out in an attempt to discover the resulting sets of social relationships?

Radcliffe-Brown raised this issue in his presidential address to the Royal Anthropological Institute in 1940. The difference of interest, he stated, leads to two kinds of study 'between which it is hardly possible to obtain agreement on the formulation of problems'. He himself was interested in society. If we set out to investigate a native community, he went on, we find a certain number of human beings in a certain natural environment:

'We do not observe a "culture", since that word denotes, not any concrete reality, but an abstraction, and as commonly used, a vague abstraction. But direct observation does reveal to us that these human beings are connected by a complex network of social relations. It is this that I regard it as my business to study if I am working ... as a social anthropologist. I do not mean that the study of social structure is the whole of social anthropology, but I do regard it as being in a very important sense the most fundamental part of the science.'[1]

In the course of ten years Radcliffe-Brown must have changed his mind. In an earlier paper he had explained the concept of social structure by reference to culture.

[1] A. R. Radcliffe-Brown, *Structure and Function in Primitive Society*, London, 1952, pp. 189-90.

'By any culture [one passage read] a certain number, larger or smaller, of human beings are united together into a more or less complex system of social groups by which the social relations of individuals to one another are determined. In any given culture we denote this system of social grouping the social structure. The life of a people is essentially made up of the collective activity of groups, which may vary from an act of religious worship to a football match, or from a war carried on by a nation to a meeting of a science congress. And the life of a people is therefore determined by their social structure, by the system of groups the various activities of which make up the total social life.' [1]

The later statement seems to have arisen directly from Radcliffe-Brown's growing dissatisfaction with the work of the so-called cultural anthropologists. He specifically criticized those Americans who regard culture as a haphazard collection of traits, 'a planless hodge-podge, that thing of shreds and patches called civilization',[2] and also Malinowski, who had referred to the effects of Western influences on native communities as 'culture contact'. To do this, said Radcliffe-Brown, 'was simply a way of avoiding reality'. The interaction is not of cultures but of individuals and groups within an established structure that is itself in process of change. What is happening in a native tribe subject to European domination can only be described by recognizing that it has been incorporated into a wider political and economic system.[3]

Many anthropologists would agree with these strictures, but

[1] A. R. Radcliffe-Brown, 'Applied Anthropology,' *Australian and New Zealand Association for the Advancement of Science*, Brisbane Meeting, 1930, p. 269. Cf.: 'Social relations are only observed, and can only be described, by reference to the reciprocal behaviour of the persons related. The form of social structure has therefore to be described by the patterns of behaviour to which individuals and groups conform in their dealings with one another' (*Structure and Function in Primitive Society*, p. 198).

[2] *Structure and Function in Primitive Society*, p. 186. The quotation is from an early work of R. H. Lowie, who Radcliffe-Brown admitted had by that time changed his views. Lowie later explained how he had come to make the statement, which, he said, had had no bearing on his anthropological theories (see R. H. Lowie, *Primitive Society*, London, 1953, p. viii).

[3] *Ibid.*, p. 202.

it should be borne in mind that Malinowski, despite his use of the expression 'culture contact', was in fact interested in social relationships. This is indicated by his continued insistence that the units of comparison between societies must be the institutions, sometimes defined as systems of activities and sometimes as groups of persons. Had he undertaken a detailed study of change, a task he never attempted, he would not have followed the cultural anthropologists who discuss the diffusion of traits: he would have concentrated on particular institutions that are in process of modification. 'The units of transformation', he wrote, 'are not traits or trait complexes but organized systems or institutions.'[1]

We can agree that 'culture' is an abstraction and also that it is hardly possible to study 'a whole culture', as Malinowski and various other cultural anthropologists had ostensibly aimed to do. But 'society' is equally an abstraction, and the description of 'a whole social structure' presents just as many difficulties, especially as 'all social relations of person to person' and 'the differentiation of individuals and of classes by their social rôle' would have to be included.[2]

'A social structure in Radcliffe-Brown's sense can be perceived but never fully described [says Firth]. When I knock into someone on the street and apologize we have a social relation. But is this to be reckoned as part of the social structure? . . . "The social structure", viewed as something within the grasp of the ethnographer's account, is a myth. Social structure is a conceptual, not an operational or descriptive tool.'[3]

Radcliffe-Brown did not acknowledge the problem explicitly, though in the introduction he prepared for a volume

[1] B. Malinowski, *Dynamics of Culture Change*, New Haven, 1954, p. 119. Cf. L. P. Mair, 'Malinowski and the Study of Culture Change,' *Man and Culture* (ed. R. Firth), London, 1957. Mair also points out that he quoted with approval Fortes's statement that culture change is not 'a mechanical pitchforking of elements of culture like bundles of hay' ('Methods of Study of Culture Contact in Africa', *International Institute of African Languages and Cultures Memorandum XV*, p. xix).

[2] *Structure and Function in Primitive Society*, p. 191.

[3] R. Firth, 'Social Organization and Social Change', *Journal of the Royal Anthropological Institute*, Vol. LXXXIV, p. 5.

C

on the political constitutions of African tribes he wrote: 'Two societies ... may resemble each other in one aspect of the total social system and differ in another. It is therefore necessary to compare societies with reference to one particular aspect ... of the whole social system, with reference to the economic system or the political system or the kinship system.' [1] When classifying Australian tribes he restricted himself exclusively to the 'kinship aspect' of the social structure.[2]

Structure and Change

The structural point of view has had such a considerable influence on British anthropology that it will be well to begin with an account of Radcliffe-Brown's theory.[3]

The members of any society are connected by the social structure, the network of social relationships seen in the system of groups, including those of kinship, neighbourhood, sex, rank, and occupation. In primitive societies membership of most groups is determined by birth and is compulsory. The range of choice is narrow, for there are few voluntary associations corresponding with our clubs, lodges, unions, and sects, which a person may join or not as he pleases. Where a person cannot withdraw from his group or change to a new one, his fellows are able to bring great pressure to bear to make him conform to accepted standards.

New members enter a society by birth or immigration, old members disappear by death or emigration, quarrels break out, and marriages and divorces occur. If the groupings and associations continue as before, the structural form of the community remains the same. On the other hand, the groupings and associations may change, sometimes gradually, sometimes, as in military conquests and revolutions, with great suddenness

---

[1] *African Political Systems* (ed. M. Fortes and E. E. Evans-Pritchard), Oxford, 1940, p. xii.

[2] A. R. Radcliffe-Brown, 'Social Organization of Australian Tribes', *Oceania*, Vol. I.

[3] See *Structure and Function in Primitive Society*, pp. 178–204; and 'Applied Anthropology', *op. cit.*

—though even then some continuity of structural form is maintained. Just as the biologist carries out research in the morphology, physiology, and evolution of animal species, so the anthropologist can investigate social morphology or the classification of social structures on the basis of similarities and differences, social physiology or the way in which social structures function, and social evolution or the changes in structural types—how one kind gives rise to various others and how simple kinds develop into those that are more complex. But the biological analogy must not be pressed too far. In an animal organism it is to some extent possible to observe structure independently of function, and morphology can therefore be separated from physiology: in society the social structure is only observed as it functions. The relationships of father and son, of buyer and seller, of ruler and subject are only visible in activities. Further, an animal organism does not in its lifetime change its structural type (a pig does not become a hippopotamus), whereas a society in the course of its history may alter its structural type without any break of continuity.[1]

The theory assumes that in every social system the parts ordinarily dovetail and work together with some degree of harmony. The rules are generally accepted, and all conflicts are capable of being either resolved or regulated. 'In order that a society may exist and continue to exist the groups that constitute it must possess a certain degree of cohesion. A people to maintain itself and its culture must possess a certain degree of social integration.' This condition Radcliffe-Brown also referred to as functional unity and internal consistency. 'Social function' he defined as the contribution that a partial activity makes to the total activity of which it is a part. The function of any particular social usage is therefore what it does in the functioning of the social system as a whole.

But social systems may on occasion be lacking in integration (or functional unity and internal consistency), and some of the

---

[1] The last sentence comes almost verbatim from *Structure and Function in Primitive Society*, p. 181. But a tadpole becomes a frog, and certain grubs become butterflies.

conflicts that arise are then incapable of resolution. The biological analogy can again be used, this time with an animal
organism suffering from disease. Radcliffe-Brown, following
the Greeks, suggested the terms 'eunomia' and 'dysnomia' for
social health and social ill-health respectively. A society in a
state of eunomia is socially integrated, in a state of dysnomia it
is disintegrating. In an animal it is possible to distinguish
healthy and pathological conditions objectively: disease is that
which threatens the organism with death or interferes with its
characteristic activities. Very few unhealthy societies, however,
have actually died. Normally they 'continue to struggle towards some sort of eunomia, some kind of social health, and
may, in the course of this, change [their] structural type': in
other words, partial social disintegration is usually followed by
reintegration. The anthropologist, as the student of societies
that are pre-literate and hence without records, has little chance
of working out the details of long processes of change of type.
His observations are largely confined to the disintegration of
social structures, though he may here and there discover some
evidence of spontaneous movement towards reintegration.

Radcliffe-Brown carried out several studies in social
morphology, though, as was mentioned, he did not deal with
whole structures. He also wrote a number of essays on details
of social physiology, here again keeping within narrow limits.
Thus he demonstrated the social function of various kinship
usages, such as preferential and forbidden marriages and the
so-called joking relationships, which in some communities en-
join teasing and horseplay between certain classes of relatives.[1]
Preferential marriages, he pointed out, help to maintain the
kinship structure, whereas those that are forbidden would, if
they were allowed, destroy it. The joking rules typically apply
in structural situations where the parties are in a position of
opposition in terms of one significant kinship relationship and

---

[1] See the introduction to *African Systems of Kinship and Marriage* (ed. A. R. Radcliffe-Brown and D. Forde), Oxford, 1950; and *Structure and Function in Primitive
Society*, pp. 90–116.

attachment in terms of another. Hostility and friendliness are incompatible, and laughter provides a way out of the impasse. Joking hence contributes towards the integration of the kinship system by keeping approved behaviour consistent within itself.

Social evolution, however, Radcliffe-Brown touched upon only incidentally, chiefly in the 1930 paper on applied anthropology. 'Any considerable change in a culture', he said, 'necessarily involves changes in the social integration, in the social structure. Social change consists essentially in processes of integration and disintegration.' One of the chief differences between ourselves and primitive peoples lies in the range of effective social relationships. Our social structure embraces millions of persons, those of the primitives hundreds or, at most, thousands. Social evolution is in effect the disappearance of simple narrow systems of integration in favour of more complex wider systems. Old groups, with their accompanying collective activities, diminish in importance as they are replaced by others.

Integration may not at a given level be effective.

'An insufficiently integrated society will usually if not always suffer from moral unrest, and this may show itself in different ways. An increase in the rate of suicide; an increase in neuroses . . .; revolutionary political movements; formation of new religious sects, particularly when accompanied by forms of hysteria or excess of emotionalism; any of these may be symptoms of lack of social integration. An increase in certain forms of criminality also may sometimes be due to this cause.' [1]

Europeans when they establish control over a primitive society always bring about changes in integration, and, unless another social structure comes into being, disintegration and its attendant evils follow. A ban on warfare, for example, may have untoward effects. Colonial officials may realize that war integrates nations, their own included, but fail to see that the

---

[1] 'Applied Anthropology', *op. cit.*, pp. 270–1.

same may be true of the small groups they have to administer. Peoples prevented from making war at times find alternative means of differentiating themselves as separate units, but the best way for a government to avoid trouble would be for it to encourage reintegration at a higher level by creating a large inter-tribal body into which they could all combine. This task is not an easy one. The new group cannot in present conditions be integrated by warfare, yet, if it is to be effective, it must have a meaning for the members and some concrete purpose.[1]

The introduction of a new legal code may also be disastrous.

'In a normally integrated society the laws are based on and are the expression of the moral consciousness of the community. Things regarded as wrong are made the subject of legal sanctions. We have a quite different state of affairs when a dominant people declare wrong in law things which the subject people have not learned to think wrong. The native may, by fear of punishment, be made to keep the law. He is more likely to take care that he does not get found out. There thus arises a divorce of law and morality. Some things are wrong; others are merely forbidden under threat of punishment. This inevitably creates a . . . pathological attitude to the law as such . . . A people's conception of right and wrong cannot therefore be changed by the mere process of imposing laws from outside, nor, indeed, can they be changed at all except by slow evolution.'[2]

[1] For an example of the difficulties see M. E. Opler, 'The Creek Town and the Problem of Creek Indian Political Reorganization', *Human Problems in Technological Change* (ed. E. H. Spicer), New York, 1952, pp. 165–80. The Creek Indians are divided into a number of tribes, each of which originally occupied a separate town. Relations between them were facilitated by an inter-tribal organization of moieties and clans, and from time to time all joined together in a temporary alliance against common enemies. The United States Government wished to set up a central political body which could speak for the Creek Indians as a whole, and to this end moved them into a central settlement. Despite a hundred years of effort, the experiment is still unsuccessful. To begin with, unfortunate early experiences made the people distrustful of the Government, and they do not wish to enter into negotiations with it. Equally important, however, is the fact that the tribes can still carry on their affairs independently. Each was allocated its own ward in the new building scheme, and the divisions between them are further reinforced by allegiance to different Christian sects.

[2] 'Applied Anthropology', *op. cit.*, pp. 274–5.

Homans has challenged Radcliffe-Brown's concept of function. The anthropologist, he points out, is in a different position from biologists who carry out experiments on animals; he is unable to alter the characteristics of a society in order to see whether it will continue to survive. True, a handful of primitive communities have died out, but what has commonly happened is comparable with the fate that overtook the Roman Empire. In Italy in the fifth century the governmental organization alone fell: Italian society survived the barbarian invasions and has maintained an unbroken continuity till today.

'When [anthropologists] talk about survival they are apt to mean the survival of a society rather than a governmental organization, yet it might seem hard to establish any but the most elementary inferences about the contribution a social institution makes to the survival of a society when so few have not survived. How can you be sure what does contribute when you do not know what does not contribute?' [1]

Homans seems to have confused populations with social structures. When the Roman Empire fell, the relationships of the Italian people to their government and to one another were altered, and their social structure thus suffered disintegration. Some elements of the old structure survived, nevertheless, and Italian society was subsequently reintegrated, in the beginning at a lower level.

Yet it must be admitted that Radcliffe-Brown's reification of society in his general statements is misleading. There is no point in saying that a certain custom has an integrative function for the society as a whole; and to state that society in a state of dysnomia always struggles towards eunomia is to cloud the issues. It is rather individual persons who combine into new groups when they find that some common aim is best achieved thereby. At the same time, Radcliffe-Brown in practice was concerned with the analysis of how social arrangements work, and in his detailed papers he tried to cover the structural bones

[1] G. Homans, *The Human Group*, London, 1951, p. 270.

with the flesh and blood of action. So, instead of being content with remarking that a particular kind of kinship behaviour, such as compulsory joking between affines, holds the society together, he sought to discover how it fitted into the kinship structure and helped to keep this in operation.

Homans also finds fault with the logic of the argument that because some recurrent activity is organically interrelated with other activities it therefore makes a contribution to the survival of the society. 'The interrelatedness of the elements of social behaviour may be dysfunctional as well as functional,' he says.[1] Magical ritual may be closely linked with economics in the sense that ceremonies are required at every stage of the principal undertakings. It is possible that the people are thereby stimulated to put forward their best efforts: it is also conceivable that the time occupied with the rites might be better spent in production.

Magical rites, however, can readily be dissected, and the functional parts, in terms of the existing social structure, separated from the parts that, in the same context, are dysfunctional. Malinowski, to mention only one writer, amply demonstrated that magic has a close connection with leadership and organization. The magician, by virtue of his knowledge of the appropriate spells, acts as the director of certain communal tasks.[2] But magic takes time, energy, and material. If a survey indicated that the people were putting so much time into ritual that cultivation was suffering and other activities being neglected and that, in addition, the authority or influence of the magician was increasing, we would be justified in concluding that some of the relationships within the society were being modified. This could only mean that the social structure was changing.

Opposition and Change

Godfrey and Monica Wilson, in their *Analysis of Social Change*, develop Radcliffe-Brown's theory of the linkage between

---

[1] G. Homans, *The Human Group*, London, 1951, p. 271.
[2] B. Malinowski, *Coral Gardens and their Magic*, London, 1935, Vol. I, pp. 66, 152.

change and imperfect integration. They begin by accepting the hypothesis that the ideal society is fully integrated.

'All objective analysis of social relations rests on the assumption that they form coherent systems, that within any one field they support and determine one another inexorably ... To deny the assumption of social coherence would be to abandon all hope of analysis in history, and to fall back on a mere chronicle of seemingly accidental and so incomprehensible events.'

In the colonial world of today, however, 'social relations are largely incoherent, pulling against and largely contradicting one another'.[1]

The Wilsons introduce a new term, 'opposition', which, they say, has two forms, distinguished as 'ordinary' and 'radical'. Ordinary opposition occurs even in well-integrated societies and relates to who is to have power over whom, who is to partner whom, and the precise application in particular cases of rules that are generally accepted. It is resolved by balance within the social structure and by social pressures. For example, friction was common in the Trobriand Islands between a boy and his mother's brother, among the Bemba of Rhodesia between a young man and his wife's kinsmen, and among the Pondo of South Africa between a woman and her husband's people. Yet the problems were never insoluble, and the difficulties could in the end be smoothed out. Radical opposition is different. It is inconsistent with itself. It is the opposition of law and law, logic and logic, convention and convention. Where radical opposition exists the society is necessarily in a state of social disequilibrium, and change is inevitable.[2]

To illustrate radical opposition the example is quoted of the present attitude of the Nyakyusa of Tanganyika to hospitality. These natives have always respected a man who entertains visitors lavishly and despised one who does not—if he is really

[1] G. and M. Wilson, *The Analysis of Social Change*, Cambridge, 1945, p. 23.
[2] *Ibid.*, pp. 124-7.

mean he is thought to run the risk of being bewitched. In order to be generous to all, a person must have help to cultivate his fields, brew beer, and serve food. The assistance used to be provided by extra wives. But today many Nyakyusa have been converted by missionaries, and are therefore restricted to one spouse. A convert who insisted on being a polygynist would lose face with his fellow Christians and possibly also with the pagans; further, he would believe that he was in danger of hell fire. He cannot be hospitable, and is thus at war with himself. The change that will probably come about will be the employment of labourers by those who can afford it and the replacement of beer by coffee, which is easier to prepare.

Radical opposition is always muddled. Each person supports concepts that are contradictory, laws that conflict, and conventions that do not harmonize. Compromise is necessary all the time, but one man's decision may differ from that of others. Order is in consequence maintained only with difficulty.

Ordinary opposition can be resolved by, for instance, changing the particular partner in a relation. But in radical opposition the partners are supported by rival systems. The behaviour of each, from the standpoint of the other, is illegal, illogical, and unconventional. Such a state of affairs the Wilsons call 'maladjustment'.

Disequilibrium and maladjustment are the result of uneven change, a failure to fit traditions to novelty, or an alteration of one aspect of a culture without alterations in other aspects. 'Disequilibrium is inherently unstable: it involves pressure to change, and so long as it continues there must be change. Disequilibrium is both a state of society and a force of change. As a force of change, disequilibrium must always press towards its own resolution, towards equilibrium.' If innovations were introduced separately, then equilibrium could be achieved— the consequent changes would follow one by one. The adoption of new things cannot now be regulated, however, and a second and a third are taken over before the first is digested.

Disequilibrium and maladjustment will accordingly continue and increase.[1]

Instability and Change

Leach is dissatisfied with this interpretation. Anthropologists, he says, are practically alone in regarding change as shattering and somehow fundamentally immoral, destructive of 'law, logic, and convention'. The people themselves often welcome the modification of their culture and structural organization, and historians and political scientists might even go as far as to judge the integrated society to be not healthy and fortunate, but moribund. The anthropologists' prejudice in favour of integration, functional consistency, and structural equilibrium, Leach argues, is the outcome of the conditions in which they work. They visit a native community for a year or two and are seldom in a position to learn much about its past or what subsequently happens to it. Their analysis, when torn out of time and space in this fashion, must be based on considerations of equilibrium, for, if it were not so, it would appear to be incomplete. But they go too far, he contends, when they assume that the equilibrium is stable. 'The confusion between the concepts of equilibrium and stability is so deep-rooted in anthropological literature that any use of either of these terms is liable to lead to ambiguity. They are, of course, not the same thing.' [2]

'When the anthropologist attempts to describe a social system he necessarily describes only a model of the social reality [Leach says]. This model represents in effect the anthropologist's hypothesis about "how the social system works". The different parts of the model system therefore necessarily form a coherent whole—it is a system in equilibrium. But this does not imply that the social reality forms a coherent whole; on the contrary, the reality system is full of inconsistencies; and it is precisely these inconsistencies which can provide us with an

[1] G. and M. Wilson, *The Analysis of Social Change*, Cambridge, 1945, p. 134.
[2] E. R. Leach, *Political Systems of Highland Burma*, London, 1954, p. 7.

understanding of social change ... Every individual of a society, each in his own interest, endeavours to exploit the situation as he perceives it and in so doing the collectivity of individuals alters the structure of the society itself.' [1]

Leach illustrates his argument with material from the Kachin Hills of Burma. The individual here is presented with alternatives in the scheme of values by which he orders his life, and structural change comes about through the manipulation of these alternatives as a means of social advancement. In politics the Kachins have two contrasting ideals before them, one the Shan form of government, a feudal hierarchy, the other democratic and egalitarian. A Kachin native may accordingly take a title to justify his claim to be an aristocrat and simultaneously appeal to the other set of principles to escape his liability to pay taxes to the chief. Communities also may oscillate between opposite types, aristocracy and democracy, or they may make a compromise. This last, described by some writers as 'the Kachin system', is only a model. It can be represented as being in equilibrium, though it is full of contradictions and hence inherently unstable.

'The description of a social system provides us with an idealized model which states the "correct" status relations existing between groups within the total social system and between the social persons who make up the particular groups ... When we refer to structural change we have to consider not merely change in the position of individuals with regard to an ideal system of status relationships, but changes in the ideal structure itself: changes, that is, in the power structure. Power in any system is to be thought of as an attribute of "office holders", that is, of social persons who occupy positions to which power attaches ... [I] assume that a conscious or unconscious wish to gain power is a very general motive in human affairs. Accordingly I assume that individuals faced with a choice of action will commonly use such choice so as to gain power ... or ... they

[1] E. R. Leach, *Political Systems of Highland Burma*, London, 1954, p. 8.

will seek to gain access to office and the esteem of their fellows which will lead them to office.'

Esteem is determined by culture, and what some admire others may deplore. In the Kachin Hills an individual may belong to either of two esteem systems, the feudal or the egalitarian, and the best course of action is seldom clear cut.[1] Leach does not advocate abandoning the traditional techniques for studying social structure. 'In practical field work situations the anthropologist must always treat the material of observation *as if* it were a part of an overall system of equilibrium,' he says, 'otherwise description becomes almost impossible. All that I am asking is that the fictional nature of this equilibrium be frankly recognized.'[2] He himself describes three *as if* systems: the aristocratic, the democratic, and the compromise. This means analysing the ethnographic facts by reference to two abstract whole systems conceived as existing in unstable equilibrium and then postulating that the third arises from their interpenetration.

The distinction that Leach draws between equilibrium and stability is important. Equilibrium implies balance, perhaps momentary, between opposing forces, stability that the thing in question is firmly established and unlikely to suffer sudden change. But if we say that a society is stable, we do not necessarily mean that its institutions are static; they may be adjustable and hence able to continue developing new stages of equilibrium. The field anthropologist can observe disequilibrium directly, as when relationships once reciprocal are so no longer, institutions fail to dovetail, and the descriptions of the norms of behaviour do not in the least tally with what is actually done. Certainly these are symptoms of instability, but to prove that the relationships and institutions are really changing or have changed the study would have to be pursued over a long period.

[1] E. R. Leach, *Political Systems of Highland Burma*, London, 1954, pp. 9–10.
[2] *Ibid.*, p. 285.

It is well for us to be reminded, too, that the stability of all pre-industrial societies should not be taken for granted. Specific examples of early societies that were unstable at once come to mind. The Greeks, to quote one case, swung backwards and forwards pendulum fashion like the Kachins between tyranny and democracy, and in ancient Tonga an incessant struggle took place between rival houses for the supreme power. Ideally a sacred king was at the head of the community with a secular king under him on the main island of the archipelago and hereditary governors in the outlying parts to perform the duties of administration. This arrangement was supported by a complicated marriage system that had the effect of maintaining the sacred king's superior rank. In fact, however, both kings and governors carried on wars, sometimes as three-cornered contests, and it was seldom certain who was supreme.[1]

But because some peasant societies are known to have been unstable, it would be unwise to assume that therefore they all were. Positive evidence justifying a conclusion either way is seldom forthcoming, but I believe that formerly many Melanesian societies were more stable than the Kachin communities. This contention is supported by experiences during some of my own field work. I first visited Melanesia a generation ago, and in the intervening years have studied various peoples, some of them slightly acquainted with Europeans and others with a long history of contact. In the areas where life was still going on much as it had done before the white man appeared, I found that the natives seldom questioned the rules of behaviour. A man who was discovered in an offence never denied the justice of the law but sought rather to excuse himself in this particular instance by calling attention to the extenuating circumstances. If he had helped himself to a neighbour's property he insisted that his action was not stealing because the goods were for some reason forfeit to him. Further, when the con-

---

[1] This information is derived in part from traditions orally transmitted and therefore possibly inaccurate; but they are confirmed by written records dating back to the eighteenth century.

stituted authorities judged him to be guilty of the crime, they allowed him to follow some standard procedure as expiation.

It seems likely that, before the Industrial Revolution, some of the small rural groups of Europe were also fairly stable. I quote the following passage from a diary of date 1774:

'This is the journal of John Smith, farrier to Sir Thomas Troke of Hampshire. My father was farrier before me, and his father afore him, and my son, the firstborn of as good and honest a woman as ever lived, is even now driving nails in the door beam as in the manner born. I serve God, I honour the king, I am the servant of my master, I work from dawn to dark to earn my daily bread, and I rejoice in a happy life.'

John Smith was by our standards grossly exploited but was satisfied with his relationships with the other members of his society.

Another point to be noted is that although a single Kachin may in his lifetime experience change only once, in the long view the swing to and fro is regular and repetitive. In such circumstances it would perhaps be legitimate to regard the society as stable. The molecules may move, but the mass remains stationary. The situation resembles that of so many matrilineal communities where a man's sons and the sons of his sisters continually bicker over his wealth. Sometimes one set of heirs is in the ascendant, sometimes the other set.

The changes to which the Kachins are subject are also restricted in scale. In Burma, and this is equally true of ancient Greece and early Tonga, the background is firmly fixed, and only in the political sphere is the social structure modified. Oscillation can doubtless take place smoothly when its scope is so limited. I again cite some of my Melanesian experiences. In what may be called the intermediate stage of contact, when Europeans are already beginning to exert some degree of influence, all sorts of other changes may occur without seriously damaging the traditional kinship system. The day comes when this also is affected, but in the period in between, which often lasts a long time, the native system of leadership can collapse and the pagan ceremonies become only a memory without kinship obligations being dishonoured. The explanation is simple. Genealogical and affinal ties provide the framework for co-operation in such essential work as agriculture, fishing, and housebuilding. If the people continue to follow the old methods when cultivating the indigenous crops, when catching fish, and when constructing their dwellings, kinsfolk are still under the necessity of acting together.[1]

The commonest type of change today, and the only type that most anthropologists have had the opportunity to study, is vastly different from that which has occurred among the Kachins. Throughout the greater part of the primitive world the swing is in one direction only, and far more than the political system is being altered. The peoples of the Pacific and of Africa are being confronted with civilization and all its trappings. They are taking over new tools, new crops, new processes, and new gods, and are also finding new opportunities for acquiring and spending wealth. They are being compelled to obey new laws and being forced to abandon customs that their forefathers had practised perhaps for centuries. They can no longer make war, carry out private vengeance, or treat the dead in a manner they hold to be fitting. A person who is involved in a cumulative revolution of such magnitude may be expected to be thrown into confusion. Leach remains sceptical when the Wilsons say that this is so; yet it is surely obvious that the native in many colonies now lives in a shifting scene and is continually faced with a series of fundamental dilemmas. Should he seek employment to earn money for the purchase of goods that are now so necessary, or stay at home to grow food for his family and care for his ageing parents? Should he carry out the instructions of the agricultural officer and gather the

---

[1] See H. I. Hogbin, *Experiments in Civilization*, London, 1939, pp. 220–2; and *Transformation Scene*, London, 1951, pp. 96–7. The point is discussed more fully in Chapter VIII.

ripening harvest in his coffee plantation, a crop his grandfather had never heard of, or fulfil his tribal responsibilities and attend the protracted funeral ceremonies of a chief in some distant village? Should he accept the judgement of his headman, who now has no power to enforce it but at least knows all the surrounding circumstances intimately, or take the charge to a European magistrate and submit to the tedious, and to him meaningless, procedure of the white man's law? Should he spend his money on a new pair of trousers, which he badly needs, or pay the traditional dues to his chief? Should he listen to the missionaries who say that he is morally entitled to choose a bride for himself, or accept the stranger selected for him according to ancient usage by his kinsmen? Should he be strictly monogamous even if his one wife is barren, or take an extra spouse to ensure the continuity of his clan? These and similar problems are cropping up all the time.

We can admit that some anthropologists of a former generation were unrealistic, even sentimental, in deploring the passing of primitive ways. They were prepared to justify native warfare, for instance, on the grounds that it was the focus of the economic life of the people, gave the warriors training in manly skills and developed their foresight, and led to a fine flowering of art in the form of images, decorated canoes, and ornamented club houses.[1] But modern anthropologists have a different attitude. They know of the losses that change has brought in its train; but they also see the gains. Tribal conflict probably had all the merits that were claimed for it, yet now that peace has been established travel is easier, and goods and ideas can be freely exchanged. Anthropologists of today accept the fact that Western technology and Western ways are spreading over the face of the globe, and it is they who have revealed that in many places the native is already more eager to accept than the European is to give. If the Wilsons say that conditions

---

[1] See W. H. R. Rivers, *Essays on the Depopulation of Melanesia*, Cambridge, 1922, pp. 84–112; and B. Malinowski, 'Ethnology and the Study of Society', *Economica*, Vol. II, pp. 208–19.

D

in the colonial world are destructive of law, logic, and convention, it is reasonable to believe not that they are foolishly exalt-
ing the past but that they are making a statement for which
there is supporting evidence. The remoulding of primitive
societies, whether it is ultimately to the advantage of the people
or not, is inevitable; and it seems to be just as inevitable that
the individuals caught up in the transition should find the process uncomfortable. Political independence is here irrelevant.
Delhi can no more alleviate the troubles of an Indian tribesman
than Whitehall would have been able to do.

It is doubtful, too, whether Leach's method of investigating
the interpenetration of two different systems is capable of
application to a situation where one of the social structures is
changing in several aspects simultaneously—when politics,
law, economics, and religion are all being altered together. He
could use it because among the Kachins the political aspect was
alone involved, and they themselves were able to describe as
separate entities each of the ideals that they alternately em-
braced. On the one hand, they had the Shan political model
and, on the other, the democratic model. As was pointed out
earlier, however, the total social structure of a primitive society
can hardly be apprehended as a unit or, indeed, as a model; and
emphatically that of European society cannot be. But even if
this were possible, nobody envisages native communities becoming either immediately or in the near future an exact
replica of a civilized State. A survey of official documents
might reveal the ostensible objectives of a government at a
given moment, the concrete proposals in the political, legal,
economic, and educational spheres; but the details of policy are
always subject to modification. The fact that theory and practice are not always in harmony raises further difficulties. In
large-scale social change, which, I repeat, is most often met
with today, we are dealing not with a rigid pendulum oscillat-
ing between two clearly marked fixed points; we have before
us a shadow, always blurred and sometimes obscured, moving
in one general direction towards some spot whose exact posi-

tion is unknown. Again, although we can all agree that the desire for power is often a motive for human action, I doubt if it has the overwhelming significance attached to it by Leach. He links it with public esteem and striving for office. Certainly everyone is anxious to have approval, and if a person wins respect he acquires prestige and may then exert some degree of influence. But where conflicting moral systems operate, as they now do in almost every colonial society, any course of action will give offence in some quarter despite the approbation it may meet in others. A man who pleases the progressives must simultaneously annoy the conservatives, if he satisfies the young he antagonizes the old, and if he secures the goodwill of the Christians he assuredly forfeits that of the pagans. Even in our own highly complex society, too, with its members of parliament, presidents of local councils, chairmen of committees, directors of companies, foremen of shifts, and leaders of gangs, the majority of us know that we will always be cast as subordinates. We keep our personal advantage in mind and are content with a small measure of recognition. Over and above this, however, is the demonstrable fact that behaviour may be inspired by motives other than power. Individuals are at times prepared to sacrifice their private interests from a sense of duty, or because they feel that a certain decision is right when judged by an objective standard. It is probable also that some persons in all societies are genuinely unwilling to accept the responsibilities of power and that there are some societies where, through cultural conditioning, nobody wants it. Ordinarily in primitive New Guinea when an old leader died the next most distinguished man in the community succeeded more or less automatically, but among the Arapesh and the Busama peoples the villagers had first to decide whom they wanted as their head and then force the title upon him. The victim, if such he can be called, was generally reluctant to accept.[1]

[1] M. Mead, *Sex and Temperament in Three Primitive Societies*, New York, 1935, p. 27; and H. I. Hogbin, *Transformation Scene*, p. 131.

Social Organization and Change

Firth emphasizes the need for a technique for investigating how individuals come to alter their regular behaviour, and hence their relationships. He suggests that this can be worked out by contrasting the aspects of the social system where choice is permitted with those where the mode of conduct is rigidly prescribed. The process of change, he says, is best analysed by reference to responses to particular situations. The situations may be similar to those that have occurred in the past, except that one of the persons implicated now perceives an opportunity for enhancing his status; or they may be quite new, brought about by external forces, and hence pose problems for which precedents supply no ready-made answers. Once an initial decision has been made, further action is called for. New choices present themselves, and in the end the structure is itself modified.

The social structure must be understood before any social process can be appreciated, Firth insists. But this is not enough.

'It is necessary to see how in any given case social activity is the resultant of a complex set of elements, including direct response to structural principles, interpretation of them, choice between them, by regard to personal interests and experience, temperamental dispositions, and the pressures exercised by other individuals striving to accomplish their own ends.' [1]

The analysis of social structure must therefore be accompanied by the examination of what Firth calls social organization.

'Generally, the idea of organization is that of getting things done by planned action. This is a social process, the arrangement of action in sequences in conformity with selected social ends. These ends must have some elements of common significance for the set of persons concerned in the action. The signi-

[1] R. Firth, *Elements of Social Organization*, London, 1951, p. 61.

ficance need not be identical, or even similar, for all the persons; it may be opposed as between some of them. The processes of social organization may consist in part of the resolution of such opposition by action which allows one or other element to come to final expression. Social organization implies some degree of unification, a putting together of diverse elements into common relations. To do this, advantage may be taken of structural principles, or variant procedures may be adopted. This involves the exercise of choice, the making of decisions.' [1]

Structure and organization can be used respectively to account for social continuity and social change.

'Continuity is expressed in the social structure, the set of relations which make for firmness of expectation, for validation of past experience in terms of similar experiences in the future. Members of society look for a reliable guide to action, and the structure of the society gives them this—through its family and kinship system, class relations, occupational distribution, and so on. At the same time, there must be room for variance, and for the explanation of variance. This is to be found in the social organization, the systematic ordering of social relations by acts of choice and decision. Here is room for variation from what has happened in apparently similar circumstances in the past. Time enters here. The situation before the exercise of choice is different from that afterwards. An open issue, with elements as potentials in several directions, has become a resolved matter, with potentials given a specific orientation. Time enters also as a factor in the development of the implications of decisions and consequent action. Structural forms set a precedent and provide a limitation to the range of alternatives possible—the arc within which seemingly free choice is exercisable is often very small. But it is the possibility of alternatives that makes for variability. A person chooses, consciously or unconsciously, which course he will follow, and his decision will affect the future

[1] R. Firth, *Elements of Social Organization*, London, 1951, p. 36.

structural alignment. In the aspect of social structure is to be found the continuity principle of society; in the aspect of social organization is to be found the variation or change principle— by allowing evaluation of situations and the entry of individual choice.'[1]

Firth gives several examples to illustrate rigidity and flexibility. In Tikopia membership of the lineage, clan, and social class is determined absolutely by birth. If Tikopia were another type of society it might be possible for a person to be absorbed by some lineage or clan into which he was not born; and it might be possible also for him, by dint of industry or thrift, to rise from the class of commoners to that of the chiefs. But if such actions were to be permitted the society would not be what it is. Movement to another settlement is allowed, however, and within a short time the man and his children are accepted as belonging to the district in which his dwelling is situated. Local alignment is thus an element in the structure where preferences can be exercised. Assignment to the lineage, clan, and class is automatic; assignment to the district automatic but optional. Choice may also, in certain instances, enter into kinship relationships. The community is small, and all persons, including spouses, are connected by a number of genealogical ties. A man after his marriage is obliged to modify his behaviour towards his wife's siblings and treat them as affines; his brothers are free to decide whether they will follow him and do likewise or continue to reckon them among their cognates.

Any theoretical framework for the analysis of change must be concerned with what happens to the social structure, says Firth; but if it is to be truly dynamic it must also allow for individual action. Each separate individual in a society is striving to attain his ends and interacting with his fellows as he does so. The behaviour of them all is to a certain extent governed by the basic relations of the social structure, which embody expectations as to what they ought to do. Individual conduct has

[1] R. Firth, *Elements of Social Organization*, London, 1951, p. 40.

therefore a complex scheme of motivations behind it. The person's own interests, recognition of the interests of the other members of the society, and recognition of the structural values that have previously guided him—all of these affect his patterns of behaviour. Yet no act is a precise repetition of what has gone before, even though it may be carried out as a response to a similar stimulus.

'The pattern then is the main theme, not an identical procedure. At any step in the action process new motivations may present themselves to the individual. These may arise from his perception of advantages to be derived from the social system hitherto unperceived by him. Or they may arise from the entry of new factors into the social environment, offering new opportunities or enforcing new ways of protection. Into the social process of an agricultural community . . . drought, flood, tempest, accidents to animals or gear, and discovery of a new crop strain present the members with problems which they can solve only by modifying their activity . . . All this demands a new adjustment by the individual . . . But he has also to maintain some orientation to the values which have hitherto held a place in his motivational scheme. He must also have regard to the ways in which other members of the society are likely to react to the new factors in the social situation, and to his response to them. The outcome is likely to be some organizational change. There will be a replanning of time, of the order in which fields will be ploughed or harvested, or the ways in which the members of the household will co-operate to carry out the daily tasks. Preferences will be different. . . . Choices will fall differently between the new range of alternatives. Activity will take new directions and form new combinations.' [1]

Firth admits that minor organizational change may not affect the social structure. Structural change occurs when the alteration of procedure at last goes so far that the basic relationships between the members of the society are modified.

[1] R. Firth, *Elements of Social Organization*, London, 1951, p. 84.

Structural change, although it may not imply a high degree of coincidence between the new motivations of any large number, means in effect a shift in the pattern of their activities and possibly also a new common orientation.

'The observer can recognize that a former basic relation has lost its magnitude, its force, its frequency. He may be able to see a new relation directly substituted for it, or several new relations may have arisen. The potato and the pig, for instance, when introduced among the Maori of New Zealand, radically altered the economic structure. They reduced the amount of labour put in on other crops and on fowling; they altered the production balance as between men and women; they gave commoners a chance of earning relatively higher incomes and elevating themselves in the social scale; they even helped to change the scheme of ritual by reducing the amount of economic magic demanded. Together with other factors, such as the musket, they were the basis of some important structural changes in Maori society.' [1]

Disintegration and Reintegration

It seems that when putting forward a theory of social change we must have in mind a pair of opposites. On the one hand, there is a society with a fully integrated social structure and also in a condition of complete equilibrium and perfect stability; on the other, an aggregation of individuals incapable because of their lack of organization of functioning as a social unit. The former corresponds with Radcliffe-Brown's eunomia, society in a state of health: the latter goes beyond his dysnomia, a society diseased, to death itself—such a collection of individuals cannot be regarded as a society at all. The two may be compared respectively with a chronometer corrected to the smallest fraction of a second and a series of watch parts lying unassembled on a workman's bench. They represent theoretical possibilities, neither of which may ever have existed.

[1] R. Firth, *Elements of Social Organization*, London, 1951, pp. 84-5.

We can only say that some of the communities of the pre-industrial era perhaps had an almost fully integrated structure; and if we want an example of a disorganized aggregate, then the nearest approximation may be the herd of slum-dwellers on the outskirts of African cities. All present-day societies of which a record is available—societies as they are in the mid-twentieth century—lie somewhere in between. They are partially integrated and to a certain extent unbalanced. Lopsidedness means a tendency to topple over, and faulty social integration also implies movement. Two sets of forces operating in different directions can be recognized, the one undermining existing social relationships, the other creating substitutes. Structural change takes place as these forces are resolved.

We can readily discern the effects of the destructive forces in our own society. The weakening of family relationships is one instance.[1] Our family in the days before the industrial revolution was similar to that of the primitives, compact and self-supporting.[2] The members farmed their land together, grew their food, wove the cloth, and fashioned their own garments; and the parents were responsible for the education and health of the children and carried out religious ritual on which the welfare of the group was believed to depend. Now that we have become industrialized the man takes employment and earns an income with which to buy the food and clothing. We are also obliged to have so much basic knowledge to make a living that the home education is inadequate. Children must therefore be sent to school for training by specialist teachers. Health, too, is no longer a matter of administering herbal tea for a stomach ache; we consider it essential for the sick to be treated by a qualified physician or surgeon and expertly nursed in hospital. Finally, many of us have abandoned the religious forms of our great-grandfathers. Almost the only activities left to the family are the sexual relations of husband and wife,

---

[1] Cf. G. Homans, *The Human Group*, London, 1951, pp. 276–80.

[2] Rural families in certain parts of England were still largely self-supporting in the nineteenth century. See the reminiscences of F. Thompson, especially *Larkrise*.

the provision of emotional security for the children, cooking, and the maintenance of the household. Social relationships do not exist in a vacuum but develop out of common tasks and interests. In earlier generations the bond between husband and wife was founded on their joint efforts and continuous co-operation. The division of labour gave them different jobs, but they toiled side by side. Today they seldom act together. The man spends the bulk of his time in an office or factory while the woman stays at home or undertakes paid employment. Often neither understands what the other has been doing, and conversation about work is difficult if not impossible. Each may accordingly have a separate circle of friends.[1] It follows that, because our social system offers them nothing else, spouses choose each other on the basis of romantic attraction. When the romance fades, as fade it must, they have only sex and companionship left. Sex is scarcely sufficient for an enduring relationship, and if the couple are to be true companions they are obliged to look for something to be companions in. The old-fashioned family did not have to contrive anything of the kind—it was given. At that period, whatever else happened, it was almost certain that the marriage would endure, at least in name. Now if a couple become bored with each other no link exists to take up the strain. The inevitable consequence is that many unions end in the divorce courts.

The wider circle of kinship is also playing a decreasing part in our lives. The choice of trades and professions is now so broad that fewer sons follow the father's calling. Further, the development of transport offers scope for the young man to go far afield to better himself financially. Couples thus tend to set up their new home miles away from their parents, often in another town or country. Kinsfolk, who, in any case, have become less numerous as the family has shrunk in size, are in consequence given only occasional opportunities for combin-

[1] See E. Bott, 'Urban Families: Conjugal Rôles and Social Networks', *Human Relations*, Vol. VIII, pp. 345–84; and R. Frankenberg, *Village on the Border*, London, 1957, pp. 51–57.

ing, such as at weddings and funerals. Grandmothers and aunts are not even available to act as baby-sitters when the husband and wife wish to attend a cinema. Again, the increasing range of expensive consumer goods on the market, many of them now considered to be household necessities, means that the majority of persons feel that they cannot afford to contribute to the support of their invalid and ageing relatives. The children may also suffer. In earlier times they were able to spread their affection on a host of kinsmen in the same village, and the emotional shock if a parent died was effectively softened. In modern conditions they have no alternative but to concentrate their love on the father and mother, and should the home break up through death or divorce they may lose their sense of security and become a social liability.

Yet new ties, despite a time lag, often considerable, are already being built up. True, the enfeebled family and kinship relationships have been left almost untouched,[1] but others are steadily taking their place. The impersonal links between the individual and the central administration, for instance, have been much strengthened. Each adult has a vote, and he can if he wishes use the government facilities for educating his children and keeping them and himself in good health. The State, too, provides pensions for the maintenance of those who have reached the age of retirement. Various groups have also come into being to take care of both old and new needs. Trade unions, of which every worker can be a member, regulate the conditions of employment and negotiate for a fixed minimum beneath which wages must not fall; municipal councils, for which all property-holders are eligible, deal with water supplies, lighting, drainage, garbage disposal, roads, and so on; building societies, which anyone can join, furnish money for the construction of houses; finance companies, which, again, anyone can approach, lend cash, for a consideration, for the purchase of furniture and other equipment; and if domestic

---

[1] It is too soon to tell yet whether the alteration of habits brought about by television will revitalize family relationships.

help is required to meet an emergency there are agencies that attempt to find someone to supply it. It may also be mentioned here, though the matter is not strictly relevant to the present discussion, that now we have come to realize that the future of the human race depends on the formation of a world society many of us are prepared to give our political leaders encouragement to support such organizations as the United Nations. Our efforts to create international relationships are as yet half-hearted, but perhaps in a decade or two all communities may be prepared to combine into a well-integrated union.

The social structures of primitive societies present a similar picture of breaking down and building up. Family relationships are being shattered by the absence of the men, and in some places of the women also, in European employment; clan and lineage relationships by the new tools that obviate the necessity of large groups co-operating (a householder can now by himself carry out in a day many tasks previously demanding a week's effort by a team); tribal relationships by the prohibition on warfare and the withdrawal of the right of criminal jurisdiction from the headman or chief; and class and age-group relationships by the adoption of a money economy. To-day almost anyone, including the humblest and the most youthful, can earn an income. Those of lowly birth can therefore enhance their status and those still immature become independent. Troubles have arisen, too, wherever the natives have been taught how to grow produce for sale. The earlier systems of land tenure, though admirably adapted to the cultivation of the indigenous subsistence crops, are generally unsuited to any other type of agriculture. Then we have the spectacle of rules that are disregarded, disputes that are never settled, factions that are always opposed, and groups that exist in name only with no activities to perform. Kinship relationships that were once reciprocal have also become unequal. Uterine nephews help a maternal uncle and in the end see the wealth that they expected to inherit pass to his sons, or the maternal uncle contributes to the support of his young nephews and later finds out that they do not intend to look after him in his decline. The fear of sorcery, too, far from diminishing, has actually increased. The people cannot now punish those whom they suspect of carrying on the black art and therefore feel that they are without protection. Again, many Christians are saddled with a permanent guilty conscience. By abandoning the forms of the pagan religion, they have lost the means of expiating actions that they still regard as wrong.

Although the social fabric of the traditional culture is being unravelled, the threads are not lying in a completely disordered tangle. Some of them have been gathered up in an attempt to weave a new cloth based on a different set of patterns. Fresh relationships include those between groups of neighbours who have pooled their resources to buy capital equipment to be shared or hired out, between members of co-operatives that undertake the processing of harvests and the marketing of produce, and between persons who belong to the same Christian mission or the same church congregation. Then, if the ties between the tribesman and his chief have declined in significance, those between the people themselves are gaining in strength through the new local legislatures and judicial bodies. Again, the aristocracy of wealth is in part replacing the aristocracy of birth, new systems of land-ownership are being tried out, and new classes of medicine men are beginning to appear as a defence against sorcerers. The effects of wage labour have also not been uniformly disastrous. Individuals from places far apart mix together and make lasting friendships, which can now be maintained by correspondence.

Even the slum-dwellers of African cities, persons drawn from dozens of different tribes, are trying to create some form of social structure for themselves. Like human beings elsewhere, they are obliged from time to time to co-operate with one another, and stable relationships and groupings provide the foundation on which joint action can be based; moreover, a person by allying himself with others probably acquires a sense of belonging and hence a measure of psychological security.

So there are trade unions, political organizations, social clubs, and strange religious sects.[1] Some individuals also operate together as gangs to carry on a career of crime, but such bodies cannot be regarded as integrative unless they prey exclusively on strangers.

Anthropologists have hitherto devoted most of their attention to the disintegration of social structures: the fact that integration is also taking place, albeit in terms of another type of structure, has been largely overlooked. The reasons for this lapse are not difficult to understand. The spread of Europeans to the distant parts of the Pacific and Africa is comparatively recent, and many workers have carried out their research only a short period after the establishment of administrative control. At this stage the disintegration is so devastating that it is readily apparent. But disintegration still goes on, even if the initial contact took place a couple of generations ago or longer. We have ourselves during the past fifty years improved our technology and revised our attitude to colonial problems, and it follows that peoples whose structures have already been modified continue to take over unfamiliar tools and continue to be forced to obey unfamiliar regulations. Relationships are therefore becoming progressively more and more disturbed. Reintegration processes, on the contrary, are, in present circum-

---

[1] See G. Balandier, *Sociologie des Brazzavilles Noires*, Paris, 1955.

E. H. Spicer, 'Reluctant Cotton Pickers', *Human Problems in Technological Change* (ed. E. H. Spicer), New York, 1952, pp. 41–54, gives an illustration of collections of individuals forming themselves into stable groups, in this instance for the duration of the war in the Pacific. All persons of Japanese descent resident on the west coast of the United States were after the attack on Pearl Harbour removed to a centre in Arizona. They came from different cities, and few were acquainted beforehand. They had no need to work, for the government provided housing, food, clothing, etc. The camp was located in a cotton-growing area, however, and, because of the call up, the farmers were short of labour. The internees wanted to demonstrate their loyalty to America and were also aware of the value of securing the goodwill of the local community. At the same time, they refused to sign on separately as labourers for fear of arousing dissension within the camp—they believed that the high incomes that the larger families would earn might cause jealousy. The authorities accordingly suggested that the wages should be paid into a general welfare fund. This also was unwelcome. Why should anyone work for the benefit of persons whom he did not know? The final outcome was to buttress the church groups and barrack clubs by allowing each of them to open a collective fund.

stances, difficult to observe. They begin at a later stage, and, as disintegration is still taking place, are not likely to have advanced far. If the old social structure of a primitive society is forty per cent destroyed, probably not more than ten per cent of the substitute structure will have been built up. (This statement is not to be taken too literally: I do not know how the disintegration or the reintegration of a social structure could be accurately measured.) New relationships, too, are necessarily experimental, and for a time there is bound to be a heavy turnover. Only after trial are any permanently accepted. Some are rejected when they unexpectedly prove to be incompatible with relationships felt to be more binding, others when the mechanism for the enforcement of obligations is found to be inadequate. New groupings, too, being tentative, may remain unnamed. People talk freely about their villages, clans, lineages, age sets, and social classes; they do not discuss an organization if as yet there is no word for it in the language. The anthropologist is therefore obliged to probe deeply to discover it. Despite the obscurities, however, and the consequent laboriousness of the task, analysis of reintegration is just as essential for an understanding of social change as the investigation of disintegration. We need both if we are to know how one type of social structure develops out of another.

Some writers in the past have been so oppressed with the symptoms of disintegration that, as has been mentioned, they have given way to despair. Europeans in contact with native peoples have undoubtedly caused great suffering by their wanton interference, even though they were often inspired by the loftiest motives. It could be truthfully said that during the nineteenth century the road to hell for many primitive societies was paved with the good intentions of missionaries. (There is also a credit side: these same missionaries studied the native languages, produced the first dictionaries and translations, and taught the people to read and write.) Yet pessimism unrelieved by hope is premature. Social structures have achieved comparative reintegration in the past, and it is reasonable to expect that they will be able to do so in the future. I have in mind now not the reintegration of the political structure alone, as when empires decay and invaders overthrow a government, but the reintegration of a total structure after the introduction of an entirely different mode of existence. The first cultivation of plants and the first domestication of animals must have brought about changes as startling, and in a sense as catastrophic, as those that are taking place among primitive peoples now. We cannot ever expect to know the details of what happened when our remote ancestors were persuaded to renounce nomadism, hunting, and collecting in favour of a settled life, agriculture, and animal husbandry, but our present society is proof that their social structure survived drastic revision. Contemporary primitives have an advantage over our predecessors of thousands of years ago. Civilized man is beginning to learn that he is not the plaything of blind fate: he is trying to stand on his own feet and accept the responsibility for planning the destiny of mankind as a whole. As Linton remarks, he at last realizes that there can be no return to the good old days and that he must go forward and create good new ones.[1]

Change and Institutions

The anthropologist viewing change with structural principles in mind is mainly interested in alterations in the network of social relationships. He observes individuals, either of their own freewill or by compulsion, disengaging themselves from social ties and entering into new ones, and he sees one set of groups disappearing and another emerging. The reshuffling may take place directly, or it may follow on as an incidental after some modification of the culture. Two examples of a direct change in relationships may be cited from New Guinea. In the areas that have as yet been little influenced by civilization the administration adopts the practice of appointing a native from each settlement as its representative. Often the

---

[1] R. Linton, 'Present World Conditions in Cultural Perspective', *Science of Man in the World Crisis* (ed. R. Linton), New York, 1945, p. 203.

traditional leader, who has perhaps been directing the opposition to European encroachment, is passed over in favour of a retired policeman, hitherto exercising no special influence. The bond between the people and their headman is thus loosened, and new ties come into being between them and the official nominee. Elsewhere, in places where the contact has been prolonged, a different scheme operates. Here the inhabitants of a village choose councillors for a central body which is empowered, subject to the veto of the district commissioner, to enact local-government ordinances and levy taxes. Adventitious changes in relationships are more common. A man acquires a steel axe, and from this act the weakening of the kinship unit begins. The new tool is more efficient than a stone implement, and he can now dispense with some of the help that he formerly demanded. Or, if he is an African, he may buy a plough. Should he then agree to work for his neighbours and accept cash for the service his bonds with them tend to become less personal.

Finding a method for the systematic study of the changing network of relationships creates a problem. If a social structure cannot be described in its entirety, clearly the attempt to assess the full extent of change within a total social structure must be doomed to failure. The alternative procedure is to take Malinowski's units of transformation, the institutions. His own definition varied slightly in different publications, but in a late volume he described them as separate entities of organized activity with a purpose behind them (in that they are directed towards satisfying a need); agreement regarding the set of underlying values; a personnel (in other words, a group); and practical, ethical, and legal norms.[1] The more important may be

[1] B. Malinowski, *A Scientific Theory of Culture*, University of North Carolina, 1944, pp. 34, 52. For other definitions see S. F. Nadel, *Foundations of Anthropology*, London, 1951, pp. 107–9. Cf. also that of Radcliffe-Brown, *Structure and Function in Primitive Society*, p. 200. He saw institutions as 'standardized modes of behaviour' that form the machinery by which the network of social relationships 'maintains its existence and continuity'. Many of his studies, as when he analysed the 'social function' of preferential marriage and joking, turn out to be a demonstration of how a particular institution holds together.

E

classified as those of kinship, law, politics, education, economics, and religion. Particular institutions include the family, marriage, courts of law, blood feuds, chieftainship, property, the market, and the church.

Firth offers a further lead. Inquiry into such questions as the exercise of choice, the responsibility for planning and making decisions, the co-ordination of manpower and resources, the basic compensations, and the enforcement of rules gives a clue to the identification of the factors making for continuity and for change. We should be able, in the light of this information, to see how within an institution the relationships, especially those concerned with co-operation, status, and authority, are likely to decay or develop.

Before I deal with institutions in detail, I propose to examine the initial stages of change and find the answer to such questions as why some innovations are eagerly adopted while others, seemingly as attractive, are rejected and why, when a government applies force to eradicate customs of which it disapproves, dependent peoples should so often offer resistance.

CHAPTER III

Voluntary Acceptance of Change

EUROPEAN traders when they first visited the islands of Melanesia in the early nineteenth century were prepared to give away axes, knives, spades, and other goods in return for sandalwood, turtle-shell, and fresh vegetables. The natives were agriculturalists, but although they welcomed the axes and knives, they displayed little interest in the spades.

An individual adopts an innovation of his own free will only when he has become convinced that it offers him some kind of a reward—perhaps greater efficiency, or more security, or enhanced status. The opinion of others, especially if they are judging the possible benefits in the light of a different background, is irrelevant, though they may possibly exert influence by pointing out some of the hidden implications of a decision. Everything new has to be paid for, however, either in money or goods or by incurring extra obligations or surrendering rights and privileges; and, in addition, fresh habits and skills are often called for. The individual must accordingly be assured that the reward is worth the cost and inconvenience. The resources at his disposal have a direct bearing on his action, and what civilized peoples can easily afford is often beyond the means of a native. The person with little to give away must be content with having only a few of his needs satisfied, and if he is wise he chooses the most important. Even then he may discover that he has made the mistake of over-estimating the returns and under-estimating the price.

The Melanesians could see the advantage of steel axes and knives over sharpened stone, bone, or shell; and a single trial revealed that the necessary techniques could easily be mastered. They therefore wanted the tools at once and willingly handed over the sandalwood and other products. The spade raised an insuperable difficulty. The natives were no doubt aware that when wielded by a well-shod European it did the work better than a digging-stick; but they went about barefoot. In this case, too, the contrast between the relative usefulness of the new and the old article was not so marked. Quarrying stone and grinding down the edges of the pieces were laborious tasks, and the finished products were still inefficient. A pole, on the other hand, could not only be cut anywhere in a few seconds, but it also made a reasonably adequate agricultural implement. The islands have a moist climate, and the soil in consequence remains permanently soft.

Values

The individual has been our starting point. As Fortes remarks, persons and not customs react under contact.[1] Yet it is also a fact that decisions about the adequacy of the reward and the reasonableness of the cost and inconvenience are in part socially determined. Resources vary from community to community but are never unlimited, and nowhere can every need be fully satisfied. If wealth, or energy, or time is devoted to achieving one particular end, then it is not available for another. All peoples, civilized as well as primitive, are obliged to make a selection and rank certain objects and certain modes of conduct as more desirable, more agreeable, or more worthy than others. Each society has such set orders of preferences, usually referred to as its system of values. (Values formally defined are preferences regarding objects and actions in their social context.) The value scales are imposed upon the members of the group by the ordinary process of social conditioning, and what attracts or repels one person tends also to attract or repel his fellows.

[1] M. Fortes, 'Culture Contact as a Dynamic Process', *Methods of Study of Culture Contact in Africa*, International Institute of African Languages and Cultures, Memorandum XV, p. 62.

Qualitative judgements of this type may be explicit or implicit. Explicit values find expression in moral rules and opinions. The persons who make up a community must always be prepared to display a measure of mutual forbearance, helpfulness, and trust; and moral systems throughout the world necessarily have a fundamental similarity, with numbers of the elementary obligations in common. A list of the cardinal virtues drawn up by an Englishman or a Chinese would closely resemble one prepared by a Solomon Islander or a Zulu.[1] Yet, despite this basic equivalence, there are many differences of detail. The extent of the field within which the rules are held to apply, for instance, is wider among civilized peoples than among primitives. We think of mankind as a universal brotherhood and believe that we have responsibilities towards the inhabitants of the under-developed areas, whereas the Melanesian villager is indifferent to the well-being of natives living fifty miles away, and the African tribesman looks upon the followers of other chieftains as his natural enemies to be plundered at will. Green, though he exaggerated the uniformity, was to some extent justified when he said that it is not the sense of duty to a neighbour which varies but the practical answer to the question, 'Who is my neighbour?'[2] Contrasting preferences are readily apparent also in the regulations dealing with sexual relations and marriage. Some societies approve of pre-marital promiscuity and others favour chastity for the young, some permit polygamy and others restrict the number of spouses to one, some maintain that the marriage partnership is for life and

[1] Cf. M. Ginsberg, 'On the Diversity of Morals', *Journal of the Royal Anthropological Institute*, Vol. LXXXIII, p. 122: 'A list of virtues or duties drawn up by a Buddhist would not differ very greatly from one drawn up by a Christian, a Confucianist, a Muhammadan, or a Jew.' This statement implies that morality is derived from the religious system, whereas many peoples in fact keep the two separate. Confucius, for example, did not seek religious backing for any of his teachings. We may therefore conclude that morality is autonomous, carrying its own authority regardless of any additional sanctions, religious or legal, that may from time to time and from place to place be attached to it. (See A. Macbeath, *Experiments in Living*, London, 1952, Chaps. XI, XII.)

[2] T. H. Green, *Prolegomena to Ethics*, Oxford, 1883, p. 220. Cf. F. Boas, *Anthropology and Modern Life*, London, 1923, p. 219.

others allow divorce. Missionaries often experience difficulty in securing converts when they insist that our own values relating to sex are an integral part of Christianity. The Trobriand Islanders, today nominally Methodists or Roman Catholics, still ignore the ban on early sexual indulgence, arguing that it is based on an extraneous gloss by Saint Paul on the statements of Jesus contained in the Gospels.[1] Food gives rise to other divergencies. Muslims hold that it is sinful to eat pork. The inhabitants of some parts of Indonesia are short of high-grade protein, but an attempt to improve the diet by introducing pigs would be doomed to failure. These peoples belong to Islam and in consequence regard the animals as ritually unclean.[2] Hindus treat cows as sacred and refuse to eat beef. One third of the world's cattle is concentrated in India, but only a quarter of the population consumes any meat, and this mainly in the form of mutton and poultry. The presence of so many cattle has the effect of decreasing the available supply of food, for cows compete with men for the grain. Even the establishment of a cheese industry to counteract the lack of refrigeration would encounter religious obstacles. The milk in processing would have to be mixed with rennet manufactured from the fourth stomach of a calf, and the finished product would hence be taboo.[3] Then some codes incorporate seemingly arbitrary prohibitions, or prohibitions that have outlived their usefulness. Mohammet could not have foreseen an invention that was to take place centuries after his death, but for a long period the absence of any mention of printing in the Koran was interpreted as a condemnation of it. The publication of books was as a result delayed in Islamic countries till modern times.[4]

Implicit values are the premises underlying action. Here also a core of similarities is frequently obscured by peripheral, but still important, differences. All peoples prize mechanical effi-

---

[1] H. I. Hogbin, *Transformation Scene*, London, 1951, pp. 253-4.
[2] See R. Firth, 'Social Aspects of the Colombo Plan', *Westminster Bank Review*, May, 1951, p. 7.
[3] *Cultural Patterns and Technical Change* (ed. M. Mead), Paris, 1954, p. 218.
[4] A. L. Kroeber, *Anthropology*, London, 1948, p. 418.

ciency and rate highly any tool that reduces effort. Appreciation, however, is within each group tempered by such factors
as cost, the wealth of the natural environment, the background
of tradition, the store of knowledge, and the level of organization. The Melanesians of today continue to employ the digging-
stick, although they know, perhaps even better than their forefathers, that a spade would be a great help in gardening. But if
they had a spade they would need footwear. No indigenous
animal supplies leather suitable for home shoe-making, and
they would be obliged to buy both items from the traders.
Their opportunities for earning money are limited, and they
reserve cash for goods considered to be more essential. The
circumstances in which they live have thus forced the spade
down near the bottom of their scale of preferences. They
appreciate its advantages as well as we do, but for them it has
a lower social value. Many Australian tribes, to quote another
case, have in their primitive state so few possessions that they
can manage satisfactorily with a numerical system that does not
extend beyond three. Clearly, in these conditions they could
not be expected to display any interest in devices requiring
arithmetical calculations. Again, the social arrangements in
Alexandria in A.D. 100 did not permit the exploitation of Hero's
steam turbine, and the invention remained an interesting toy.
Our forbears of 200 years ago faced a similar difficulty when
Morrison produced the first telegraph.

Other foci of implicit values include security, freedom, comfort, and prestige. If other things were equal, most persons
would like to feel safer, enjoy wider liberty, live an easier existence, and win greater respect from their fellows. But conditions
are not equal—the hard facts of poverty, of varying tradition,
of insufficient knowledge, and of inadequate organization are
always obtruding. The range of preferences accordingly differs.
Primitive peoples living in a harsh environment generally protect themselves by training everyone in the use of arms and setting a high value on military prowess; those occupying more
favoured regions often rate warlike achievements low and

concentrate on the accumulation of riches, which enable them either to keep their more aggressive neighbours at bay with tribute payments or else to engage mercenaries to fight battles on their behalf. The relative emphasis on one or other set of values is also inconstant. At one period security may be stressed at the expense of freedom and at another freedom at the expense of security. During the feudal era in Europe the serfs were willing to sacrifice freedom for security. Later, during the seventeenth, eighteenth, and nineteenth centuries, freedom became the paramount consideration of the new middle class. Nowadays we are prepared to surrender some of our freedom, this time for the security offered by the Welfare State. Again, status sometimes comes before comfort and sometimes after. European women desirous of winning a reputation as leaders of fashion have on several occasions during the past few hundred years been forced to choose extravagant clothing that made sitting down in public practically impossible.[1]

Not all social values, however, are universal within a particular community. Generally the members of one section of the society have special interests. These persons share the majority of values with the rest of the people but maintain some that are peculiar to themselves. Even in the tiny groups of Melanesia, where formerly the villagers mostly chose their own leaders, the older men as a body were accustomed to exercise a number of privileges. On the island of Malaita, in the Solomons, they alone possessed large establishments with several wives and alone had the right to perform the more important rituals. It is scarcely surprising that in the early days the main hostility to missionary endeavour should have come from them. The majority remained steadfast to their ancestral faith long after their sons had been converted, and some were still pagan at the time of their death. In Melanesia also men's and women's activities are rigidly separated by strong social barriers. The few high schools are open to males only, and men alone are eligible for employment by Europeans. The

[1] D. L. Moore, *The Woman in Fashion*, London, 1949.

women remain at home, where their life is largely centred on the hearth. As a rule they own little property, and in native eyes they are minors for whose conduct a guardian—the father, brother, or husband—is responsible. The female half of the population is in consequence conservative and less ready than the male half to accept innovations. Men long ago gave up beaten bark cloth as a pubic covering in favour of a cotton loincloth, but women almost everywhere, even if they have a dress on top, continue to wear a grass skirt. The men, too, enjoy a meal of imported rice, though many women will not touch it. Again, more men than women are prepared to accept hospital treatment.[1]

Sectional differences in values are still more noticeable when the social system is based on a well-defined class structure. The nobility, jealous of their standing, place the established order high on their scale of preferences and decline anything new that may endanger their position. The commoners, in contrast, are less satisfied with existing conditions and welcome changes in the hope of bettering themselves. It is a commonplace that missionaries and religious revivalists always make most headway among the downtrodden. Christianity did not appeal to the Roman patricians, nor does it today to the Brahmins of India. The new teaching is as successful now among the lower castes as it was earlier among the slaves. Wesley drew his congregations from the slums of industrial England. Guam provides an interesting paradox. The upper classes were converted first and have come to regard Christianity as a mark of aristocracy. They in consequence resist its introduction to their social inferiors.[2]

As societies grow more complex, so they become less and less homogeneous. The nucleus of values to which all subscribe remains, but the magnitude of the subsidiary differences increases. There are now not only sections with their own interests,

---

[1] In other places, where Europeans regularly take native mistresses, the women are possibly more important than the men as innovators. This would be true of north-west Australia.

[2] H. G. Barnett, *Innovation*, New York, 1953, p. 305.

but subsections and fragments of subsections. Further, the web of traditions may now be made up of strands from several sources and in consequence be full of contradictions. In our own community many persons defend capital punishment, while others just as genuinely detest it, some advocate birth control while others condemn it, and some urge that the grounds for divorce should be widened while others argue that marriages are too easily ended already.

The Priority of Technical Change

Change begins when an individual seizes the chance of realizing an accepted value in a new way. It may be one of the general values of the community or one peculiar to a section, such as an age, sex, or class group. This readily happens with material objects, and improved tools and similar items diffuse much more rapidly than modifications of the social system.[1] The Melanesians' recognition of the superior efficiency of the steel axe marked the first alteration of their way of life. The other changes all came later.

Tools are always judged according to one standard. Everyone, regardless of his previous experience, agrees that a steel axe is better for cutting down trees than a stone axe. Customs, on the contrary, are judged according to different standards. If natives have believed for generations that polygamy is right, a missionary who thinks it is wrong faces a hard task in bringing them round to his point of view. Then ideas that are capable of practical demonstration are inevitably easier to grasp than those requiring explanation. The European, because he has been brought up as a Christian, knows what he is about when he takes part in a Communion service or a baptism, but pagan natives must serve a long apprenticeship before they can understand the symbols of the ritual.

Tools are also impersonal and make no counter demands on the user. He can experiment with them and, if he tires of them, throw them away. Disengagement from social usages and the

[1] H. G. Barnett, *Innovation*, New York, 1953, pp. 374-7.

accompanying relationships is more difficult. Again, each individual is free to accept a simple tool without consulting his fellows. If he requires no assistance in purchasing or handling it he can exercise his discretion and either take it or spurn it as he pleases. This situation may be contrasted with the introduction of a new word to the vocabulary. The innovator must here secure general agreement—the expression would be useless if other people did not know what it meant. The approval of others is equally necessary for changes in law, politics, kinship, or religion. A man who decides to set aside the established rules of inheritance, for example, soon finds his action contested by those adversely affected. An instance from Hanuabada is instructive. Many of the residents have had a good schooling and are fully literate. They could earn high wages if they would accept employment on the government outstations, but as soon as anyone volunteers his kinsfolk step in and bring various pressures to bear to keep him at home. These relatives are unwilling to lose the constant daily assistance to which they feel entitled.

Efficiency

All peoples esteem mechanical efficiency, as was mentioned, and see merit in appliances that reduce the amount of work. In pre-industrial societies the foremost consideration is the saving of effort, though other factors count. The new device makes an additional appeal if it is more durable than the old, or, should it be something portable, if it is lighter and less bulky. No group of which we have a record has failed to respond to an offer of matches. These are convenient, cheap, reliable, and much easier to use than a cumberous fire-plough or set of firesticks. Priests may continue to light their sacred temple fire in the old-fashioned way, but for them tradition is of greater value than utility.

A saving of time is not in general so significant. Native concepts of the time dimension are in several respects different from ours. In particular, they are less precise. Primitive peoples frequently possess a calendar by which agricultural and other seasonal tasks can be regulated, and some of them even give names to the nights of the moon; but, unless there are age sets, the years go by unrecorded, and nobody knows how old he is. Again, nothing comparable to our divisions of hours, minutes, and seconds exists, and periods are measured simply as long or short. An unfamiliar tool that enables a week's job to be completed in a day or two certainly arouses admiration, but one that cuts the period by something like half a morning may not produce any comment, favourable or otherwise. The clock is by no means the most sought after of our complicated machines. A native adopts a timepiece only after he has been subjected to a good deal of Western influence and accumulated a fair amount of money. Even then he takes it more to prove his sophistication than for its usefulness. Once, indeed, I saw a primitive Solomon Islander in a very remote settlement with an alarm clock—but he was using it as an ornament. Its white face and shining metal cover attracted him, and he had placed it in the lobe of his ear, which was already pierced by a large hole. The piece of elaborate gear that today is ubiquitous is the sewing-machine. It has followed close behind cotton clothing and is now found in the farthest corners of Africa and the loneliest Pacific Islands. Why I shall explain later.

Despite the universal appeal of efficiency, various peoples have declined superior apparatus. One instance is provided by the aborigines of Arnhem Land in northern Australia. These natives during earlier days received regular visits from Indonesian voyagers and yet retained their old simple technology.

Arnhem Land has a heavier rainfall than many other parts of the Continent, but at this period, before Europeans had brought in domestic animals and crops that could be cultivated, the people, like the rest of their compatriots, survived only by following a nomadic existence as hunters and collectors. There were no indigenous herds that might have been tamed, no seeds or roots that might have been regularly planted and harvested. Possessions that are too heavy to be carried about are useless to a nomad, and of necessity the material equipment of the aborigines consisted of bare essentials. They had no cooking vessels and roasted all their food on open fires, and their canoes were clumsy affairs hastily constructed from the bark stripped off a convenient tree. Such craft were fit for crossing the crocodile-infested rivers or for fishing close to the shore but would have been dangerous in the open sea.

The Indonesians came to north Australia to trade. They sought pearls, pearl-shell, sandalwood, and trepang and were prepared to give in exchange steel tools, tobacco, and rice. They remained in the area for the duration of the monsoon season only and interfered with the natives as little as possible. They did not want land and never attempted to found colonies. At the same time, they taught the natives two things—how to make clay pots in which to boil the rice and how to fashion dug-out canoes for visiting the reefs where the pearl-shell was to be found. The voyages were eventually stopped in 1907 by the Australian Government, and recent research has revealed that in the technical sphere the culture was practically untouched.

The aborigines kept the axes and knives and still smoke tobacco, which on this coast grows wild, in a pipe of Malayan design. But very few of them went on cutting dug-out canoes. The construction demanded joint effort, and the owner had to persuade his companions to stay in one place for some time till the task was finished. A bark canoe, on the contrary, can be made in a few minutes and discarded without regret after it has served its immediate purpose. Pot-making was also abandoned. The vessels were too fragile and burdensome for a community that was constantly moving about from place to place.

The influence on aboriginal ritual was rather more marked. The Indonesians removed the mast from their prows on arrival in Australian waters and did not replace it till they were about to depart. Stepping the mast thus came to symbolize farewell. At funerals the corpse is now lifted up to an erect position as though it were a pole while the mourners chant a dirge in pidgin Malay. It is probable also that the local cult of an earth mother is indirectly of outside origin.[1]

Many communities have also refused the modern steel plough. The explanation is sometimes readily apparent. The Melanesians are too poor to buy anything so expensive, and, even if they were richer, they have no draught animals. But what of India? In the United Provinces the wooden plough is still in general use despite the fact that some of the peasants could afford improvements. The reason is to be found in the structure of the rural society. Craftsmanship is transmitted with wealth, and the tradesman hands on his special knowledge to his sons. Each village includes several carpenters, and these men and their families are traditionally bound to a series of farming families in a relationship of mutual dependence. The carpenters have the task of keeping the ploughs in good order and in return are invited to feasts, when the womenfolk are presented with saris. Thus the farmers look to the carpenters for the maintenance of their implements, and the carpenters look to the farmers for entertainment and for clothing for their wives and unmarried daughters. If the farmers were to buy steel ploughs this social bond would be broken. Further, they would have no one to carry out repairs. Training the farriers to do the job, a procedure that would seem to be eminently reasonable, would not provide a solution. There are fewer farriers than carpenters, and as a rule not more than two or three are to be found in each series of villages. The roads are bad, and carting the ploughs to the blacksmith's shop would be an onerous business. To add to the difficulties, the ploughing season is short, and any delay might be disastrous. The extra weight of the steel plough would raise other problems. Stronger oxen

[1] W. L. Warner, 'Malay Influence on the Aboriginal Cultures of North-Eastern Arnhem Land', *Oceania*, Vol. II, pp. 476–95; R. M. and C. H. Berndt, 'Discovery of Pottery in North-Eastern Arnhem Land', *Journal of the Royal Anthropological Institute*, Vol. LXXVII, pp. 133–8; R. M. Berndt, *Kunapipi*, Melbourne, 1951; and 'Pottery in Arnhem Land', *Man*, Vol. LIV, No. 258; and P. M. Worsley, 'Early Asian Contacts with Australia', *Past and Present*, April 1955.

would be needed, and these in turn would have to receive more fodder.[1]

Objects are frequently adopted before the techniques for their manufacture. The Melanesians have not even begun to learn how to make the steel tools that they now handle daily. As a preliminary they would need to acquire some knowledge of mathematics, geology, mineralogy, physics, chemistry, and engineering; and they would also have to build a totally new social structure based on a division of labour with specialization.

The spread of bronze in prehistoric times provides a parallel. In northern Europe the belongings of the dead unearthed in tombs dating from the Stone-Age cultures frequently include bronze daggers imported from the south. A lengthy period was to elapse before the northerners could fashion these for themselves. Almost any adult in a stone-using society could pick out the raw material for his tools. Suitable rocks were selected as they occurred in Nature and then hammered, chipped, or ground into shape. Working with bronze was not so easy: the people had to learn all the different processes of metallurgy. First it was necessary to recognize the ores, which do not in the least resemble the metal extracted from them. These were then smelted, and afterwards the pure metals were mixed in the correct proportions to produce the best alloy. Finally, the alloy was forged or cast in the desired shape.[2]

Objects designed for a specific task may also be unacceptable in their original form or for their proper purpose. The Pacific Islanders were accustomed to smoothing their planks with an adze, and at first the carpenter's plane did not impress them. Then they discovered that the blade was not a fixture. The piece of flat steel, once it had been provided with an

---

[1] *Cultural Patterns and Technical Change* (ed. M. Mead), p. 209. For an account of the social effects when changes occur see D. G. Mandelbaum, 'Social Organization and Planned Culture Change in India', *India's Villages*, Development Department of West Bengal, undated (1955?).

[2] R. L. Beals and H. Hoijer, *Introduction to Anthropology*, New York, 1953, pp. 245-7.

elbowed handle, could be used in the familiar way and quickly replaced the inferior stone adze. Safety-pins, too, offered no appeal as fasteners to peoples who lacked clothing. But they were frequently sought after as ear ornaments.

Where a community has a class structure, and a consequent divergence of social values, the reluctance of some of the members to take to a new appliance can affect economic advancement profoundly. The system whereby the honest and able man loses money if he works for the government is peculiar to Western countries. In pre-industrial class societies the persons belonging to the higher strata usually owe their wealth in part to a right of appointment to administrative posts that carry great financial rewards. Their salary is far higher than the earnings of craftsmen and traders, and they can often supplement it by organized graft. Mechanics and those engaged in business therefore occupy a lowly place in the social hierarchy. If a foreign expert arrives on the scene to implement a developmental policy he finds that the educated few, who for this reason are the best fitted for training, despise mechanical toil and will not be taught. The upper classes, who alone can afford to send their sons to good schools and overseas universities, prefer to have them follow white-collar occupations. Even the youth who has by chance gone into engineering will as a rule have chosen theory rather than practice and still consider manual work degrading.[1]

Security

The Christian missionary, confident that his is the only true faith, offers converts the assurance both of life eternal after death and present peace of mind amid everyday troubles. He tells them that if they accept Christ sincerely and abide by the precepts of the Church they will be enveloped forever in heavenly love and have no serious cause for future worry. Here, indeed, is a promise of full security.

[1] R. Linton, 'Cultural and Personality Factors affecting Economic Growth', *Progress of the Underdeveloped Areas* (ed. B. F. Hoselitz), University of Chicago, 1952, pp. 84–5.

Few native peoples have been immediately stirred, and many of the early missionaries were murdered. Yet in the end the message prevailed. Today practically every Pacific Islander below middle age who has had ten years or more of European contact is a member of one or other of the Christian sects. He is a Roman Catholic, an Anglican, a Lutheran, a Methodist, a Congregationalist, a Presbyterian, a Baptist, a Seventh-Day Adventist, or a Mormon.

Why did the natives without any objective proof believe the missionaries? And why did they abandon so much of what had hitherto served to orient their lives? Their pagan religion had guaranteed a measure of security, but they dismissed these beliefs as superstitions, ceased attending the ceremonies, treated their priests with disrespect, burned the images or sold them to museum collectors, and allowed the temples to fall in ruins. There were also consequential losses outside the field of the sacred. The early cults had been closely associated with the social structure, and this link was now broken. The different groups—extended families, lineages, clans, hamlets, and villages—were no longer identified with private gods and private rituals, and the political leaders could not now appeal to the myths as precedent for their secular authority. Any rule of conduct incorporated in the old religious system was also robbed of its former supernatural sanction. The natives were even obliged to revise many of their moral values. They had to learn to condemn certain actions formerly encouraged and to encourage others formerly condemned. Our problem in this instance is thus to account not for an unexpected rejection of an innovation but for a surprising acceptance.

The answers to our questions must differ according to the circumstances. The earliest converts on the island of Malaita in the Solomons, to take one case, treated the Christian God as though He were more or less an equivalent of their ancestral spirits. The latter were supposed to possess supernatural power with which they could influence mortal affairs. It was assumed that a descendant who honoured them duly with appropriate

F

sacrifices would be awarded success, but that if he committed certain offences he would be afflicted with misfortunes. These first Christians had for the most part become disgruntled either because their offerings had not been followed by prosperity or because their blameless conduct had still not saved them from disasters. They decided to experiment in order to see whether God exercised similar power and would give them a better deal. They hoped by attending church services to secure His goodwill but were prepared, or so they said, to accept punishment for violating any of the ten taboos set forth so clearly in the Commandments. Many of them felt that the subsequent results justified their action. They then went further and substituted prayers for the old magical spells with which they had sought to cure disease and secure good harvests and satisfactory hauls of fish.[1]

At a later stage, after more prolonged contact with the West, numbers of the natives were prepared to trust the missionaries more and consider their sayings closely. These missionaries, to begin with, were members of the politically and economically superior group, and for this reason inevitably acquired some status. Like the other white men, they also appeared to be rich, owned so many possessions, and obviously knew so much. In addition, they were in a position to win more personal respect and even love. They alone of the permanent foreign residents in the colony followed a calling that compelled them to live side by side with the native community and learn the vernacular tongues. They visited the afflicted, tended the sick, and were interested in the humblest villager and prepared to work for his well-being. In conversations they discussed many other matters besides religion, and some of their statements could be put to the test and proved right. The converts made the transfer and concluded that therefore everything must be correct. Many of us follow the same false reasoning when an acknowledged expert in physics or chemistry makes a pronouncement on social affairs. We conclude that because he is a scientist in one field

[1] H. I. Hogbin, *Experiments in Civilization*, London, 1939, Chap. IV.

his thinking will be scientific also in others in which he knows no more, and possibly less, than the average citizen.

Today the missions can also offer the Melanesians a concrete reward. The natives want economic equality with the whites, and many of them have come to recognize that education is a necessary preliminary. The village schools, however, are controlled and staffed by the Churches. Christians alone therefore have the opportunity to learn reading and writing. The abandonment of pagan ways is not considered to be too big a price to pay.

Finally, there are natives who become Christians to satisfy their ambition. Church elders, catechists, and teachers all exert some influence in the village, and such offices are in consequence thought by some to be desirable.

Tangible rewards of a different kind had earlier contributed much to the conversion of the islanders in the central Pacific. Missionaries in the first half of the nineteenth century were often prepared to distribute arms, thus enabling the natives to carry on their old feuds under the guise of a crusade against the heathen. The Tahitian chief Pomare, by rights the overlord of one small district, succeeded with mission guns and ammunition in extending his sway over the whole population.[1]

Negative rewards can have almost as strong an appeal. Many religious observances are burdensome, and a declaration by a missionary that those connected with pagan beliefs were unnecessary sometimes served as an excuse for neglecting them. The conduct of persons related in certain ways was in the Huon Gulf region of New Guinea governed by regulations that were in part supported by supernatural sanctions. Cousins of a particular type and also kinsmen-by-marriage were required to show mutual respect, and to this end were forbidden to eat together without covering their mouth from sight by a mat or to address one another by name or by a kinship term. An individual who inadvertently broke the rules was obliged to offer heavy damages to regain his reputation but was still

[1] Ari'i Taimai (T. Salmon), *Memoirs*, Paris, 1901.

believed to be in danger of illness inflicted by the spirits. The missionaries maintained that such restrictions were ridiculous and advised the Christians to pay no attention to them. The natives ignored the counsel, until at length, with more extensive contact, the relationships began to be modified and the old code became increasingly oppressive. Nobody at this stage was aware that Christianity demands obedience to other rulings that may be equally irksome. The practising Roman Catholic, Anglican, or Lutheran, for instance, must cleave to his spouse no matter how incompetent or faithless she may be; and even if she proves to be barren he still cannot take a second wife.

Other factors operated in New Zealand. The appeal of the new religion here was primarily for its shielding and protecting influence. The Maori received firearms from whalers and traders and, like the Tahitians, used them mainly against their traditional tribal enemies. Minor quarrels, which previously might have been settled after a trivial skirmish, developed into bloody wars of extermination. The first European settlement took place on the north-eastern coast, and the natives of this region thus had the advantage over the peoples of the interior and the south. The northerners, indeed, killed or captured so many that ordinary economic life came to a standstill. The missionaries secured the release of the captives, indoctrinated them, and then sent them as catechists to their relatives and friends.[1]

South Africa furnishes a similar example. Early missionary work synchronized here with a great native upheaval, and to this fact most of the fruitful results can be attributed.

'Petty intertribal wars, with little bloodshed, had been common enough among the Bantu, but when the missionaries came to the country it was just one great battlefield [writes Eiselen]. The tribes of the Free State and the Transvaal had been reduced to terrible straits by the wars of Tshaka and his emulators and by the ensuing years of famine. Starving remnants of once

---

[1] Apirana Ngata and I. L. G. Sutherland, 'Religious Influences', *The Maori People of Today* (ed. I. L. G. Sutherland), Oxford, 1940, p. 339.

powerful tribes were wandering aimlessly about the country in constant fear of attack by some band of cannibals, or they were eking out a miserable existence in some mountain refuge. To these harassed people the missionaries came like so many Good Samaritans. Their faith in the ancestral gods had been badly shaken, and they were ready to open their ears to a message of love and hope.'

In striking contrast was the attitude of the victorious tyrants Dingaan and Mzilikazi. 'They showed little liking for the Gospel and its teachings of brotherhood and tolerance. In fact all those tribes which emerged with flying colours from the Zulu wars of the early nineteenth century—the Zulu, the Swazi, and the Amandebele of Mapoch—did not in the beginning befriend the missionaries.' [1]

Comfort

Greater comfort means in effect improved food supplies and expanded public services, particularly those connected with preventive and curative medicine, transport, and education. Normally wealth must be increased to cover the additional expenditure. The metropolitan powers during the past decade have paid growing attention to expanding production in the under-developed countries, and experts have gone out to furnish the inhabitants with schemes giving the best methods of procedure. These efforts have met with indifferent success, and too often the advice has been disregarded. With certain notable exceptions, then, the simpler peoples have tended to reject innovations that might have made their life easier.

Such inertia puzzles those who imagine that we ourselves are ever ready to improve our conditions. In fact we often hesitate just as much as the natives. Thus those of us who live in places subject to recurrent catastrophes can rarely be

[1] W. M. Eiselen, 'Christianity and the Religious Life among the Bantu', *Western Civilization and the Natives of South Africa* (ed. I. Schapera), London, 1934, p. 68. Cf. B. Hutchinson, 'Some Social Consequences of Nineteenth Century Missionary Activity among the South African Bantu', *Africa*, Vol. XXVII, pp. 160–77.

induced to move elsewhere. In Italy the farmers go back to the slopes of Mount Vesuvius after each eruption, and in New South Wales the residents of towns built on rivers that are liable to flooding always return when the waters have receded. One stream has broken its banks six times during the last ten years, on each occasion causing loss of life and damage to property. Clearly much of this destruction would have been avoided had the settlements been resited at an earlier date on higher ground. The chief obstacle was, and still is, expense. No insurance to cover flood damage was available, and the municipal authorities lacked the capital required for constructing new roads, power stations, reservoirs, sewage disposal plants, and so forth. Individual householders, even if they had had the money, were naturally unwilling to rebuild their dwellings in a spot which, though safe, was miles away from their work and out of reach of normal amenities.

Raising living standards must always be a long-term project, with advancement proceeding stage by stage. If the basis is to be agriculture, then the planners would do well to carry out intensive research to determine the potentialities of the region. Should they fail to do so, and in consequence tender bad advice, they may never be trusted again. The British Government, discouraged by the groundnut fiasco in East Africa, is unlikely to try out any other large-scale farming enterprise in the colonies even if scientists bring forward incontrovertible evidence that a certain area is suitable. Native peoples react similarly. An unsound suggestion may cause them to turn away from all counsel, even the best.[1]

Economic progress can thus be compared with a hurdle race, where the obstacles to be surmounted are arranged in strict order one behind the other. There are no optional jumps and no short cuts. If the runner omits a hurdle and tries to pass from number one to number three he must either go back or

---

[1] In Burma the introduction of deep ploughing into rice cultivation without a preliminary survey had the unfortunate result of breaking up the clay band that held the water (see J. S. Furnivall, *Colonial Policy and Practice*, Cambridge, 1948, p. 327).

else lose all chance of being allowed to continue. The pre-industrial peoples are like a contestant who is so obsessed with reaching the winning-post that he wants to go towards it by the most direct route. They do not understand that they would then be disqualified as soon as they started. If they agree to abide by the rules, as some do, they are apt to become discouraged by the difficulties and lack of immediate rewards and to retire after the first few leaps. As an inducement they need small prizes at various interim points in the race.

Technical aid programmes for some of the Asian countries face an additional problem. The authorities here usually give a higher priority to changes unrelated to economics. The Indian government recently decided for political reasons to replace English with Hindi as the *lingua franca* and language of instruction. Hindi has its roots in the Indian past, and its use will help to remove the memory of conquest, foster national unity, and break down the barrier separating the educated and the poorer classes. Development, however, will be retarded. Those who do not now speak Hindi will need time for learning it, and all text-books will have to be translated. Further, foreign experts will no longer be able to find assistants who can understand what they are saying, and Indian students will fit less easily into occidental universities.[1]

The future will be full of interest should other peoples after securing their independence place the same high value on eradicating the reminders of their domination by foreigners. If the Irish succeed in suppressing English in favour of Erse, till recently almost a dead language, perhaps we shall see the day when Africans will want to give up maize, now in many areas the staple crop although it was introduced from America by the Portuguese.

Adjustment to the existing culture is so automatic, especially after generations of poverty, that many peoples do not recognize its inadequacy. They are satisfied provided a bare

[1] Cf. M. E. Opler, 'The Problem of Selective Cultural Change,' *The Progress of the Underdeveloped Areas* (ed. B. F. Hoselitz), pp. 126–27.

sufficiency of nourishment can be produced, a small measure of health maintained, and the lives of a few children saved. Their preference in consequence is for coping and patching rather than for adventuring and exploring. The approach of general famine has at times been so gradual that when at length it arrived the population was too weak to take any action, and the situation was thus beyond remedy. The writers who refer to the potato not as the blessing of Ireland but its curse—had the Irish been reduced to starvation earlier, it is argued, they might have thrown off the English yoke then—are possibly over-estimating the effect of an empty belly. Instead of revolting, the peasants might have died out.

This conservative outlook is sometimes reinforced by religion. The concept of progress is in primitive societies unknown, and among such groups the golden age is placed not in the hypothetical future but in the past. Natives may thus ignore suggestions regarding better agricultural methods even when the intention is not to introduce a new crop for sale but to grow more of the indigenous crop for internal consumption. They will not listen because they believe that tilling the ground in a manner unsanctioned by ancestral usage is morally wrong. Corn cultivation in Yucatan is not simply a way of producing food, Redfield and Warner tell us, but a form of worship.

'Before a man plants he builds an altar in the field and prays there. He must not speak boisterously in the cornfield: it is a sort of temple. The cornfield is planted as an incident in the perpetual contract between supernatural beings and man. By this agreement the supernaturals yield part of what is theirs— the riches of the natural environment—to man. In exchange men are pious and perform the traditional ceremonies in which offerings are made to the supernaturals. These ceremonies are a dramatic expression of this understanding.' [1]

[1] R. Redfield and W. L. Warner, 'Cultural Anthropology and Modern Agriculture', *Farmers in the Changing World; 1940 Yearbook of Agriculture*, United States Department of Agriculture, Washington, 1940, p. 989.

Similar statements might be made of a number of communities.

Here and there a particular doctrine, peculiar to one or more societies, may serve as an added check. On Manam Island, off the north coast of New Guinea, the natives think that a person who ate the food that he himself had helped to grow would be liable to supernatural punishment. They say that he would become seriously ill and might perhaps die. Housewives after cooking the evening meal accordingly make exchanges with one another before serving their families. A man would need a big inducement to produce a heavier crop if his neighbours were alone to reap the benefit.[1]

Unfamiliar types of seed giving a bigger yield may also be resisted perhaps on general religious grounds, or on account of some special religious tenet, or for æsthetic reasons. In Dobu, an island off eastern New Guinea, each person eats only taro corms that are the progeny of suckers inherited from his or her matrilineal ancestors. So rigid is this rule that the women cook for themselves and their husbands separately.[2] The Spanish–American farmers of New Mexico actually tried out an improved variety of maize offered to them by government agricultural experts; but they abandoned it after only a season's trial. They were satisfied with the harvest, which was larger than usual, but their wives objected. Corn pancakes are here the main food, and the flour ground from the new grain was heavier in texture, yellower in colour, and different in taste from that made from the old.[3]

Pastoral tribes are often as reluctant as agriculturalists to accept advice given in their own interest. Many African peoples have refused to reduce the size of their herds despite the poor

[1] He would only do so if success in gardening was so highly valued that he could acquire extra prestige from growing an abundant crop. The best gardeners in the Trobriand Islands are always highly esteemed, but each man is obliged to give away a large portion of his harvest to his sisters and their children (B. Malinowski, *Crime and Custom in Savage Society*, London, 1926, Chap. VII).

[2] R. F. Fortune, *Sorcerers of Dobu*, London, 1932, pp. 18, 102.

[3] A. Apodaca, 'Corn and Custom', *Human Problems in Technological Change* (ed. E. H. Spicer), New York, 1952, pp. 35–9.

quality of the beasts and the growing worry of soil erosion caused by overstocking. Milk is generally an important item of the diet, but the animals are chiefly desired for other reasons. Marriage is not legal unless the kinsfolk of the man hand over several head of cattle to the kinsfolk of the woman, court fines must be paid in cattle, cattle are killed to provide a feast for high-ranking visitors, and cattle also serve as offerings to the ancestors for securing their protection in worldly affairs. One beast is usually regarded for such purposes as equivalent to any other, and each man therefore aims at owning as many as possible regardless of their condition.[1]

Primitive peoples are even more averse to growing new crops than to adopting unfamiliar methods to produce a greater supply of the old one. The traditional food is bound up with so much of the culture that a change in the one is likely to result in a change in the other. This food is always the focus for emotional associations and also acts as a channel for interpersonal relations. It is the only offering fit for the gods, and as a gift from one man to another it signifies love, trust, or approval, depending on the social context. The killing of someone who has shared the family meal is looked upon almost universally as a heinous offence.

The inhabitants of Mentawai, off the west coast of Sumatra, set a high value on their festivals, which they celebrate with feasts of taro. Their Malayan neighbours cultivate rice and have more to eat, but the Mentawai refuse to copy them because if they did so they would be forced to give up the festivals. Rice is not only considered to be inappropriate for formal occasions, but it also demands unremitting attention. Work in the taro gardens, on the other hand, can be so arranged that no serious loss results when it is from time to time neglected.[2] Some of the highland peoples of New Guinea display similar stubbornness in clinging to the sweet potato. They imagine that this vegetable, the staple, is the chief source of

---

[1] Cf. G. and M. Wilson, *Analysis of Social Change*, Cambridge, 1945, p. 94.
[2] E. Loeb, *Sumatra; Its History and People*, Vienna, 1935, p. 163.

energy and believe that if it were not available they would lose their vitality.[1]

Further objections have to be overcome before a people will undertake the cultivation of a commercial crop. New uses of land, manpower, time and material demand a reassessment of preferences. Land is apt to create some of the worst difficulties. The rule of inheritance in many communities provides for the division of ground on a man's death among a number of heirs, sometimes all his sons, sometimes the sons of all his sisters. Such a system leads to fragmentation, to many small plots scattered over a wide area. A primitive gardener, producing perhaps taro or yams, is not much inconvenienced, but for modern farming and the efficient use of machinery consolidation is essential.

Co-operation also raises new issues. In primitive conditions, although much of the work is done by the family, lineage mates and fellow clansmen are called in for the heavier jobs, like clearing, fencing, and harvesting. A person is born into a lineage or a clan, and this mutual aid in agriculture is incidental to a multitude of other duties. The co-operative units of an industrial society are different: they are set up for a specific purpose.

Re-allocating time and material resources is a further problem. Peasant farmers have little capital, a lack to some extent overcome by increased application of labour, which appears to cost nothing. In the Caribbean Islands the most popular crop with small farmers is maize. No cash outlay is called for, and the return, though only seven cents for each hour worked, is speedy. Sugar would yield twenty-three cents, but the canes would first have to be bought, and the harvest would not be ready for over a year. In this same region much time and land are also wasted. If fodder were to be planted the seed would cost money. The farmers therefore deliberately leave large areas uncultivated from which they can collect the wild grasses.[2]

[1] I observed this myself in 1944. Mr M. J. Meggitt tells me that the same belief was current in 1957.

[2] A. L. Jolly, 'Small-Scale Farm Management Problems', *South Pacific*, Vol. VIII, p. 84.

A bigger income does not in itself guarantee higher living standards. These will remain as they are at present unless schools, libraries, and centres of adult education are provided. Many peoples who have more money to spend today squander it through ignorance. Some of them buy fripperies, and others beggar themselves by giving larger feasts on the traditional pattern. The Spanish American farmers of New Mexico even make a practice of hoarding their gains in silver dollars.[1]

But general education by itself is still not enough: methods of birth control must also be adopted. Technological advance, unless accompanied by restrictions on breeding, in the end will depress living standards. In earlier times, when the death-rate was high, the population figure probably remained almost stationary. Today, thanks to modern hygiene and medical practice, it is everywhere increasing. Yet large families go on being encouraged. Social status is often still bound up with the number of children, and many peoples continue to believe that a person's happiness in the world to come will depend on his descendants offering sacrifices to his shade. Such anachronistic attitudes may not be easy to eradicate.

Status and Prestige

Fame is everywhere a qualification for social distinction, and all peoples approve of those who achieve an outstanding success. We respect our leading figures in sport, the professions, science, and the arts; and natives look up to their chief warriors, craftsmen, and magicians. The pursuit of enhanced prestige in these fields may at times lead to social change, as when a noted warrior like the Zulu Tshaka seeks to raise his reputation still higher by adopting a new weapon (in this instance the assegai) and inciting his companions to undertake an expedition against other communities.[2] Few persons are born with the necessary talents for winning renown of this sort, however, and such incidents are probably rare.

---

[1] *Cultural Patterns and Technological Change* (ed. M. Mead), p. 202.
[2] E. A. Ritter, *Zulu Shaka*, London, 1955, pp. 25-31.

Birth also merits esteem if an hereditary upper class is recognized. Persons of humble origin then try to acquire extra privileges by stressing any remote or obscure relationship with the nobility. In parts of Polynesia, where the male line is usually emphasized, a man whose mother is higher in rank than his father generally chooses to trace his descent through her. The Maori of New Zealand and the Hawaiians had few scruples about actually falsifying their genealogies if by so doing they could advance themselves.

Possessions that are the sole prerogative of a nobleman are accepted as a sign of his social superiority. If then for some reason they become more easily accessible, the lower orders may make an effort to obtain them. In earlier days in Germany the aristocracy alone owned saddle horses, which they used for riding around their estates to supervise the workmen. The German peasants who migrated to southern Brazil found that there a hack was cheap. The argument that saddle horses were in this environment unnecessary carried no weight, and each new arrival bought one.[1]

This urge to purloin the symbols of rank can soon lead to changes in social relationships. Unless the members of the upper class succeed in adopting something else as their special mark the social division between them and the commoners becomes blurred. The Elizabethan writer Phillip Stubbes, as was mentioned earlier, feared that the artisans of his day, by taking to the fine clothing hitherto reserved for the gentry, might soon create general disorder. He thought that the structure would crumble if a gentleman was no longer easily recognizable by his appearance. Yet there have been cases of commoners refusing to take advantage of new-found opportunities. Ashanti peasants will not imitate the dress of the royal clans. This is fashioned from hand-made cloth decorated with certain patterns that Lancashire manufacturers can easily duplicate. The people consider that the sale of such material is in bad taste

[1] E. Willems, 'Acculturation and the Horse Complex among German Brazilians', *American Anthropologist*, Vol. XLVI, pp. 153–61.

and decline to buy it.[1] We might react similarly if our shops were to offer us replicas in rayon and rabbit of the Queen's silk and ermine ceremonial robes.

The influence of the aristocracy of birth, where it existed, is now diminishing, and the aristocracy of wealth is tending to become paramount. Mere ownership of a banking account, or its equivalent, is insufficient as a recommendation for prestige, nevertheless, and misers are invariably the subject of mockery. The riches must be spent in a way approved by the society. Among ourselves the type and quantity of a man's possessions are the hallmark of his status—though if he has plenty of the right things and is also of aristocratic descent he may be doubly respected. Most of our suburban householders are ready to incur heavy debts in their efforts to outdo one another. Each aims at having the most ostentatious furnishings, the biggest television set or record-player, and the car with the largest area of chromium plating. If he succeeds at one level he can always go higher by moving to a more exclusive street and undertaking more lavish expenditure on such items as schooling for his sons, and furs, jewellery, and fashionable clothing for his womenfolk. Social change occurs as fresh goods come on the market and living habits are thereby modified. Manufacturers are well aware of the appeal of prestige, and many advertisements stress not the practical utility of the commodity but the fact that the man who buys it will rise in status. The cartoonist in a recent issue of the *New Yorker* might have been repeating an actual statement when he had a salesman asking a prospective customer, 'Can you afford to let the people next door think you cannot afford this automobile?'

Wealth and money are to us synonymous, but among many primitive peoples this was formerly not so. They had nothing that might have served as a liquid asset capable of being devoted to any one of a wide variety of ends. The principal valuables of many of the Melanesians, for example, were foodstuffs, notably root vegetables, coconuts, and pigs. Except in one or

[1] M. Herskovits, *Man and His Works*, New York, 1951, pp. 559-60.

two areas there were no social classes, and the whole population carried out the same kind of tasks, cooked the same sort of meals, and dwelt amid the same style of household furnishings. A man could neither eat his surplus wealth nor spend it on anything immediately useful and therefore derived no direct benefit from it. Yet custom provided a method whereby he could use it to raise his prestige. There were frequent opportunities for hospitality, and he advanced himself by preparing more and more feasts at which larger and larger quantities of taro, yams, nuts, and pork were distributed among the guests.

Melanesian economy is based on reciprocity. Every service rendered and every gift presented has in theory to be returned by a counter service or a counter gift. A man desirous of erecting a new house, for instance, enlisted the help of a number of his neighbours, and the job proceeded as a co-operative enterprise. But he was obliged to feed the workers at the end of each day and at appropriate intervals to invite them to a feast. If he gave them more food than usual, they repaid the compliment by enlarging the house and making it as fine as possible. They fastened extra sheets of thatch to the roof, chose timber of good quality for the walls, and widened the veranda. Often, too, they carved the barge-boards and attached wooden images to the ridge-pole. A superior dwelling thus signified that the owner was wealthy and hence socially prominent.

Public buildings, such as the men's club-houses, demanded the collaboration of several villages. The host community was then under the obligation of furnishing a very large feast indeed. The size of the completed club was always directly proportional to the amount of food supplied. Neighbouring settlements were frequently in friendly competition, each striving to outdo its rivals.

The association of prestige with better housing largely accounts for the extensive use in present-day Melanesia of corrugated iron. Provided the settlement is near the coast, and transport presents no great difficulty, many natives try to have at least the roof of their dwelling made from sheet metal. This material is more durable than the old sago-leaf thatch, but it is less comfortable to live with. The day temperature of the interior of the house is hotter by several degrees, and at night the moisture condenses on the under surface of the metal and falls on the bedding.

The residents of each settlement today also do their best to put up the most imposing church in the vicinity. One small New Guinea congregation, when the average wage for a native labourer was 7s. per month, paid £400 for iron and sawn timber alone. The hideous edifice when finished was as hot inside as a baker's oven and would have held a group three times the size, but everybody was proud to boast that there was not another church so grand within a day's sail by canoe.

At times an entire society acquires status from its great wealth. In some of the mountain areas of New Guinea the natural resources are meagre in the extreme, and here the natives have always considered themselves to be raw provincials by comparison with the more fortunately situated peoples of the coast and riverine plains. The mountain dwellers in the past were glad to take their dance forms and religious rituals from the lowlands, and now Western goods and Christian beliefs follow the same pathways.[1] Adolescents in Europe and Australia have a similar attitude to Hollywood. They look upon the film centre as a model and adopt the accent, slang terms, and fashions in clothing of the favourite stars of the moment.

A situation of this kind gave rise to one of the rare recorded instances of direct rather than consequential changes in social relationships. Certain of the aboriginal tribes in Australia deliberately modified their kinship system and marriage rules to bring themselves into line with others whose customs they admired.

Indonesian traders, as well as visiting Arnhem Land, made regular voyages for many years to the Kimberley coast of

---

[1] M. Mead, 'The Mountain Arapesh: I, An Importing Culture', *Anthropological Papers of the American Museum of Natural History*, Vol. XXXVI, Part 3, New York, 1938.

north-western Australia. Why the first changes took place we shall now never be able to discover, but the aborigines of the region, as a result of contact with the outsiders, adopted circumcision, sub-incision, tree burial, a cult involving cave paintings, and the grouping of kindred into eight intermarrying subsections. These people, possibly because they also owned the first steel tools, were so envied by the tribes nearby that they came to be treated as the purveyors of more advanced customs. Field workers in recent years have traced the fanwise spread of the new fashions, which moved independently and at different rates, to the south, south-east, and east. Subsections reached Arnhem Land in the period between 1912, when Spencer reported that they were not present, and 1947, the date of an expedition by Ronald and Catherine Berndt.[1]

Throughout Australia persons who co-operate in any way can always assume a genealogical connection. They refer to one another by kinship terms and model their conduct on the pattern considered appropriate to the particular relationship. Everyone is also provided from birth with a number of potential spouses, to all of whom, again, a genealogical connection can be postulated. No new terms are applied after a marriage has taken place, and husbands and wives, parents-in-law and children-in-law, and brothers-in-law and sisters-in-law continue with those used previously. Behaviour, too, except that of the married couple, remains basically unaltered.

Subsections represent a considerable elaboration of this social system. Extra kinship terms must be introduced, new patterns of behaviour worked out, and the rules of marriage changed. If there are no subsections the correct partners are cross-cousins; if there are subsections the partners are the children of cross-cousins.[2] The problems connected with the

---

[1] A. P. Elkin, 'Complexity of Social Organization in Arnhem Land', *Southwestern Journal of Anthropology*, Vol. VI, pp. 1–20; and A. P. Elkin, R. M. and C. H. Berndt 'Social Organization of Arnhem Land', *Oceania*, Vol. XXI, pp. 253–301.

[2] The expression 'cross cousin' is used for the children of the father's sisters and of the mother's brothers. The children of the father's brothers and of the mother's sisters are known as 'parallel cousins'.

G

switch over taxed the ingenuity of the aborigines. We know that the elders worked out solutions at joint conferences during the big inter-tribal meetings, though there is no information on how the decisions were enforced. It is of interest that the sub-sections of western Arnhem Land bear the same names as those of the southern tribes, where the languages are different, and that here the re-grouping already has support from the mytho-logy, which in theory never alters.

Foreign customs often enjoy great prestige in a group sub-ject to the early stages of political domination. Most of the Melanesians, who previously wore very little clothing or none at all, today regard shirts as a mark of social distinction. During the Pacific war, when they and the army labour corps were fre-quently engaged side by side at the same task, the European soldiers worked for comfort's sake in trousers alone while many of the natives sweated in an upper garment. Here we have the explanation of why sewing-machines are more popular than clocks. A man with a machine of his own—and most of them are worked by men rather than by women—can make the clothing now regarded as so essential: a clock he still thinks of as a luxury.

One final point must be noted. It should not be assumed that the prestige motive always works for change: it may operate in the reverse direction and prevent change taking place. The white Australian male is proverbially casual in his dress, and in the tropics of his own country, in northern Queensland, he is content to go without a jacket. But if he moves a few miles closer to the Equator, to New Guinea, and has social ambitions, he garbs himself almost as though he were living in the tem-perate zone. He does this partly because the conventions are of greater significance among the few thousand Europeans of a colonial outpost, partly because he wishes to accentuate the social distance between himself and the natives. For the same reasons he also likes his wife when attending formal functions to wear gloves.

Focal Interest

Brief consideration of a theory put forward by Herskovits and, independently, by Linton will form a fitting conclusion to this chapter. Every society, they maintain, focuses attention on one aspect of its culture at the expense of the other aspects, and change occurs here much more readily than elsewhere.[1]

'The fact that the interests of a people tend to concentrate on a given phase of their culture has been established by studies reported in many monographs', says Herskovits. He cites as an example the overwhelming importance that we attach to technology, the Australian aborigines to kinship, the East African tribes to cattle, the Toda of southern India to rituals associated with the dairy, the Polynesians to status arising from birth, and the Melanesians to prestige derived from economic activities. The things that mark a culture outstandingly, he continues, tend also to dominate the lives of the members of the society concerned.

'Because such matters are important to them, people will think and talk a great deal about personalities, events, and possibilities lying in this aspect of their culture. As a result of this interest and the concomitant discussions that are carried on, possibilities for realignment will emerge, and emerge with enough frequency so that the resistance to the idea of something new would be lessened. It is apparent that a suggestion of change in a phase of life that is taken for granted and seldom discussed will meet with greater resistance than in one where the phenomenon is under common discussion, and various possibilities in its form and function are thus constantly being suggested. In the former instance, the seed falls on barren ground; in the latter, the soil is fallow. Therefore, we can state that the greatest variation in custom can be looked for in the

[1] M. Herskovits, 'The Process of Culture Change', *Science of Man in the World Crisis* (ed. R. Linton), New York, 1945, pp. 143–70; and *Man and His Works*, pp. 523–60; and R. Linton, 'Present World Conditions in Cultural Perspective', *Science of Man in the World Crisis*, pp. 201–21.

focal aspects of a culture, and this represents either potential or achieved social change.'[1]

In support of his argument Herskovits quotes the case of the American negroes. Religion provided the focal interest in their original home in West Africa, and with it as their guide they were able to fashion a culture suited to their new social environment.

Religion underlies the West African political structure, Herskovits assures us, and agriculture, trade, and the practice of various crafts all demand the carrying out of religious ceremonies. The local arts are also based on religion. Sculpture, painting, and music are concerned with honouring the gods, and the folk literature consists of tales about the adventures of these beings in the world of men.

'Native psychology, as revealed in discussions of their culture by the West Africans themselves, underscores the interest these people have in the [focal] aspect of their culture. . . . A conversation on kinship terminology turns on the place of the ancestors in the lives of their living descendants. A description of agriculture inevitably entails a discussion of how the farmer assures himself that no places sacred to the supernatural beings are violated when he breaks the ground for a new field.'[2]

Religion, because it was 'focal and thus encouraged experimentation and the acceptance of innovations', enabled the negroes to give meaning to their life as slaves. 'In West Africa gods had been freely borrowed, and there was no reason why the Christian concept of the universe and the powers that rule it could not equally well be incorporated into the system of belief.'[3]

---

[1] M. Herskovits, *Man and His Works*, p. 544. Cf. the following: 'Inventions which are along the lines of a society's dominant interests have a much better chance of being accepted and incorporated into the culture than those which are not. People feel that even a slight improvement along these lines is worth the trouble of readjusting other parts of the culture. The same thing holds for borrowing from other societies, one of the most important processes of cultural growth. People will borrow things that they are interested in while blandly ignoring other things seemingly of greater obvious advantage.' (R. Linton, *op. cit.*)   [2] *Ibid.*, p. 552.   [3] *Loc. cit.*

Critical examination of the theory at once reveals a difficulty. How is the focal aspect of a culture to be located? Counting the number of pages allotted by the author of an ethnographical report to each separate part—kinship, economics, religion, and so forth—could be misleading. It might well be that he had given greater attention to what he and not the people found fascinating, or he might have felt that certain activities, because of their complexity or unusualness, demanded more detailed treatment than the rest. The kinship systems of the Australian aborigines are exceedingly intricate, and the linkage between the terms used and everyday behaviour is also closer than is customary. It follows that in all general monographs on Australian tribes the account of kinship is of disproportionate length. We would not be justified, however, in saying that therefore kinship is the focus of aboriginal culture. This may be so, but a decision could only be reached on the basis of more positive evidence.

The advice Herskovits offers is no better. He says that the focus can be deduced from the frequency with which given themes crop up in conversation. In the course of field work I myself have known days and even weeks when the one topic was on everybody's lips, but the reason was always obvious. A great feast or an important ceremony was contemplated, or a suspected case of sorcery had aroused fears that were normally dormant. Native peoples in ordinary conditions discuss all sorts of subjects, and the opinion of an ethnographer about which predominates is likely to be highly subjective. Few workers to date have been supplied with recording machines and sufficient tape to provide the material for statistical analysis. But even definite proof that the members of a certain community talk about some matter constantly would still not establish beyond doubt that this was the focus of their culture. If we are to believe Herskovits, Western cultures revolve around technology. White Australians, nevertheless, have an overwhelming interest in what is locally called 'sport'; that is to say, gambling, horse- and dog-racing, and watching specialists play such competitive games as football, cricket, and tennis. Most of the governments of the individual states conduct lotteries, five out of the nine main radio networks devote their full programmes on Saturday afternoons to 'sporting' services, all the national newspapers publish large 'sporting' sections daily, and much time is spent in arguing about betting odds and the form of animals and teams. It appears that some Australians even regard 'sport' as of greater value than security. During the War an emergency measure banning mid-week horse-racing was much criticized. A possible explanation for the discrepancy is that these Australians take machinery so much as a matter of course that they no longer give it a thought. Their dark compatriots react in a similar manner to kinship. Field workers state that the aborigines, except when changing over to subsections, scarcely mention kinship at all.

We can actually envisage a situation in which a people would speak less about their main interest than about other topics. If the members of a community value warlike prowess above the satisfaction of hunger and regularly neglect agriculture in order to raid their enemies, then the chances are that the frustrated desire for nourishment will colour many of their conversations. Australian soldiers during World War II, as soon as they moved to forward areas and were deprived of customary meals and the society of women, talked about food and sexual indulgence with monotonous regularity. On the other hand, there are times when social taboos forbid the mention of something that is uppermost in a person's mind. These same soldiers were willing to admit afterwards that they had often been frightened, but so long as the danger persisted they uttered no word of fear and were careful to make no audible calls for help from the Deity. The American chaplain who is reported to have remarked of his fellow countrymen that there were no atheists in foxholes might have judged that few Australians were anything else. Such a conclusion would have been wrong.

A further objection is that it is not at all clear why, even if the focal interest were apparent, this part of the culture should be especially susceptible to change. The sceptic could point out that individual men and women fight to defend what they hold to be sacred and that in consequence the dominant aspect of a culture is more likely to persist unaltered.[1] He would be able to cite as supporting evidence such facts as the unwillingness of Australians to modify the racing rules and the football, cricket, and tennis codes and their indifference to any unfamiliar game, such as lacrosse. The instance of religion serving as a continuing focus for the American negroes can also be disposed of. What else but beliefs could slaves take with them?—certainly not kinship, or a legal system, or economics, or political organization. Moreover, as was mentioned earlier, persons who are unable to take practical steps to alleviate the misery of their present life are especially prone to grasp at the promise of a better existence in the world to come.

The theory might have had some appeal had focal interest been carefully defined. The fact that several distinct types of phenomena were being grouped together would then have been apparent. Herskovits's foci include bonds between persons, items of wealth, and religion. He thus confuses relationships, cultural objects, and institutions.

Relationships can on occasion provide the basis for a whole social system. If these change, the structure of the society is no longer the same. Examples would be the administration preventing a chief from exercising his customary authority and the members of a matrilineal group deciding to hand their property to their sons rather than to their nephews. Cultural objects are never of such direct structural significance. The cattle of the pastoral peoples of Africa, for instance, serve as a means of expressing relationships indirectly. As was indicated, they are exchanged when a marriage takes place, when compensation is

---

[1] Mr M. J. Meggitt informs me that, although he does not consider the pig exchange to be the focal interest of the Enga of the New Guinea highlands, these natives certainly devote much attention to the activities connected with it. Government officers disapprove of the exchange because supplies afterwards are seriously depleted. The transaction continues to be carried out, nevertheless, and, as well as the pigs, all sorts of Western goods now change hands.

paid after an offence, and when peace is concluded between two opposing factions. Modifications of the structure may occur if fresh methods of using the beasts are introduced or if money is substituted for any of the customary payments, but such changes are consequential. Institutions are different again. Although the Toda devote much of their time to dairy rituals, it is conceivable that the details could suffer much interference without any major structural loss.

Herskovits has also failed to analyse focal interest in terms of values. Earlier in this chapter I said that change begins when an opportunity presents itself for realizing an established value in a new way. We want to know how the dominant relationships are then affected. In former times a native of Guadalcanal, in the Solomons, was obliged to help his maternal uncles in order to satisfy his basic needs. They welcomed him as a clansman in return for this assistance, gave him land to cultivate, and protected him in time of trouble. Today he can earn a livelihood by accepting employment with a European. If part of his time is occupied in working for wages, then less is available for assisting his uncles. Their obligation to him is diminished, and they are free in consequence to devote more attention to the welfare of their sons. Dominant relationships may also be upset when the achievement of one value comes into conflict with the achievement of another. Throughout most of Melanesia in earlier days the elders acquired both prestige and a reasonable chance of living at the maximum standard of comfort available by handing out the traditional valuables as bride price for their young kinsmen. People honoured them for their generosity, and the young men paid back the debt by offering their labour for various tasks. Where bride price is still offered but cash has taken the place of the old type of wealth the senior men are in a quandary. They could derive prestige from contributing, but they do not have much money, and by using it in this way they deprive themselves of the means of purchasing European goods. The tendency is therefore towards a loosening of the ties binding the two age groups together.

A hypothesis that depends on the identification of something and fails to provide a means for its recognition cannot be regarded as helpful. When it also omits detailed definition and avoids analysis, we may perhaps be pardoned for ignoring it.

CHAPTER IV

Enforced Change

F EAR of punishment can be as strong a motive for modifying conduct as the promise of a reward, and changes have
often been brought about by the passing of new laws and regulations backed up by such penalties as hanging, imprisonment,
exile, or the confiscation of property. To be effective, of course,
any threat of retribution must be capable of enforcement. The
Maori of New Zealand paid no attention when the first official
British Resident, James Busby, arrived among them alone and
told them to stop fighting. They nicknamed him 'The Man-o'-
War without Guns' and went on killing one another.

Social values must again be taken into account, however,
and if people rank certain conduct high on their scale of preferences they may refuse to behave differently. Even when no
change is contemplated many persons are prepared to suffer for
the ideals of the group and willingly make personal sacrifices in
pursuit of objectives held to be worthy. They undertake
rituals involving fasting, curtailment of liberty, mutilation, and
torture in order to ward off misfortune or gain enhanced reputation by retaining their composure throughout the period of
ordeal. If commanded to do something they have learned to
regard as wrong they may go further and choose death rather
than obedience. The Roman emperors failed in their efforts to
stamp out Christianity, and in sixteenth-century England
Queen Elizabeth I was equally unsuccessful when she tried to
eradicate Roman Catholicism. In both cases every martyr gave
the survivors added strength and made them more determined
than ever to hold on to their faith. Elizabeth to attain her end

would have been obliged to kill every Catholic in the country, the method employed in an earlier age by the papal forces to root out the Albigensian heresy. Politically powerful minority groups have at times been rebuffed, too, in the endeavour to impose their own sectional values on the population at large. The prohibitionists in the United States are an example.

It should also be noted that on occasion governments have forcibly prevented changes from taking place. Many more Japanese might today be Christians had the authorities not expelled all the European missionaries during the seventeenth century, and Communism could well hold an appeal for some of the natives of New Guinea if the administrations were to stop shielding them from its influence by restricting the issue of permits of entry into the colonies to persons approved by the Australian Security Service. Governments may also decline to introduce changes held by some to be desirable. Thus the Ministry of Territories in Canberra refuses to sanction the establishment of native courts in New Guinea similar to those already existing in the Solomon Islands and parts of Africa. Such institutions would have their origin in the past, but many new features would be called for if they were to function effectively as a means of punishing criminals and settling disputes.[1]

The difficulties associated with blocking change are similar to those encountered in bringing it about. An innovation to which a high social value is attached may be so attractive that the attempt to place it out of reach proves unavailing. Protestantism became deeply entrenched in Tudor England, and the

[1] 'The [United Nations] Mission heard requests ... for the establishment of recognized indigenous courts. ... The Mission understands and appreciates the anxiety of the administration and judiciary lest the premature establishment of native courts, without sufficient preparation and training, should start off on the wrong foot. But it is bound to express the view that the authorities are being excessively cautious in their approach to this question.' (*Current Notes on International Affairs*, Department of External Affairs, Canberra, Vol. XXVII, p. 406.)

For an account of the Solomon Islands courts see H. I. Hogbin, 'Native Councils and Native Courts in the Solomon Islands', *Oceania*, Vol. XIV, pp. 257–83. Proposals for similar courts in New Guinea are outlined in H. I. Hogbin, *Transformation Scene*, London, 1951, Chap. IX.

Marian persecutions were too late to have any lasting effect. Mary's efforts to make the old religion universal once more were indeed as futile as the subsequent activities of her sister on behalf of the new faith. In India also the movement for independence was so strong that the leaders were assured of greater prestige and influence each time they served a gaol sentence. The resources of post-War Britain were probably insufficient to enable her to retain control, though the fact that British public opinion would scarcely have tolerated the setting up of a police State was an additional complication. Moral attitudes to imperialism are today different from those of 1857, when the first Indian rebellion was suppressed.

The reforming process is positive when the governing body is primarily concerned with introducing new practices. Probably the chief interest of the Indian conqueror Tippu Sultan, for example, was the conversion of the vanquished peoples to Islam. They were mostly Hindus, and he ordered them on pain of death to eat beef and submit to the rite of circumcision. They were so ashamed afterwards that they never returned to the old gods.[1] The process is negative when the governing body suppresses practices that it dislikes. The Bechuanaland chief Lentswe, head of the Kgatla tribe, on becoming a Christian issued a decree banning the payment of the traditional bride price, considered to be a mark of paganism. The prohibition coincided with a rise in the divorce rate, which his successors attributed, on insufficient evidence, to this one cause. They accordingly decided to restore the custom in modified form.[2] In general both positive and negative processes operate simultaneously. The colonial administrations in Melanesia have forbidden head-hunting raids as a means of settling disputes and now urge the parties involved in a difference to refer the matter to a court for judgement by a European magistrate.

Innovations that a community accepts voluntarily are only potentially disruptive. The people are active agents and may in

[1] A. C. Mayer, *Land and Society in Malabar*, London, 1952, p. 21.
[2] I. Schapera, *Married Life in an African Tribe*, London, 1940, p. 85.

consequence be able to achieve social integration without a violent disturbance of their social system. Certainly the guns the Tahitian chief Pomare took from the missionaries enabled him to embark on a campaign to subjugate the whole island; but matches had no further effect than saving the natives a slight expenditure of time and energy. Innovations forced upon a society almost invariably cause serious social disintegration. The administration generally fails to understand that consequent readjustments are necessary, and the people, being now passive agents, are not in a position to take the initiative themselves.

An Example of Enforced Change

The Makah of Cape Flattery, the north-western tip of the United States, provide an illustration of deliberately engineered transformation. The government assumed direct control of the tribe in 1863, when white Americans still took it for granted that the Indians were irresponsible children who must be compelled to accept civilization. 'Force is what we need,' an official report stated, 'not only to carry out the wise regulations of the [Indian] department but to make [these people] receive the benefits that we desire to bestow upon them.' Successive Indian agents were empowered both to issue any instruction that they deemed fit and to call upon the army, stationed less than a day's journey away, to see that these were observed. The administrative officers made the natives send their children to a central boarding school, where the teaching was carried out in English; prohibited them from celebrating pagan ceremonies and feasts; and ordered them to live in separate family dwellings instead of large communal houses.[1]

If the present trend continues, the Makah within another generation will be distinguished as a separate community solely by their status as wards of the government and their joint ownership of the land that formed the original reservation. Their settlement is now like any other small American town,

[1] E. Colson, *The Makah*, Manchester, 1953, pp. 9, 101.

the economy is based on money, and the whole tribe is Christian. Even the old language is fast disappearing. The younger adults find English more useful, and the children reserve the vernacular for cursing in the classroom, where the teachers, if they understood the insults, might punish them. Tribal memories linger, but although no one is aware of it, these are constantly being revised as conditions change. Tradition is thus to be considered less as history than as a form of mythology justifying present conduct. Almost the sole behaviour carried over from the past consists of certain kinship loyalties and the remnant of a custom known as the potlatch. The Makah realize that they attach more significance than is usual among Europeans to genealogical relationships and have felt obliged to take special precautions lest the legal system should be endangered. An English judge does not hear a case if one of his relatives is involved, but no extra appointments are made on this account. These people, although the community is small, have a chief judge and three associate judges. The potlatch was a form of feasting that enabled the extended families to acquire social prestige by destroying valuable property and overwhelming their rivals with gifts. Wedding parties now serve a similar purpose, except that the status is today secured not by groups but by individuals. The host, usually the bridegroom's father, advances his claims to social pre-eminence by supplying a lavish meal, and the guests retaliate by presenting the couple with packages of money.[1]

The task of remoulding the Makah presented relatively few obstacles. They never numbered more than 600, and their territory was not extensive. Further, they lived in compact villages along the shore, and the resident agent could readily keep them under surveillance. As they were fishermen without any knowledge of agriculture, they could not fly to the dense forests of the interior, where the difficulty of the terrain might have guaranteed them a measure of freedom. Then they had no need to learn a new form of subsistence to raise their living stan-

[1] E. Colson, *The Makah*, Manchester, 1953, pp. 3, 54, 195, 223, 294.

dards. The fast-growing cities in the vicinity provided a ready market for any fish not required for local consumption, and all that was necessary was an improvement in techniques and a gradual replacement of the canoes with powered trawlers. Thus, although the Makah were dominated politically, prevented from carrying out their customs, and regularly separated for long periods from their children, they were able to compete with whites on the terms that the whites themselves laid down.[1]

A civilizing policy can only be fulfilled in its entirety in such circumstances as these. The governing powers must be able to apply unlimited force over a period of three or four generations and have sufficient faith in their aims to abate any scruples when the occasion arises for using it. They must be prepared to incur heavy expenditure on inaugurating, developing, and maintaining public services, including education for the adults as well as for the children. The people themselves, in their turn, must be living in conditions that permit the exercise of discipline. Either they should be assembled in closely knit settlements, or, if the houses are scattered, communication should be unimpeded by such hazards as deserts, mountain ranges, or dense forests. The change-over will always proceed more easily and smoothly if, as among the Makah, the traditional occupations furnish a foundation for the new economy. Yet, provided the geographical environment is favourable, the difficulties involved in introducing another form of economic life need not be insuperable. Once the physical problems have been overcome—good roads constructed, water supplies assured, and so forth—the chief requirements are encouragement, proper instruction, and endless patience.

Success was rarely achieved even in America. Some of the tribes were so widely dispersed that regimentation proved to be impossible, some had already been broken by wars with the whites, some had been pushed into tiny reservations, and some had lost their basic resources. The Plains Indians, for example,

---

[1] E. Colson, *The Makah*, Manchester, 1953, pp. 283-5.

depended in earlier times almost entirely on the buffalo, and when the herds vanished they could no longer support themselves. The Indian department attempted to turn them into agriculturalists, but the effort failed. The officers chosen for the experiment were untrained and not only neglected to teach the people how to carry out the unfamiliar tasks but also selected crops that were unsuited to the soil and climate. The tribesmen therefore had nothing to live on but the meagre rations supplied by the government. They began looking back to an idealized vision of the past and were soon endeavouring to recreate it by magical means.[1]

In many countries the natives suffered a still worse fate, and in some places, such as south-eastern Australia, they practically died out. The Australian continent, as has been pointed out, provided neither crops for cultivation nor animals for domestication, and the aborigines in their primitive state were of necessity hunters and collectors. They were divided into small clans, each of which owned a separate area. The members of the group had exclusive rights within this territory but none at all in any other part of the country. The whites, when in the late eighteenth century they settled on the east coast, took all the best land for themselves. The people who were dispossessed, even if they had been familiar with the interior, would have been killed by the other tribesmen had they migrated thither. They thus had no alternative but to linger on the fringes of the settlements, where they fell a prey to the diseases attendant on poverty and malnutrition. They might have been taught to become valuable citizens of the young colony, but in those days universal education for the whites had not been thought of, and the few schools were mostly of poor quality.[2] Not until the present generation have aboriginal children been admitted to ordinary State schools on the same

---

[1] E. Colson, *The Makah*, Manchester, 1953, p. 282.

[2] A Commission appointed by the government of New South Wales in 1854 to advise on education reported that of the 202 schools visited 'few are worthy of the name'. Nearly half the marriage certificates issued at that time to white Australians bore crosses, indicating that the parties were illiterate.

footing as children of European descent, and the establishment of good schools in the outlying areas, where aborigines alone are found, is still more recent.[1]

Force and Evasion

Today the amount of force that the majority of colonial governments can bring to bear on the native communities under their care is decidedly limited. The chief reason is lack of funds. The local revenue is inevitably small when the territory is not yet developed and the inhabitants are still technically backward, and even if the metropolitan power makes supplementary grants the total figure remains comparatively insignificant. The income of the New Guinea administrations from all sources for the year 1955, for example, was approximately £7,000,000: Australia, with only six times the population, produced a government income 150 times as large. Colonial expenditure has in consequence to be kept to the minimum, and the needs of no one government department are ever fully met. Public health, public works, education, agriculture, and the rest all suffer, and the number of staff retained for the maintenance of law and order is always less than would be considered safe in a civilized state. Further, the senior officers alone are Europeans, and the native constables in the lower grades are often more in sympathy with their fellow countrymen than with their superiors. These men are trained to help in the task of preventing the cruder forms of violence, but, even if there were more of them and communication were easier, they could hardly be trusted to supervise the changes desired by the administration in the ordinary life of the villages.

Natives in the initial period of contact, once they realized that the white man possessed guns and through these exercised power, were at first inclined to believe that he could compel them to do anything. They now know that he has less authority than they imagined and that many of his orders can be disregarded with impunity. In the meantime, however, certain of

[1] Up to the present no aboriginal has graduated from a university.

H

their social values have changed, and observance of some of the rules can be secured with fewer threats. Thus a reputation for military skill and valour is today not greatly appreciated. Although in the beginning the leaders gave up organizing warlike expeditions reluctantly, they are no longer so anxious to fight. They have learned to enjoy the advantages of living peaceably, without the constant fear of attack, and prefer to go on doing so. In places like southern New Britain, too, where the people thought that a wife ought to be one with her husband even in death, life has come to be more highly esteemed than the fulfilment of the terms of the marriage contract. Widowhood has ceased to be looked upon as shameful, and protective measures to save the woman from being strangled at her spouse's graveside are unnecessary. Then European goods exert such a strong attraction that the natives, in those few places where an indigenous crop can be sold for cash, do not have to be coerced into extending the area under cultivation. The inhabitants of north-eastern New Britain and New Ireland, who at an earlier stage were most reluctant to carry out the order to grow extra coconuts, today run their own plantations on commercial lines.

European social values have also during recent years undergone revision. We of the Anglo-Saxon countries have begun to doubt the political wisdom of imposing our will at all times on others, and, in addition, a tender conscience is leading many of us to question the extent of our moral rights. We are still prepared to employ force in order to give native peoples greater physical security, and we still aim at fostering their economic and political advancement, but we now consider that many of the rules framed by the colonial governments of earlier days were an unjustified interference with personal liberty. The Makah Indians, if they were making their first acquaintance with civilization at the present time, would almost certainly not be compelled to give up their pagan ceremonies or to abandon their traditional secular festivities. Nowadays, too, we do not conscript labour, even for the benefit of the community, unless some grave crisis has occurred. The methods adopted for the opening up of New Guinea prior to 1914 may be compared with those of today. At that time the natives had to build roads without payment, and if the district officer found that the surface of a particular stretch was unsatisfactory he insisted that the offending villagers should lift him in his carriage over the bad patches: now more highways than ever before are under construction, but the workers are engaged on a voluntary basis, treated like other employees, and given the usual wages. It should also be mentioned that an old New Guinea regulation setting out the clothing that natives may wear, although it remains in the statutes, has not been invoked for at least two decades.

Yet despite the fact that native scales of value and our own are at some points drawing closer together, at others they remain far apart. Many of the old conflicts accordingly continue unabated. The inhabitants of all the primitive parts of Melanesia still oppose the regulations designed to prevent the spread of infectious diseases. Differing theories about the causes of illness are at the root of the problem. We mainly base our conclusions on the findings of bacteriology and pathology, new sciences about which the members of simple communities know nothing; moreover, many years must pass before the information will have seeped downwards to the village level.[1] The natives, on the other hand, are still convinced that sickness is brought about by supernatural forces set in motion either by sorcerers or by spirit beings. Ritual to counteract the evil magic or win back the approval of the spirits is hence in their view the chief need. They dismiss instructions about such matters as the disposal of the dead, the use of latrines, the handling of animals, and the improvement of housing as pointless, possibly impious, or even potentially harmful. Unless the government has a fully educated and responsible agent on the spot continuously—and in the remoter areas this is out of the question—it

---

[1] Our æsthetic standards, which differ from those of other peoples, may also be of some slight importance.

has literally no chance of securing obedience. In our society a handful of inspectors succeeds in ensuring the health standards of our eating-places by bringing prosecutions against the few proprietors whose premises are found to be unsatisfactory. But we know all about germs and would not willingly patronize an establishment known to be dirty; and the *restaurateur* is aware that his personal reputation among his friends will suffer if he is judged guilty of a criminal act. In Melanesian societies the inspectors are lacking, cleanliness is less of a virtue, and the man who is fined or imprisoned for breaking laws for which no one can see any valid reason is held to be a martyr rather than a rogue.

The people of Wogeo, when I was living with them during the period 1934–5, had been described as fully under control for the previous twenty years. The island is separated by many miles of open sea from the nearest administrative post, patrol officers paid brief visits only at rare intervals, usually about once annually, and no policeman had ever been stationed there. Contact with the outside world was maintained chiefly by plantation owners seeking labour for their estates, but few of these ever went ashore. The young men were so anxious to enter employment that they paddled out in canoes as soon as a schooner dropped its anchor. Even the missions had paid no attention to the people until towards the end of my stay, when a native teacher at last landed to begin the work of conversion. The result was that although raiding had ceased and steel tools had taken the place of those made from stone, the population conducted most of its affairs in the same manner as in the past. A murder, unknown to the administration, had been committed shortly before my arrival, my presence almost certainly prevented another, and I learned subsequently, when I went back again in 1948, that others had followed my departure, also without coming to the notice of the government officers.

The traditional Wogeo method of dealing with the dead was burial in a shallow grave beneath the floor of the house. The stench was nauseating, but the occupants of the dwelling believed that by subjecting themselves to such unpleasantness they were displaying their respect and affection. Patrol officers banned the practice and ordered the residents of each hamlet to set aside a plot of ground as a cemetery. The islanders carried out the command, and when I reached them every settlement had its enclosure. This was protected from the ravages of the domestic pigs by a stout fence, and the individual graves inside, with decorative shrubs at the head, were all neatly bordered with shells or blocks of white coral. But they were without exception fakes. Only once had a body actually been placed in a burial ground. This incident occurred when a man died during the course of a visit by a government official. Later, after the officer had embarked for the return journey to the mainland, the relatives exhumed the corpse and reinterred it in the more usual place.

Latrines are throughout much of New Guinea treated in similar fashion. The natives dig a deep hole at the back of the house because they know that the patrol officer on his inspections will look to see whether the work has been done and punish them if it has not. Yet they seldom if ever use the excavation for its intended purpose. Busama, the scene of my most recent field work, provided the single example within my experience of one person reporting another for defecating in the bush alongside the village. Such a charge would not have been made in distant Wogeo, but Busama is situated a few miles from the European centre at Lae, and the government office is within easy reach. The accuser, however, could hardly be said to have been outraged. He harboured a grudge against the man concerned and hoped that he would cause him some inconvenience. The latter, too, showed neither shame nor embarrassment at the revelation. He knew that everyone else was alike guilty, and his sole reaction was a burst of anger at having to appear before the court.

The chief reasons for the resistance to latrines are old habits and continuing ignorance.[1] Why when space is plentiful, the

---

[1] The Near East Foundation reported in 1948 that after a campaign for latrines lasting for fifteen years in the rural areas of Greece only two per cent of the farmers

people ask, should anyone bother to walk the few extra paces? They are as a rule careful to avoid the banks of the streams that supply drinking water but have no hesitation in squatting anywhere else in the bush to relieve themselves. They are unaware that parasites from the fæces can penetrate the skin of the feet and cause hookworm or that the swarms of flies may carry dysentery. In some areas an additional argument is put forward. Here the natives fear that sorcerers, by performing rites over stolen excreta, can do them harm. In such places a person feels safe only if he defecates in secrecy. The inhabitants of one mountain region in New Guinea take the exceptional course of always using certain streams so that the fæces will disintegrate rapidly. The coast dwellers lower down are unaware of which rivers have been contaminated.

The government of Uganda was more fortunate in that here the people's dread of sorcery could be utilized. Medical officers convinced the natives that if the latrines were deep, and each person threw in a shovelful of earth after he had used one of them, the matter would be beyond the reach of any magician.[1]

Fear of sorcerers is at times a serious bar to medical research involving the examination of fæces. Lambert, of the Rockefeller Foundation, had the greatest difficulty in securing any specimens at all in Malekula, an island in the New Hebrides. In Rennell, one of the Solomon Islands, his action in enclosing the first specimen in a tin precipitated a panic. Later, after much persuasion, each man who brought in excreta waited until the investigation was finished to make certain that the material was then carefully buried.[2]

The Melanesians are mostly just as reluctant to take steps to keep the domestic pigs out of the villages. (Health officers prefer the animals to be at a distance because their presence en-

---

had installed them (*Culture Patterns and Technical Change* (ed. M. Mead), Paris, 1941, pp. 242–3).

[1] G. Gillandis, 'Rural Housing', *Journal of the Royal Sanitary Institute*, Vol. LX, p. 231.

[2] S. M. Lambert, *A Yankee Doctor in Paradise*, Boston, 1941, pp. 52, 226, 295–6, 304.

courages the flies.) They build a fence around the settlement but leave gaps here and there which they close as soon as they have news that an officer is out on patrol. In the Solomons an order that all the pigs must be confined in sties had to be countermanded when it was learned that the natives chose rather to kill the animals. The pigs when free can forage for much of their food: had they been enclosed the people would have been obliged to feed them night and morning.

Again, in the hill country in New Guinea and the Solomons the natives refuse to live in houses with a raised floor. These are in some respects healthier than those built directly on the ground, but few persons can afford blankets, and the chill night air creeps in through the crevices between the planks. In some areas the space underneath is thought to increase the danger of sorcery in that the magician can crawl in and carry out his rites there. The threat of imprisonment may impel the householder to erect a dwelling of the approved design, but he and his family crowd into a hut alongside, ostensibly the kitchen.[1]

Instances of similar evasion occurred during the War. The members of the labour corps and the refugees from the bombed villages accepted the tins of tomato juice included in the army ration scale but always threw the contents away. The authorities made no explanation of the bodily need for vitamin C, but it is doubtful, had they done so, that the natives could have understood. The addition of sugar would have rendered the juice palatable, or the dieticians might perhaps have imitated the methods of Captain Cook. He adopted a subterfuge to induce his men to eat sauerkraut, thereby preserving them from scurvy, till that time one of the major causes of death on long voyages.

'The men at first would not eat it [he wrote in his journal] until I put in practice a method I never once knew to fail with seamen—and this was to have some of it dressed every day for

[1] Cf. D. L. Oliver, *A Solomon Island Society*, Harvard, 1955, pp. 15-17, 125.

the Cabin Table, and permitted all the officers, without exception, to make use of it, and left it to the option of the men to take as much as they pleased, or none at all; and this practice was not continued above a week before I found it necessary to put every one on board to an allowance, for such are the Tempers and Disposition of seamen in general, that whatever you give them out of the common way, although it be ever so much for their good, it will not go down, and you will hear nothing but murmurings against the man that first invented it, but the moment they see their superiors set a value on it, it becomes the finest stuff in the world, and the inventor is an honest fellow.' [1]

Peoples who are still unfamiliar with modern medicine also dislike hospitals, and if there is little risk of discovery they ignore the penalties for failing to bring in the sick for treatment. In the first place, they regard most drugs as useless. The newer antibiotics, the results of which are so spectacular, have won some favour, but the rest are held to be aimed at dealing with symptoms rather than with the real cause, conceived as supernatural in origin. Then the nearest post may be miles away, and the task of carrying a patient thither, over steep mountain trails or through trackless swamps, would be extremely arduous—indeed, he might not survive the journey. When a man is ill, too, he feels that he needs the protection and comfort of his kinsfolk. If he were in hospital he would be surrounded by strangers, all of them possibly sorcerers. He might even find that no one could speak his language. Other specific objections are the unaccustomed routine, the unfamiliar food, and the handling of bed-pans containing excreta by persons who might use such matter for their own nefarious purposes.

Schweitzer, in describing his hospital in the French Congo, brings out other points. The fact that some patients arrived alive in the evening and were taken out dead in the morning gave rise to the suspicion that the doctors were human leo-

---

[1] Journal of Captain Cook on H.M.S. *Endeavour*, under the date April 13, 1769 (quoted by A. Kitson, *Life of Captain James Cook*, London, 1911, pp. 243–4; and by C. Lloyd, *Voyages of Captain James Cook round the World*, London, 1949, p. 8).

pards. The people were both afraid of anæsthetics and despised the anæsthetist, who, they thought, constantly failed in his efforts to inflict lasting death. Dysentery, which involved the sufferer being placed under close supervision, was usually concealed, but, if it was discovered, the other patients disregarded the rule against sharing the man's food. 'Better be with my brother and die than not see him', one man remarked in excuse. Again, Schweitzer's humanity in helping the dying led the people to distrust him. They contrasted his behaviour with that of their own medicine men, who refused to waste their skill on those past healing.[1]

The Navaho Indians, it is said, hate hospital treatment because they are 'unaccustomed to a bed, to living by the clock, to staying in one place continuously instead of wandering around, and to efficient impersonal attention'. They miss the individual care that a medicine man gives and cannot see why they should be fed on gruel and milk when, if they were at home, they would be given as much of the choicest foods as they could eat. In addition, the relatives, after travelling several miles to make a visit, are often told that they have come on the wrong day.[2]

Eradicating Sorcery

A discussion of the tenacity with which native peoples cling to the belief in sorcery is relevant here, though the problem is somewhat different from that arising out of the deliberate evasion of general administrative measures. Colonial governments have partially succeeded in preventing the natives from punishing convicted sorcerers but have completely failed to eliminate the fear to which sorcery gives rise; indeed, the evidence suggests that the apprehension from this cause is everywhere increasing. Various unforeseen changes have also taken place in sorcery practices as a result of official actions.

[1] A. Schweitzer, *The Forest Hospital at Lambaréné*, New York, 1931, pp. 28, 38, 110, 117, 160.
[2] A. H. and D. C. Leighton, *The Navaho Door*, Harvard, 1944 (quoted in *Cultural Patterns and Technical Change* (ed. M. Mead), p. 225).

Europeans in touch with natives constantly point out to them that they would be invulnerable if only they would cease being so credulous. Government attitudes differ, however, and whereas in British Africa legislation is mainly aimed at punishing anyone who accuses another of sorcery, in most of the Pacific islands, though not all, regulations provide for the imprisonment of persons who can be proved to have performed the rituals of black magic.

Natives universally attribute disease and death to supernatural agencies, as has been indicated, yet their views about the way in which the forces of darkness operate differ from community to community. In some places sorcerers are most often blamed, and in others the avenging ancestors are held responsible. Then there are places where the sorcery is real and others where it is probably a figment of the imagination. Again, the identity of the magicians may be known to all, or they may themselves be ignorant of their powers until the information is made public by a diviner or oracle. Finally, they may be highly respected citizens or so hated that their lives are always in danger.

These variations are correlated with diversity in the social structure. Thus sorcery tends to diminish in significance as the central government becomes stronger. In the Trobriand Islands black magic was an integral part of the still poorly developed political system, and the chief maintained a somewhat uncertain authority by virtue of his knowledge of spells that he could recite if his subjects displeased him. The Bemba of Rhodesia, on the other hand, lived under an autocratic chief who could freely order any commoner to be beaten or mutilated. He was therefore so powerful that he had no need of sorcery. The presence or absence of organized judicial procedure can also affect the incidence of sorcery. The Bantu peoples of Africa are as a rule free to obtain redress for grievances in tribal courts, whereas the Melanesians, mostly lacking in such formal institutions, are forced to fall back on magic. Again, in some communities individuals or groups are linked by such burdensome obligations that a state of tension is created. Such an atmosphere is especially favourable to suspicion and hence leads to frequent charges of sorcery. Throughout the greater part of the Pacific a woman at marriage joins her husband and becomes so much a part of his local group that his kinsmen, realizing that her interests and their own are identical, would never dream of accusing her of bewitching them. The Melanesians of Dobu Island, however, have the custom of bilocal residence, and here married couples are required to live for one year with the kinsmen of the husband and for the next with the kinsmen of the wife. The population of a village is in consequence never the same for two consecutive seasons, and nobody can ever be absorbed into a stable working party. It is no accident that Dobu is one of the most sorcery-ridden communities of which we have a record.[1]

The subject would become unduly complicated if I were to go far afield, and I shall confine myself to two or three groups in the Pacific. Ontong Java will provide the first instance of the many forms of sorcery beliefs.[2] I have said already that this is a coral atoll inhabited by Polynesians lying some 200 miles to the north-east of the Solomons. The original settlement took place many generations ago, and the people, until the arrival of Europeans, had few contacts with the outside world. Traditions tell of an occasional canoe drifting in from Melanesia, Micronesia, or central Polynesia, but the Ontong Javanese were at no time face to face with a foreign community, where the mode of life was different, with which they might have had regular relations, either friendly or hostile.

The social structure is based on segmented patrilineages. Each of the patrilineages of intermediate size, those with a depth of five or six generations, is largely autonomous. The members learn to trust one another and carry out the bulk of their tasks together under the general direction of the man of

[1] B. Malinowski, *Argonauts of the Western Pacific*, London, 1922, p. 64; A. I. Richards, 'A Modern Movement of Witch-Finders', *Africa*, Vol. VIII, pp. 417-18; and R. F. Fortune, *Sorcerers of Dobu*, London, 1932.

[2] See H. I. Hogbin, *Law and Order in Polynesia*, London, 1934, Chaps. II, III, VI.

senior kinship status. Quarrels are rare for the simple reason that everyone depends on the help of his fellows and dares not risk offending them. When somebody is guilty of outrageous conduct the rest try to ignore his action: to punish him would not only do violence to their kinship loyalties but also deprive them of his valued services. Yet it is thought that the ancestors, observing all, will sooner or later intervene and cause the wrongdoer to become ill. These beings are regarded as the watchdogs of patrilineage morality, and most illnesses are ascribed to their anger. The relatives carry the patient to the house of a spirit medium, who discloses in a trance how exactly he has offended. Few persons, if any, lead a blameless existence, and gossip is often able to hazard a number of helpful suggestions. Perhaps he has disobeyed his leader, or neglected to take part in some communal activity, or struck a brother in anger, or interfered unduly in his nephew's affairs. Once the particular sin has been ascertained, an attempt can be made to expiate the offence. Recovery is accepted as an indication of ancestral pardon, death as proof of their unrelenting vindictiveness. The victim's kinsmen may feel resentful, but other members of the community are prepared to argue that he has paid the price of his folly.

The Ontong Java chief (sometimes referred to as the king) in earlier times had overriding authority in the relations between the different lineages. Although at this period personal retaliation was usual for injuries committed by members of other groups, he had the duty of exercising supervision and seeing that justice was done. The offending party could choose between direct action and causing black magic to be carried out against the wrongdoer. Several sorcerers were available, and one of these was generally ready, for a suitable fee, to perform a public rite that everyone believed would cause the person at whom it was directed to fall ill. The people imagined that he would be sure to grow gradually worse and eventually die unless he confessed his fault and made reparation. If the compensation was acceptable the now satisfied accuser asked the sorcerer to neutralize the effects of the earlier magic. It follows that sorcery was given out as the reason for a death only when the ritual was known to have been employed. In such circumstances the dead man was usually considered to have deserved his fate. The sorcerers were men of standing, with a reputation to keep up, and it was felt that they would scarcely be likely to have upheld an unjust claim. They were looked upon, in other words, as the supporters of law and order. If they abused their position, as a few from time to time apparently did, the chief stepped in and ordered them to be punished. Stories are told of one or two such who, by his orders, were bound hand and foot and thrown into the sea.

The Busama have a different social system and another interpretation for their misfortunes.[1] These natives live together in a single compact village, which in former times was politically independent. The settlement, instead of being isolated in the open ocean like Ontong Java, is located on the mainland of New Guinea amid a series of separate communities similarly constituted. The trade carried on with some of these leads to friendships and a certain amount of intermarriage. Other villages, which possess nothing useful to exchange, were earlier regarded as enemies. The Busama population as a whole is bound together by ties of kinship, and general collaboration takes place for all the larger undertakings, including housebuilding, canoe construction, and the celebration of certain festivities. There are also two sets of smaller groupings, one determined by matrilineal descent and the other by the more or less fortuitous siting of the dwellings around the club houses where the men meet in the evenings. The members of the matrilineage own land in common and carry out their agricultural work together, and those of the club group engage in other tasks in company. Social prestige in pre-European times was determined not by birth, but by the ability to give feasts. The two or three leaders who had outdone everyone else in generosity were finally chosen as the headmen of the

[1] See H. I. Hogbin, *Transformation Scene*, Chaps. VI, IX, XI.

community. These men exercised a limited authority in village affairs and represented the settlement in negotiations with other groups.

The same factors that served to preserve harmony within the Ontong Javanese lineage operated in Busama to maintain a general state of peace. The villagers refrained from quarrelling partly because they had been trained to respect their kinsfolk, partly because they were all forced to rely on one another's assistance. The usual method of securing redress when a man felt that his neighbour had injured him in some way was to carry out a mild form of sorcery in secret. Each of the minor diseases that the natives recognized, such as headache, toothache, pains in the abdomen, boils, and so forth, had an associated system of magic, with spells to cause the illness and spells to cure it. Everyone knew at least one of these systems and if annoyed had no hesitation about using it. Yet he was careful not to allow his intended victim to suspect what he had done lest the man be offended and afterwards decline to help him. The Melanesian islands are unhealthy, and there is a good deal of sickness. This mild form of sorcery accordingly appeared to be effective, and the magician could usually have the satisfaction of believing that his efforts at securing vengeance were successful. The patient felt no serious cause for alarm and did not try to locate the companion who might have been responsible. He was content to seek out someone who knew the curative spells and to have these recited. Natural resistance as a rule triumphed over the infection, and on recovering he thought no more of the matter. If the illness continued he could always take other measures. First he pondered over his movements during the previous few weeks. Trespass, even when done unwittingly, was believed to arouse the anger of the guardian spirits of the owners of the land, and if he remembered hunting in an area that he had no right to visit or entering gardens without asking permission he sent a gift to the members of the matrilineage concerned and asked them to offer it up as a sacrifice. They never refused, and if his health now began to improve he was sure that he had at last discovered the source of his troubles. A third line of conduct was indicated where he still remained unwell. The Busama believed that contact between the sexes, natural though it might be for men and women to want to be together, was fraught with danger for both. Menstruation served to cleanse the women of male influences, but men were obliged to take positive steps to rid themselves of female contamination. It was agreed that they ought to purge the impurities from their blood by gashing the penis at regular intervals of about a month. The operation had to be performed with due ceremony, and the patient was forced to take various precautions, including secluding himself for a day or two and avoiding certain foods. Ordinary work was therefore interrupted, and the majority of persons kept on postponing action for as long as possible. They waited either until they were jolted into recognition of their neglect by a severe indisposition or until they were about to set out on some dangerous enterprise, perhaps a raid or an overseas voyage, for which ritual purity was advisable. Only when a man's sickness had resisted curative magic, sacrifice to the guardian spirits, and the gashing of the penis did he conclude that he must be a victim of the lethal kind of sorcery. By that time he was usually on the brink of death. Once he had died, the relatives conducted a magical inquest to find out the culprit. They conjured a spirit into a small inanimate object, such as a piece of bamboo, which one of them then held lightly in his hand. This person asked a series of questions, all so framed that the reply could be a plain negative or affirmative. 'Did the sorcerer come from the south?', he enquired, 'Did he belong to such and such a place?', 'Was it so and so?' The spirit indicated 'no' by keeping the object still, 'yes' by rolling it about. Manipulation, though it obviously must have taken place, was probably unconscious. In almost every case the name that emerged was that of a resident of some hostile village already suspected because he harboured a special grudge against the dead man. A meeting of the elders followed to decide on the appropriate form of revenge—

direct action by a raiding party or counter sorcery. The answer largely depended on the status of the deceased. If he had been socially important the people were generally prepared to risk becoming involved in a vendetta, which sometimes led to open warfare; but if he had been comparatively insignificant the matter was left in the hands of the headmen, most of whom were thought to be sorcerers. One of these then carried out rites in secret against the suspected culprit.[1]

Busama reactions were clearly derived from the solidarity of the independent village and the consequent opposition to similar groupings. The charge of sorcery, once voiced, intensified the antagonism and thereby increased the chances of the next death being treated as a further act of hostility.

The Solomon Islanders of Malaita, with a third type of structure, combined the attitudes of the Ontong Javanese and the Busama.[2] They believed that a man was safe from harm provided he retained the goodwill of his ancestors and that, even if he offended them, he would still be secure unless he was bewitched. They thus construed every death as the outcome of both ancestral displeasure and sorcery.

Malaita is divided into named areas a square mile or so in extent each containing a sacred grove where formerly the dead were buried and their spirits worshipped. A man has the right to erect a dwelling and cultivate the soil in every area in which an ancestor is buried. All lines of descent are of equal importance, and the connection may be traced through males, through females, or through a series consisting of both males and females. The local group is therefore made up of a number of persons descended from an ancestor or set of ancestors common to them all. Membership may vary through the years as a result of minor differences of opinion or continued ill fortune. The unit is largely self-sufficient, and everyday tasks are car-

---

[1] One rare type of sorcery was carried out publicly but was directed against the whole of a hostile community rather than against a single individual. Its use was mainly confined to occasions when rival groups were preparing to attack each other, and it should perhaps be considered as a special form of war magic.

[2] See H. I. Hogbin, *Experiments in Civilization*, Chaps. I, III, IV.

ried out in collaboration under the direction of a headman. At the same time, a man engaged in a big undertaking can always reckon on his kinsmen from outside coming along to lend a hand. The obligation he then incurs is later discharged when they in turn take on some heavy job. As with the Ontong Javanese lineage and the Busama village, these reciprocal ties in earlier days guaranteed the cohesion of the kindred and the absence of serious quarrels. If anyone for some reason became aggrieved with his fellows he could fall back on a system of non-lethal sorcery as a safety-valve for his annoyance. This did no real harm because it was always carried out privately. Minor illnesses, in any case, were believed to be amenable to curative magic. A patient who failed to improve examined his conscience to see whether he might have angered the ancestors. He thought that if he had neglected the sacrifices due to them, omitted the proper precautions when mixing with the members of the opposite sex, or infringed the rules defining the correct behaviour towards relatives they could perhaps have withdrawn their protecting arm. The procedure to regain their favour was a public admission of guilt followed by an offering, which was presented through a priest at a shrine within the sacred grove. Recovery, as in Ontong Java, was accepted as a token of forgiveness, death as proof that the spirits were determined to make the sinner a terrible example. But it was also maintained that the man would not have died but for the performance of the more serious form of sorcery. The kinsmen were accordingly still under the obligation of avenging him. A magical inquest took place for the purpose of finding someone who could be blamed. Like the Busama, these natives generally picked on a foreigner from a distant area and either murdered him or else carried out counter sorcery against him.

The administration of the Solomon Islands, unlike the other colonial governments in the western Pacific, makes no provision for the punishment of persons judged to be guilty of trafficking in black magic. The natives are dissatisfied and argue that the officials are indifferent to their welfare since they will

I

neither bring sorcerers to justice nor allow the wronged parties to take the law into their own hands. They say that evil now stalks abroad unhindered and that they have far more reason to be afraid than their forbears. The pagans have adapted one of the old ceremonies in an effort to meet the impasse. After a dead man has been buried the priest of the group offers the sacrifice of a pig. As the kidneys are being incinerated he prays to the ancestors and urges them to combine in striking the sorcerer down. The person's name is mentioned if he has been identified, but this is not regarded as necessary, and, in any event, it is not broadcast, and only those present hear it. Everyone now hopes that the evildoer will die. The Christians take no action openly lest they should incur the displeasure of the church leaders. Many of them confess, nevertheless, that after the loss of a loved one they have followed the example set by various characters in the Old Testament and prayed that God would smite the enemy responsible. It thus appears that both the pagans and the Christians have substituted one form of sorcery for another.

The authorities in New Guinea have followed the course that is more usual in the Pacific and framed regulations to secure the imprisonment of men proved to be sorcerers. This method is effective in dealing with those communities where, as in Ontong Java, the magician is something of a public official and makes no attempt to conceal the fact that he has performed his rites. Such a man is readily deterred and before long goes out of business. It is useless, however, for coping with societies of the Busama type. I emphasize again that these natives not only attribute every death to sorcery but are also agreed that the ritual is ordinarily carried out by stealth. If a man were prepared to kill his enemy openly, they explain, he would ignore the consequences and do so with a spear-thrust. The spells may, indeed, be recited at times, but any statement about the frequency with which this is done can only be a guess. I believe myself, though I have no positive proof, that the charges made are more often than not baseless.

The production of evidence acceptable in a European court of law against a man who takes care to close his door before engaging in the black art is obviously impossible. Yet in a New Guinea gaol that I visited some years ago seven men were serving sentences for sorcery. Their conviction had been secured by perjury. In every case the same sequence of events had occurred. Somebody had died, and the relatives had then carried out an inquest in the traditional magical way to find out which of their foreign enemies was responsible. They knew that a charge against the person whose name had been revealed would be dismissed unless eye-witnesses came forward, and they accordingly manufactured a story, a pure fabrication, telling how they had seen him at work. This action was not to them immoral. They firmly believed that the accused was guilty but lacked an alternative means of ensuring that he would be punished.

An incident that took place in Wogeo during my stay there is instructive in this connection. The island is divided into several politically independent districts, some of them traditionally friendly to one another, others traditionally hostile. Shortly before the occasion in question a woman belonging to an important family had died in a hamlet close to the one in which I was living. As is usual at such times, nerves were on edge, and sorcery formed almost the sole topic of conversation. One morning the wife of a neighbour of mine set off for the gardens on the hillside behind the settlement. She was expecting her husband to follow close behind her, but at the last moment he was delayed. She told me later that she was walking along the path thinking of her work when suddenly the dog, which was trotting on ahead, began barking. She ran back at once, screaming 'Sorcerers!' at the top of her voice. She had seen no one, and in all probability the dog had barked at a wild pig, but everyone concluded that the quick retreat had saved her from being bewitched. I accompanied the men who set out, all fully armed, to investigate whether the sorcerers had left any trace of their presence. The path was muddy, but we saw no strange footprints, and, although the forest alongside was so dense that a knife would have been necessary to hack a passage into it, not one branch was cut or broken. My companions assured me that sorcerers are adept at covering their tracks, but I am positive that nobody had been there and that the woman's disturbed state of mind, following on the recent death, was responsible for her fright.

The news quickly travelled around the district, and that afternoon someone came along with the statement that he had earlier in the day seen two men from one of the hostile areas walking in the hills. The reasonable explanation was that they were either out hunting or else keeping an assignation with a couple of young girls, but suspicion fell upon them at once, and within three days people were saying openly that the woman had observed them trying to bewitch her.

My presence on the island was a restraining influence, and the woman's relatives did not attack the alleged culprits, but her husband told me that if a patrol officer was to make a visit, or if he could at that season make the crossing to the mainland by canoe, he would lay a charge against them. Had he done so I have no doubt that as many persons as were necessary would have come forward and supported him with the usual tissue of falsehoods.

Punishing the sorcerer by law, apart from the encouragement to perjury, has further effects. Administrative officers may urge that they are taking action against him solely on account of his fraudulent claims, but the natives begin with different premises and reach another conclusion. They interpret the move as confirmation of their fears. If Europeans hold that the man is a danger, then he clearly must be, and their alarm was justified. Imprisonment for a sorcerer is thus equivalent to the award of a diploma of his competence. In the old days the residents of his own village could laugh at the verdict of the inquest, which they were not invited to attend, and say that it was based on malice. Now they look upon him after he has emerged from confinement as a figure of dread, to be avoided if possible or, if this should prove difficult, at all costs placated.

Sorcery fears have also been augmented indirectly. The Melanesians regard every stranger as a potential evil magician waiting to do them harm, but in former times their movements were circumscribed, and they seldom went far from home. Even when on a trading voyage they followed a familiar route, travelled in company, and chose as host a man whom they could trust. Today, on the contrary, the youths spend several years in employment, and both the elders and the women make occasional visits to the government station or a commercial centre. Each plantation draws its labour force from several sources, and although the men from the same village generally arrange to go away in batches of three or four, working teams are always made up of a variety of groups with pidgin-English or some other *lingua franca* as their sole means of communication. New friendships cutting across cultural barriers are fairly common, yet each of the labourers is bound to feel uncomfortable with some of his workmates and, in consequence, to distrust them. He spends large sums, which he can ill afford, on the purchase of protective magic, amulets, and charms (if he is a pagan he may buy a cross or a Saint Christopher medal from a Christian native), but these, instead of strengthening his confidence, seem rather to undermine it. If he becomes ill his first thought is that these men have bewitched him, and cases have been known in which employees suffering, according to medical experts, from mild complaints have literally died of fright.

European contact has led, too, to extra tensions within the small village community itself, and persons who would once have presented a united front are now separated by resentment and jealousy. Constant friction, as has been explained, is a fruitful breeding ground for misgivings, which too often bring a charge of sorcery. Thus distant kinsmen still feel that they are bound together but may have difficulty in discharging their mutual obligations. A man who is away in employment obviously does not help his remote cousins as he would have done earlier, and his earnings when he returns are much too precious to be squandered on indiscriminate gifts.

In Europe the general growth of knowledge led to the gradual elimination of the belief that illnesses are supernaturally caused. Among the natives, although contact has brought advancement in some spheres, the schooling available is so inadequate that others have been left untouched. I referred in the first chapter to the man from Hanuabada who represented his people at an international conference. He is a third-generation Christian, speaks excellent English, and has read widely. A few years ago he submitted a plan to the director of native affairs in New Guinea for handling the problem of 'evil magic'. 'All the Christians who believe wholeheartedly in Christ also believe wholeheartedly in sorcery', he wrote. 'You will find them preaching the Gospels and worshipping like angels, but if you were with them in their homes, especially at night when someone is ill, you would still find them talking about sorcery.' He suggested the appointment of a 'prophet' to smell out the guilty ones, who would then be confined without further trial on a small island in the care of a special police force. This attitude may be expected to continue until the people are better informed all round and nearer our own level of education and experience. At that point they will also have a more rational attitude to the public-health measures that are now so difficult to enforce.

CHAPTER V

Chain Reactions and Changing Institutions

STANDARDIZED behaviour patterns may not interlock perfectly, but the adjustment between them is such that changes in one always have indirect effects on others. When the fountain pen was invented people altered their writing habits, and the manufacturers of steel nibs and office inkwells were threatened with bankruptcy. To remain solvent they had to spend capital on switching production to different commodities. Each secondary consequence of this kind may be followed by still further reactions. The former nib-makers had to retrain their workers or find others to replace them, draw their raw materials from new sources, and seek fresh markets. A single novelty, indeed, has at times led to a major social upheaval. The motor-car is an example.

In 1900 the motor-car was a joke. It was smelly, dirty, uncomfortable, and far less reliable than the railway train or horse and carriage. But within a few years improvements had been made, and, despite some initial hesitation, ordinary householders began saving on other items to buy a car. Gigantic industries, employing millions, came into being. Foundries were established to produce the steel; workshops to fashion the engine, body, tyres, and accessories; tanneries and mills to process the hides, wool, and cotton for the upholstery and carpet; garages to carry out distribution and repairs; refineries to treat the fuel; schools to teach the drivers; and insurance offices to underwrite the losses arising from theft and other hazards. The roads were widened and improved, and before long a network of new highways spread across the countryside. The rural shopping centres then began to decline as more and more business flowed into the towns. The railways also suffered, and branch lines that could no longer pay their way were closed down. The volume of traffic went on increasing, and today the inner streets of the great cities are so choked with cars, buses, and trucks that the pedestrian makes quicker progress than the passenger. Perhaps within a decade or so the concentrated metropolis, suitable for Victorian and Edwardian commerce, will have ceased to exist. Meantime various aspects of our lives less intimately associated with transport have been disturbed. Daughters are not now chaperoned as they were in the days before it became customary for a boy and girl to go out driving unaccompanied; land values have altered as the suburbs sprawl farther and farther afield; the need to provide housing for the car has modified architectural styles; and each year more people become maimed or die in accidents. While these changes have been going on among ourselves others of comparable magnitude are occurring in the backward territories from which oil and rubber come. Petty chieftains grow powerful with the riches acquired from the royalties paid by the great international cartels, and primitive tribesmen forsake their old tools for Western goods bought with the money obtained by tapping trees in the tropical jungles.

So little is known of the internal changes in native communities while they were still primitive that we can usually only guess at the chain reactions. Hawaii is in this respect exceptional, and even there, though the destruction of the religion as described in an earlier chapter was spontaneous, the readjustments had scarcely begun when the arrival of Christian missionaries complicated the issues. Yet the taboos gave support to the monarchy, and their abolition probably contributed in no small way to the diminishing importance of the sovereign and the establishment of a republic in the years immediately preceding the annexation of the islands by the United States.

A tentative reconstruction is sometimes possible when a body of migrants, like the New Zealand Maori, have established a colony in another environment. Polynesia is one of the most favourable regions for investigation, for the traditions preserved independently by different peoples indicate that numbers of the outer archipelagoes were settled from Raiatea in the Society Islands. The cultures are similar everywhere—the dialects are variants of one language, as close to one another as southern English and Highland Scots, and priority of birth and gradations of rank are always recognized. But Raiatea is rich and tropical, and conditions in some of the other islands are as dissimilar as those of New Zealand. Easter Island, for example, is arid and almost treeless. The dwellings and even the chicken-houses, which elsewhere are of timber construction, have here to be built of stone. Wood was in fact so highly prized that it was carved into neck pendants. The canoes were flimsy and unseaworthy, and little food could be obtained from the ocean. The result was that the fishing god sank into oblivion. Eggs, especially those of the sooty tern, became the principal source of protein. Flocks of these birds visit the island annually during the breeding season, and the rites associated with their arrival replaced the normal harvest festival, when the earliest yams were presented to the gods. A new cult arose, the leading deity of which was always represented in rock carvings with a human body and a bird-like head. A race took place for the first egg, and the fortunate chief whose follower won was treated with the highest honours and elevated, for the space of a year, till the next breeding season, to the office of high priest.[1]

Documentation on the chain reactions following on the adoption of foreign items is as a rule easier to come by. Toynbee cites several instances from the Oriental nations. 'In a cultural encounter,' he says, 'one thing inexorably goes on leading to another when once the smallest breach has been made on the assaulted society's defences.' The Ottoman governor-general

[1] P. H. Buck, *Vikings of the Sunrise*, New York, 1938, Chap. XVII.

of Egypt in the early nineteenth century, Mehmed Ali Pasha, wanted to equip himself with effective armaments, especially a navy. He advertised for experts, but found that they were unwilling to come unless their wives could accompany them; and they refused to bring their wives without the assurance of medical care. The experts, their wives and families, and a number of doctors all arrived together. An arsenal was installed at Alexandria, and the doctors duly attended the sick. They still had time to spare and determined to help the Egyptian community. Maternity work seemed to be the greatest need, and a lying-in hospital arose within the naval establishment. Muslim etiquette forbade the mingling of females with the males of any household but their own, and the experiment at first seemed doomed to failure. The Egyptian women, however, set a higher value on their survival in childbirth than on the code of manners, and within a short space of time hosts of them began taking advantage of the skill of the infidel obstetricians. This ignoring of the notion of decency in the relations between the sexes was the indirect result of the Pasha's decision to equip a navy. The change was succeeded by others until the Islamic Church, which hitherto had reigned unchallenged over the whole field of Muslim life, was finally disestablished.[1]

Toynbee also draws attention to the Canute-like attitude of Gandhi in trying to stop the tide of industrialization in India. Gandhi realized that if the Indians wore cloth woven in the West they would soon begin importing machinery to make the material by similar methods. They would then forsake their fields to work in the factories. After they had become accustomed to spending hours of toil at Western jobs they would want to devote their leisure to Western amusements. Eventually they would become fully Westernized and forget how to be Hindus. He therefore set the example by spending a certain time each day spinning and weaving Indian cotton by hand in the old-fashioned way. Severance of the economic ties between India and the West, he believed, was the only sure means of

[1] A. Toynbee, *The World and the West*, Oxford, 1953, p. 76.

preventing Hindu society from being Westernized body and soul.

'There was no flaw in the Mahatma Gandhi's insight. The Westernization of India that he forboded and sought to avert was, and is, fast developing out of the grain of cotton seed; and Gandhi's remedy for India's Western infection was the right one. Only the prophet failed to induce his disciples to follow him in preserving India's cultural heritage at this price in economic austerity. The wearing of machine-made cotton goods could not have been renounced by the Indian people in Gandhi's generation without lowering the Indian peasantry's already intolerably low standard of living, and without putting out of business altogether the new class of Indian cotton operatives and Indian mill-owners that had already sprung up from India's soil.' [1]

Cultural Drift and Historical Accident

Herskovits applies the term 'cultural drift' to accumulated changes that are heading in a definite direction towards some final end. He cites the history of the necktie as a simple illustration. The indications are, he says, that this item of clothing will soon disappear. It began as a large kerchief, which people wore on all occasions. Gradually the cloth became smaller, and its removal on the sporting field and in hot weather in offices was permitted, and already manufacturers are producing shirts for daily wear with collars that can be worn either buttoned for a tie or left open. This appears to be a special form of chain reaction and is in consequence best considered now.

Every culture contains the germs of its own future, Herskovits maintains. The influence of the cultural setting is so strong that it generates within itself the situations from which discoveries derive. Such a view reduces the rôle of the individual to a minimum: 'it makes of culture an independent force whose carriers are its creatures rather than its masters'. A

[1] A. Toynbee, *The World and the West*, Oxford, 1953, pp. 79-81.

discovery, Herskovits suggests, is made only when the circumstances call for it, and as soon as the circumstances do in fact call for it, it is certain to be made. He quotes the simultaneous statement of the evolutionary hypothesis by Darwin and Wallace and argues that, if these two had not come forward at that time, someone else would have done so. A discovery made too soon, on the other hand, is always ignored. Mendel's findings on the mechanism of heredity, although published in a scientific journal of wide circulation, lay neglected for more than three decades until the biological sciences were ready for them. Various students, each working by himself, ultimately became interested in the same phenomena, and Mendel's experiments at last gained the attention they deserved.[1]

The theory was developed from Sapir's account of drift in language.

'As we look about us and observe our current usage, it is not likely to occur to us that our language has a "slope", that the changes in the next few centuries are in a sense prefigured in certain obscure tendencies of the present and that these changes, when consummated, will be seen to be but continuations of changes that have already been effected', Sapir had written. 'We feel rather that our language is practically a fixed system and that what slight changes are destined to take place in it are as likely to move in one direction as in another. This feeling is fallacious.'

The significant changes in language begin as individual variations, yet linguistic drift cannot be understood by listing these alone.

'They themselves are random phenomena, like the waves of the sea, moving backwards and forwards in purposeless flux. The linguistic drift has direction. In other words, only those individual variations embody it or carry it which move in a

---

[1] M. J. Herskovits, 'The Processes of Cultural Change', *Science of Man in the World Crisis* (ed. R. Linton), New York, 1945, pp. 153–4; and *Man and His Works*, New York, 1951, pp. 580–5.

certain direction, just as only certain movements in the bay outline the tide. The drift of language is constituted by the unconscious selection of those individual variations that are cumulative in some special direction.'

In English a number of expressions now in daily use will in
course of time be dropped. Sapir discussed the accusative form
'whom'; the words 'whither' and 'whence', 'thither' and
'thence'; and 'hither' and 'hence'; and the adverbs ending with
'ly', such as 'quickly' and 'badly', and gave convincing reasons
why they are likely to disappear. The sentence, 'Whom did you
see?', for instance, violates our speech habits in a number of
ways. Except for the personal pronouns, where the nominative
and accusative forms are so different that confusion is unlikely,
English has dropped inflexions; the accusative form of the personal pronoun is never placed at the beginning of a sentence
(we do not say, 'Him I saw'); the other interrogative words,
like 'what' and 'where', are invariable; and the phonetic
arrangement of a long vowel followed by a labial consonant
and then by a short tripping vowel sounds clumsy. Many persons already habitually say, 'Who did you see?', and in due
course others will accept such usage as preferable until in the
end grammarians will be forced to sanction it, just as they now
approve the popular, 'It's me'. 'The man whom I referred to'
at present causes less conflict, but once 'whom' has disappeared
in one context we are bound to substitute 'who' everywhere.
The leaders of the fashion will at first be regarded as wrong,
but the rest of us, or our descendants, moved by the same logic,
will ultimately fall into line.[1]

Sapir was speaking here of those linguistic changes that are
apparently unwilled and, at the time, unobserved. Even within
such a narrow field, however, the conclusions cannot always be
forecast. The gradual modification of English pronunciation is
an example. In Middle English such words as 'kind' rhymed
with our modern 'seemed', but the diphthong replaced the

---

[1] E. Sapir, *Language*, New York, 1921, p. 166.

pure vowel so slowly that there is little likelihood that anyone was aware what was happening. The development of the separate Australian and American dialects may also be mentioned. Any prophesying at this stage about their eventual form in a later generation would be extremely hazardous.

It should also be noted that many of the changes in language are not of this type. Thus new words are deliberately introduced as discoveries and inventions occur and unfamiliar concepts are put forward. A philologist of the mid nineteenth century could not possibly have guessed that we would all today be using such terms as 'camouflage', 'garage', 'aeroplane', 'uranium', 'fascism', and 'apartheid'. Another instance of willed change is the disappearance of the double negative. The grammarians of the eighteenth century condemned as illogical this hitherto acceptable construction and set about eradicating it from educated speech.

Can we say, nevertheless, that the analogy with linguistic drift is helpful for an understanding of particular forms of social change? Certainly the list of discoveries and inventions made practically simultaneously is impressive. Galileo, Fabricius, Harriott, and Scheiner discovered sunspots in 1611; Newton devised the calculus in 1671, Leibnitz in 1678; Rutherford identified nitrogen in 1772, Scheele in 1773, and in the following year Scheele and Priestley identified oxygen; Jouffroy, Rumsey, Fitch, and Symington invented steamships in the period 1783–8; Henry, Morse, Steinheil, Wheatstone, and Cooke produced the telegraph in 1837; Daguerre and Talbot made the first successful experiments in photography in 1839; and Bell and Gray theirs with the telephone in 1876.[1]

Yet it cannot be assumed, as a bald statement of the cultural-determinist point of view would seem to imply, that the appearance of each of these discoveries was foreordained from the beginning. If this were true we would be at a loss to account for the discoveries that were made before they could be utilized.

---

[1] W. F. Ogburn and D. Thomas, 'Are Inventions Inevitable?', *Political Science Quarterly*, Vol. XXXVII, pp. 83–99.

Mendel was as surely stamped with the marks of his culture to the same extent as Darwin and Wallace or Bell and Gray. European civilization is also today ready for a number of discoveries that are still out of reach. Research institutions in England, America, Australia, and elsewhere have for many years been trying in vain to find a cure for cancer—they have spent more of their resources on this project than on that for the remedy for poliomyelitis. The destruction of Hiroshima is also relevant to the question. In 1945 the Allies knew more about atom bombs than did the Germans but less about large rockets. The difference is to be accounted for not by the times calling for one weapon in English and American society and for another in German society, but by the strategic requirements of the respective governments. Numbers of British and American scientists were encouraged to work on the atom: German scientists concentrated mainly on rockets.

Sapir was careful to frame his theory in terms of current speech habits. These may be regarded as the equivalent in language of social values. He said, in effect, that 'whom' would vanish because it is opposed to a number of our established preferences. The word fails to measure up to the logical, grammatical, and æsthetic standards that we regard as desirable. The concept of cultural determinism becomes meaningful only if values are in this way taken into consideration.

Individual action is largely conditioned by the preferences current in the society, and as soon as a discovery in line with these can be conceived within the framework of existing knowledge its early appearance is probable. Sunspots could not have been reported until after the development of the scientific spirit, the exploration of the theory of optics, and the acquisition of skill in fashioning lenses. These conditions were achieved in the first years of the seventeenth century, and the observations of Galileo, Fabricius, Harriott, and Scheiner then followed. Again, when the telegraph had been in use for some time people began to think about the advantages of transmitting the voice direct by wire. The principles of electromagnetic induction and sound vibration were already appreciated, and the idea of the telephone was therefore bound to occur to a number of workers. Bell happened to be the first to produce a satisfactory device, but Gray or someone else might have preceded him.

The theory of cultural drift must not be allowed to obscure the importance of historical accident as a cause of change. The use of this phrase, as Herskovits is careful to emphasize, does not imply the absence of causation.[1] It is a recognition rather that the sequence of events could not ordinarily have been expected. The term 'accident' as commonly employed has precisely this meaning. When we speak of a man 'accidentally' falling downstairs we are not suggesting that the incident had never been thought of as a possibility. We indicate only that persons who go up or down stairs do not normally lose their balance. But we know that they may readily do so if a shoelace comes untied, the light fails, the carpet frays, or children leave toys on the landing.

Just as language is subject to drift, so also is it to historical accident. Any comprehensive study of English through the ages would have to take account of the effects of successive invasions. An informed observer, had such existed, could have foretold the arrival of the Danes, and he might have guessed that, once they had gained a foothold, they would burn the libraries, thus causing the dispersal of the Anglo-Saxon scholars. But the destruction can still, in the long view, be described as accidental. The Normans followed the Danes, and the educated classes now concentrated on French and Latin. Nobody bothered as yet to make any formal investigation of the vernacular, and English grammar remained unstandardized till a comparatively late date. The drift towards simplification may well have begun when an increasing body of the foreigners discovered that, in order to make contact with the common people, they would be obliged to learn to speak to them. Like many Europeans who today try to talk native languages, they

[1] M. J. Herskovits, *Man and His Works*, p. 588.

probably omitted the unstressed syllables and ignored the elaborate inflexions.

A typical historical accident in the social field was the death of the children of Queen Anne and the consequent succession to the English throne of a sovereign, George I, who spoke only German. This paved the way for various changes in the political system.

Isolated Chain Reactions

The different stages of a chain reaction that can be viewed in comparative isolation may with profit be examined separately. Something new appears, perhaps as the result of a discovery by a member of the society, perhaps through contacts with persons of some other community: if the device is in line with accepted values and is therefore attractive, at once an unfamiliar situation is created: precedents furnish no guidance, and values must now be balanced one against the other for the establishment of a fresh set of preferences. After the choice is made the group finds itself for a second time in an unaccustomed predicament with still further possibilities for action opening up. The values have again to be examined and the preferences reallocated. This sequence goes on until the reaction has worked itself out. The events following on the introduction of the steel axe to the Yir Yiront aborigines of Cape York Peninsula will serve as an illustration.[1]

Like the other Australian tribes, the Yir Yiront originally possessed no metals. The environment also lacked supplies of stone for tools, and the natives were obliged to import rough pieces of unshaped material from further south. The opportunity to effect exchanges presented itself during the great fiestas that took place when a collection of contiguous hunting bands assembled to initiate a batch of youths. Tribesmen living far and near attended, and the Yir Yiront offered their particular speciality, spears tipped with the spine of a sting-ray, in

[1] See L. Sharp, 'Steel Axes for Stone-Age Australians', *Human Problems in Technological Change* (ed. E. H. Spicer), New York, 1952, pp. 69–90.

K

return for various commodities from elsewhere. Each adult male had a series of trading partners with whom he carried out his transactions. He received the stone and fashioned the axe, which, when finished, remained his exclusive property. Women and children frequently borrowed the tool but always sought permission first. Ownership was thus a mark of the men's status. Every request was an acknowledgement that the petitioner admitted his or her social inferiority.

A few steel axes had reached the natives earlier, but they became available in quantity only after 1915, when missionaries opened a station on the edge of the territory. From then on anyone, male or female, young or old, could earn an axe as payment for working for a few days at the mission.

The change-over to steel presented no technological difficulties. The metal blades when blunt could be sharpened, and a broken handle was easily replaced. As the new tools were so much more efficient than the old and so much more durable, everybody wanted them as soon as possible. Yet because the natives lived in such a poor area and were entirely without European education, they were not equipped to use the time saved for improving their living standards. They simply carried out their former tasks quicker and slept longer.

The older men, whose habits were already confirmed, disliked mixing with the whites. They kept aloof themselves but, because they were so eager to have the axes, encouraged their sons and daughters to seek employment. They may have expected that the young people would later hand over the tools to them but if so were disappointed. The youngsters satisfied their own wants first and only then thought of the elders. Many of the seniors therefore found that they now had to borrow from the juniors. A small handful without families were even obliged to prostitute their wives. Thus although work was considerably lightened, age, sex, and kinship rôles became confused. The elders lost their undisputed authority and were reduced in certain situations to a position of subordination.

The next effect was the curtailment of the fiestas. This led in turn to a further decline in the prestige of the older generation. In earlier times the senior men had taken the youths to the bush for initiation and given them instruction in their various obligations. In particular, they had trained the boys to be obedient on all occasions. Such lessons were the more impressive, and hence the more likely to have lasting results, because of the elaborate ceremonial with which they were surrounded. One of the main motives for outsiders attending, however, was to undertake the all-important economic exchanges. As soon as Europeans began supplying steel axes these transfers became unnecessary, and more and more persons stayed away. The ceremonies speedily ceased to be exciting—and accordingly were less attractive—and nowadays, if they are performed at all, it is only in the most perfunctory manner.

These ceremonies were vital to the clan system, which determined a person's name, his land rights, the direction from whence his bride was to come, and his place in the world of the supernatural. The culture heroes of the past, so it was thought, laid down the pattern of social life and the correct modes of behaviour. In the course of so doing they were believed to have divided the tribe into exogamous clans, all with a definite area of country, and allotted to each one a special portion of the natural environment as a distinguishing mark or totem. Totems included the useful animals and plants, phenomena such as the sun and the rain, activities like fighting and swimming, and stone axes and other manufactured objects. The members of the clan expressed their loyalty to the traditional ways, and also their own corporateness as a group, by performing, on such occasions as initiation ceremonies, a series of rituals involving the re-enactment of the doings of the culture heroes in relation to their own totem. The introduction of the steel axe at once caused a complication. To which clan should it be assigned? Some argued for the original stone-axe group, others for the ghost group on the ground that it came from the missionaries who had a pale skin, while a considerable number, with more reason, said that as the steel axe was an importation it could not possibly have anything to do with the local heroes. No agreement could be reached, and a significant part of the people's lives now lay outside the religious system. Then gradually, as the tribal meetings came to be less and less well attended, the other representations were neglected. The link with the sacred past was weakened, and the concept of a moral order in the universe sank into the background. The old ways, that is to say, are no longer regarded as pre-ordained and beyond questioning. Further, the groupings cannot now be so readily identified, and the rules relating to such matters as land tenure and marriage are in a state of flux.

Chain Reactions in Series

The chain reaction set going among the Yir Yiront by the steel axe can be traced out step by step because the implement came in alone. The tribe has so far taken over almost nothing else from the West. The region is not suitable for commercial exploitation by Europeans, and the missionaries, whose efforts at spreading Christianity have been abortive, are the only permanent settlers. Costs have prevented the establishment of a proper school, but it is difficult to see how the natives could profit from training unless they were moved to a more favourable location. If they continue living in their ancestral homeland they must either remain nomads, and hence restrict their possessions, or else subsist on charity.

Civilization has usually impinged on native society to a far greater extent. The majority of primitive communities had something to sell that Europeans wanted to buy—land perhaps, or labour, or a local product, or a crop recently introduced. The money earned was then available for the purchase not only of axes but of an extensive range of goods, each of which by itself was a potential disturber of the traditional economy. If stone tools and clay pots were no longer made on the spot, for instance, more time could be spent in leisure or in the practice of remunerative pursuits. On the other hand, where objects formerly obtained from outside were now bought in shops, native exchanges came to an end. The sale of land, labour, or produce also had other effects. The people were often forced to redistribute the remaining areas, sometimes to the detriment of groups that had hitherto enjoyed special advantages; or they found that, when a large proportion of the adult males were away in employment, work had to be reorganized; or they were obliged to learn fresh agricultural techniques. Again, most backward peoples have been subjected to closer governmental supervision than the Yir Yiront. Fighting has been stopped, alien laws enforced, and different methods of settling disputes and punishing offenders introduced. In some places the native leaders have lost all their powers, and in others their rights and obligations have been misunderstood and they now exercise more authority than in earlier days. Missionaries, too, have as a rule made a deep impression. They have seldom achieved their professed aim of turning the natives into model Christians but have frequently managed to discredit the pagan gods and destroy some of the old sanctions regulating conduct. They have also founded schools and taught the natives to read and write, thereby improving communication and facilitating the spread of new ideas.

In general, then, we have before us not a single chain reaction by itself but several operating simultaneously. Disentangling them is always difficult and sometimes impossible, and for this reason alone, apart from the others referred to in the final section of Chapter II, the more rewarding task is to look rather at the various institutions on which they are converging. By examining the institutions successively in the light of the repeated onslaughts made upon them we can see how each has already been modified and perhaps reach the point where the direction of future changes will be discernible.

Changing Institutions

The recent survey of marriage in Africa is an instance of this type of study.[1]

Throughout primitive Africa the polygynous household, consisting of the husband, his wives, and their offspring, was the ideal, and the man with several spouses was assured of social distinction. His dependants were also his helpers, and he grew richer and more influential as their number increased. Yet although the proportion of available females, owing to their lower age at marriage, was always in excess of that of the males, the normal distribution of the sexes meant that many men could not achieve polygyny and were obliged to be content with remaining monogamous.

Each household was part of a series of wider groupings, often a village section, a village, and a district. Membership in every case was determined by kinship, which was most commonly traced in one line only, either through males exclusively or through females exclusively. Such units formed a set of patrilineages or matrilineages of extending depth and widening span. The largest included several of intermediate size, each of these was made up of others of smaller dimensions, and so on. Solidarity was emphasized by collective ceremonies, the focal point of which was as a rule a sacrifice to the original ancestor or to some other spirit.

The individuals of any lineage were called upon to accept various mutual obligations and to combine for all sorts of activities. Lineages of narrow span were associated with such things as daily work, while those that were wider were concerned with defence. The seniors of the group had the right to punish their juniors not only directly but also indirectly. Thus they could omit the name of an offender when praying to the spirits and even call upon them to inflict him with disease or some other misfortune. Discipline was also maintained by the

[1] L. P. Mair, 'African Marriage and Social Change', *African Marriage and Family Life* (ed. A. Phillips), Oxford, 1953, pp. 1-155.

puberty rites to which the youths were forced to submit. At this time they also received formal instruction in their tribal duties as well as in matters relating to sex and marriage.

The choice of a partner was as much the concern of the lineage as of the boy or girl. The elders were sometimes in sole charge of the arrangements, and even when this was not so their approval had always to be obtained. They argued that, as their judgement was detached, they were more likely to select a spouse who would prove suitable. The match itself was sealed by the husband's senior relatives handing over to the senior relatives of the bride a quantity of valuables, cattle in certain areas, goods such as hoes in others. This payment was in no sense a purchase, and the woman was never reduced to the position of a slave. Pecuniary considerations may have had some influence, and parents probably preferred to receive a greater rather than a lesser amount; but this was incidental and not essential to the system. The transaction was mainly important in that it made the union legal and legitimized the children. In certain circumstances it also helped to keep the marriage stable. In some tribes the people insisted that if the couple separated the payment had to be returned. The persons who had received a portion were unwilling to give it back and therefore exerted pressure to have any differences settled.

Numerous European observers, especially missionaries, have deplored the low standing of the wife in tribal society. They have justified their conclusion by reference to the prevalence of polygyny, to the procedures that permit the disposal of daughters against their will, to the bride-price payments, and to the division of labour that allots some of the heavy work to women. The wife, however, always had certain guaranteed rights; sons no less than daughters could be married off without their consent; and the fact that the woman contributed extensively to the subsistence of her family meant that the man was as much dependent upon her as she was upon him. Yet it must be admitted that females had the legal status of minors and were usually expected to be submissive to the husband, who, if he thought fit, could always administer a beating.

Many of the present trends are related to the increasing freedom from control observable in all aspects of native life. The African village is no longer an isolated self-contained world surrounded by enemies, and the inhabitants do not depend so much on one another's goodwill. Peace has been established, travel is safe, and most men can now earn a cash income. In consequence they rely less and less on co-operation with their kindred for the satisfaction of their ordinary needs and more and more on money. One outcome of this situation is that the young people do not allow the elders to select their partners. The older Africans give the large number of foolish choices as one reason for the greater instability of the marriage relationship.

Cash, supplied mainly by the young man alone, is being increasingly substituted for the cattle or goods of the old marriage payments. A mercenary element is thus creeping into the arrangements.

'The new attitude may be summed up in the generalization that anyone who is entitled to receive anything will tend to take it in cash, and at the highest valuation possible, and, having received the cash, will spend it, probably, on personal gratifications rather than on making a new marriage, as used to be the case with the cattle payments and some others. Fathers will tend to ask for the highest payment attainable, with the result that it may be difficult for the young men to marry, that they will have to incur debts to do so, and that the period involved in producing the amount is unduly extended.' [1]

In those areas where income is mainly derived from wage labour the high cost of marriage and the further expense of maintaining a wife and family have practically eliminated polygyny. Large households are now common only in those

[1] L. P. Mair, 'African Marriage and Social Change', *African Marriage and Family Life* (ed. A. Phillips), Oxford, 1953, p. 153.

regions such as West Africa where money is obtained through the sale of farm produce on overseas markets. Here each wife is an extra worker whose labour supplements both the husband's food supply and his earning capacity.

It is not clear whether the divorce rate is generally rising, but there can be no doubt that many of the sanctions against marital infidelity are not now operative. The adulterer or wife stealer has no need today to fear a direct attack by the injured husband, and although in many places wives may still be beaten, they can never be held by force; moreover, they do not risk capture by slave traders or enemies if they run away. The belief in supernatural punishment for sexual transgressions is also beginning to lose its force.

Pre-marital conception is becoming more common. The Africans place most of the blame on the curtailment or abandonment of the instruction given in the initiation ceremonies. Probably more important are such factors as the freedom of the young people, the ease with which the seducer can escape the consequences of his seduction by entering European employment, and the prolongation of the betrothal period necessitated by the added cost of the marriage payments.

The weakening of the family and marriage ties has gone furthest around the great towns of central and southern Africa. The long separation of husbands and wives is the main cause. The men are obliged to go away to work in order to provide their families with what are now regarded as the necessities of life, and most of them consider that an urban slum is not a fit place for women and children. The wives left at home grow weary of waiting and accept the advances of others. The few couples who migrate together are cut off from their kinsfolk and thus deprived of assistance in inculcating in the rising generation a feeling for the accepted rules and values. Often the father and mother both have to take jobs to support themselves, and the children grow up with almost no home care.

Studies comparable to the survey of African marriage, though less broad in their scope, have been carried out with reference to the institutions involving matrilineal descent. Even in pre-industrial conditions a stress on the female line created fundamental conflicts, and change is often taking place today on a considerable scale.

Most primitive communities insist upon exogamy, that is marriage with a person from a different kinship unit. When the rule operates in conjunction with matriliny the people are faced with the situation of the woman being united with a man from another group but bearing children for her own. If she leaves her place of birth and joins the husband, then her kinsmen are obliged to contrive some means of retaining control over the offspring, who are legally identified with them. Her brothers, located at a distance, find themselves dividing their authority with the father, who is there all the time. The position is no less confused when the reverse procedure is adopted, and the husband leaves his kinsfolk and takes up residence with his wife. Her brothers will also have moved away to the places where their respective spouses belong and are still not on hand to give continual supervision in the upbringing of the children. A further difficulty is that men rather than women mostly exercise authority both in the household and in the wider political sphere. The husband who is a stranger among his wife's people is accordingly the dominant partner in the union and yet in a position of subordination. He usually finds his bonds so irksome that he takes every means within his power to escape.[1]

The solution generally followed in Melanesia was either the localized fraternal extended family or else the sub-clan locally centred, with all the married males living in the same hamlet or village. The brothers or fellow sub-clansmen held their land in common and exercised full authority over their own small community, but the sisters, together with their young children, were scattered. They resided in several settlements, each with her husband. Sons and daughters remained with the father and

---

[1] See A. I. Richards, 'Some Types of Family Structure among the Central Bantu', *African Systems of Kinship and Marriage* (ed. A. R. Radcliffe-Brown and D. Forde) Oxford, 1950, pp. 246-50.

mother till puberty or a little later. The boys, once they realized that they had no rights in their father's ground, turned more and more to the maternal uncles and other senior males of their own group. They eventually took up permanent residence with these men, leaving the father, who by then had his own uterine nephews to depend on. Girls normally went straight from the father's house to the husband without spending an interval under the care of a maternal uncle.

Trobriand Island society still operated on these principles early in the century, when Malinowski carried out his field work. He recorded that the natural affection of a father for his sons made him resentful of having to hand on his wealth to his nephews. Nobody could avoid the correct transmission of his land rights, which were held jointly by members of the sub-clan, but all sorts of subterfuges were resorted to so that a share of the movables and similar property could go to the sons. The result was that the nephews were always on guard to prevent themselves from being defrauded. Bad feeling was general and quarrels frequent.[1]

Matrilineal Guadalcanal, in the Solomons, during 1933 had many features in common with the Trobriands. I lived with the islanders during that year, and several times after a death had taken place saw a nephew attack a son while the corpse still lay unburied. 'All the dead man's baskets belong to me, and you must hand back what he gave you', the nephew would shout. 'He gave me nothing', the son would reply. 'Everything I have came from my maternal uncles.' In Busama also, although the present rule is that land rights alone pass to the sisters' sons, the natives insist that this is a fairly recent, but pre-European, development. Earlier, they say, everything went to the nephews, but the fathers revolted and began giving personal possessions to their sons. Whether or not this tradition is authentic scarcely matters. The fact of its existence bears out the contention that matrilineal systems tend to be poorly integrated.

[1] B. Malinowski, *Crime and Custom in Savage Society*, London, 1926, pp. 100–11.

Today movables are coming to be prized more and more. They now include not only native valuables but also money and Western goods, in some cases such capital equipment as sewing-machines, motor-trucks, and boats. Further, customary restraints are losing their force, and the natives feel fewer scruples about following their private inclinations. In many parts of Melanesia nephews have already ceased to count on inheriting anything save land rights from their maternal uncles.

Commercial agriculture raises additional complications. In the past a man often owned a few coconut palms or fruit trees that were growing on ground belonging to other persons. In those days no one was much inconvenienced. Ample land for gardening was available, and the patches temporarily occupied by an intruder were always small. But nowadays coconuts can be made into copra and sold to traders, and in some places cocoa has been introduced as a cash crop. Palm and cocoa groves, because they are a financial asset, are becoming more extensive. A native usually chooses his own land for planting and then insists that, although the title to the soil may go to his nephews, the trees upon it must pass to his sons, who will often have helped him with the work. Suitable areas for crops of this kind, as distinct from those for the ordinary food crops, are usually limited, and the nephews may suffer hardship. Disputes are of everyday occurrence, and at times the legal tangles cannot be sorted out.

In the district around the town of Rabaul, in New Britain, where European influence has been active for over seventy years, the matrilineal system is on the point of collapse. The available evidence suggests that regular rules of residence and inheritance no longer exist. Some men live with their matrilineal kin, some with their patrilineal kin, some inherit from their maternal uncles, some from their father. Many of the natives are themselves in doubt about where they stand, and recently one of the official councils passed a resolution urging the district commissioner to make a ruling that in future all forms of property, including land, must be transmitted in the male line. As the motion went through on a majority vote, and several speakers had expressed opposition, he has not yet made a final decision.[1]

Another solution for the matrilineal puzzle was the extended family consisting of sisters and their male and female descendants in the female line. The women of the group lived under one roof, but in some communities the brothers regularly resided with their sisters and visited their wives, while in others they resided with their wives and visited their sisters. All forms of property were held jointly, and the senior male member, whether he was resident in the household or not, acted as manager of the estate. Such an arrangement could be worked satisfactorily only in areas of dense population, where the dwellings were so close together that a person could discharge his separate functions of brother and husband without grave inconvenience or serious clash of interests. This requirement was met among the Nair of Malabar, the Malays of Negri Sembilan, and the Menangkabau of Sumatra.

Nair law had always provided for the breaking up of the extended family, and the consequent splitting of the property, when the group became so large as to be unwieldy. The decision, nevertheless, rested solely with the manager. His prestige was to some extent bound up with the number of his followers, and as a rule he delayed taking action for as long as possible. When the opportunities for earning money began to increase the younger men became restive. They wished to use the cash for themselves and their children and disliked paying it into the estate for the benefit of all their matrilineal kinsfolk. At length, in 1933, the legislature passed an act permitting the division of the extended family on the request of a majority of the members, with or without the manager's approval. Almost every group has since then divided. It would be inaccurate to say that the old type of structure has disappeared, for many of the new units, though small in scale, are modelled on the

---

[1] No recent information on the Rabaul natives has been published. This summary of the situation is based on conversations with a number of government officers.

traditional pattern. At the same time, the trend is towards fragmentation, and already some groups consist of a single simple
family. Individualism is being further nurtured by the par-
tition of the land. Six households each of five persons take up
more space, and together are more costly to run, than one
household of thirty persons. Some of the present holdings are
so tiny and so cut up into widely scattered strips that they do
not suffice for the support of their owners, and the menfolk are
driven to enter employment in the towns. Sometimes they then
decide to sell in order to obtain capital. The cash derived from
the transaction has on occasion been spent in ways of which we
would approve, as, for example, when it was used for defraying
the cost of education; but it is often frittered away on objects of
no lasting worth, and the people become paupers.[1]

Changes in the extended family of Negri Sembilan were precipitated by the world demand for rubber. Originally the
people had an interest only in the swamps where rice could be
grown. They cultivated plots there and depended on the produce for most of their food. Any surplus was sold, and the
money then went towards the purchase of the few extra essentials. Each group had its own areas, and although small sections were occasionally sold such permanent alienation took
place with the consent of all the members.

When Europe and America began buying rubber the forests
at once assumed importance. Individual men now began clearing patches of jungle to plant rubber trees. They argued that
the latex belonged to them, to be sold for their personal gain,
and that the land should go to their sons. These forest areas
soon became so valuable that Chinese and other Malays sought
to purchase them. A split now developed between those who
wanted the direct return and those who felt that, in the interest
of future generations, the rubber lands should be incorporated

---

[1] A. C. Mayer, *Land and Society in Malabar*, London, 1952, pp. 99–104. If a man
leaves his wealth to his children, and no further division takes place, it ultimately
passes to his daughters' children, and matrilineal inheritance is thus restored. (Cf. the
situation among the Yao as described by J. C. Mitchell, 'An Outline of the Social
Structure of the Malemia Area', *Nyasaland Journal*, Vol. IV, No. 2, p. 44.)

into the ancestral estates. Religious values also came into the discussions. The Malays, as Muslims, are obliged to respect the *Shari'a*, a system of rules supposedly ordained by divine will for the guidance of the faithful. Human custom is in theory valid only if it can be shown to fall within the scope of the sacred law. The *Shari'a* originated in a society with a patrilineal bias, and despite some provision for the rights of women, none at all is made for matrilineal groups as the holders of property. The religious authorities, aware of the problem at last, are in favour of wholesale changes in the method of inheritance, and a clash of opinion has arisen on the extent of their proper rôle, and that of religion generally, in a modern Muslim State. The future of the extended family, to judge from Nair experience, is already precarious, and if more attention comes to be paid to the orthodox view a speedy disappearance may with some confidence be forecast.[1]

The Bemba and some other tribes of central Africa found still a third answer to the matrilineal question. The country here was too sparsely settled, with villages many miles apart, for the men to move backwards and forwards easily between the two households. The usual economic unit consisted of a man and his wife, their daughters, and the daughters' husbands and children. At marriage the bridegroom's relatives handed over bride price on his behalf, but his parents-in-law expected him to join them and spend several years at their side. Not until he had completed this period of service was he allowed to return to his own kinsfolk. The young husbands cleared the agricultural land, hunted, and carried out any necessary building and repairs under their father-in-law's orders, and at the end of the day the wives served them a meal that had been cooked on the mother-in-law's hearth. The father-in-law was even responsible for the time being for the husbands' spiritual welfare. It was part of his duty to offer sacrifices to the spirits on behalf not only of his daughters but also of his sons-in-law. When eventually a couple moved to the village of the man's

[1] R. Firth, *Elements of Social Organization*, London, 1951, pp. 107-8.

maternal grandfather or uncle he co-operated with his affinal relatives there, but, as these persons were strangers, he was their superior. He also sent his wife to cook with his own female relatives. At a later date still, as his daughters grew old enough to marry, he set up an establishment of his own, either in the settlement of his matrilineal kinsmen or in a village that he himself established. Sons went with their father each time he changed his place of abode and remained with him till their marriage. They were affiliated, nevertheless, with their maternal uncles, who alone had the obligation of helping them to pay any fine imposed by the chief. An uncle had the right, indeed, in certain circumstances, to sell his sisters' sons into slavery.

The crucial factor in the present situation is that wage labour in the European towns is the sole source of cash income. The seniors have too many responsibilities to leave home and are therefore dependent for money, and all that it will buy, on the younger men. A husband who is away in employment cannot also work for his father-in-law, and money is accepted as the equivalent of the old period of service. The older men may prefer that this should be so as they have no other means of obtaining Western goods. The payments, however, are an alternative to, and not a substitute for, the contribution to the food supply, and in many parts of the Bemba territory agriculture is suffering. The young man on returning, if he has paid his father-in-law a sufficient sum, may insist on taking his wife away at once; or, if he has not seen her for some years, he may abandon her in favour of the sister of one of his workmates. Desertion thus occurs more often than in the past, and the extended-family groups break up much earlier.[1]

I intend to follow on the lines suggested by these studies from which I have been quoting and give some account of the institutions of the present-day Melanesians with whom I am personally most familiar, namely the inhabitants of eastern

[1] A. I. Richards, *Bemba Marriage and Present Economic Conditions*, Rhodes-Livingstone Papers, No. 4, 1940.

New Guinea, the Bismarck Archipelago, and the Solomon Islands. But first it will be necessary to say something about native life in the days before European contact began and also to discuss the different agencies that are operating to bring about the changes.

CHAPTER VI

The Background to Social
Change in Melanesia

THROUGHOUT Melanesia in earlier days large concentrations of population were impracticable. One reason was the difficulty of communication. Hundreds of languages have been recorded, each associated with a culture that differed in details from the rest. Some of the dialects were spoken all over an extensive region, but the majority were confined to a small strip of territory. The 40,000 inhabitants of the island of Malaita, which is only 1,500 square miles in area, were, for example, divided into eighteen linguistic and cultural units. Transport was a further problem. The main islands all have a backbone of lofty ranges, with peaks running up to 16,000 feet; and, as the rainfall is heavy, the rivers are swift, dangerous, and seldom navigable. If a plain intervenes between the mountains and the sea much of it is impenetrable swamp infested with crocodiles. Again, few of the indigenous food crops could be stored for long periods. They were grown on a system of shifting cultivation, with the plots left to lie fallow for a decade or longer, and each family therefore needed at least ten times the amount of ground under cultivation during any given year.

It follows that Melanesian societies were inevitably minute in scale. The widest community with a coherent system for the maintenance of internal order rarely exceeded three hundred members and was often much smaller. These persons lived together in a village, or they occupied a collection of contiguous hamlets or a series of neighbouring homesteads. The land boundaries between the settlements were fixed, and the residents were always ready to defend themselves from encroachment. Every group was united in friendship, nevertheless, with certain others. People so linked invited one another to festivities, and some of them even intermarried, thus strengthening the bonds and facilitating the formation of temporary alliances in warfare. Such relationships were not dependent in any way on identity of culture, and it often happened that a particular unit was friendly with two or three each speaking a different language and hostile to one having the same speech as itself.

The economic life was fairly uniform, and most of the natives were subsistence horticulturists and pig-keepers. Taro, yams, or sweet potatoes supplied the bulk of the carbohydrates, though bananas, coconuts, and other nuts were important. The swamp-dwellers were something of an exception. Not much of their land was above flood level, and they had to depend to a great extent on starch extracted from wild sago palms. The peoples living on the coast or alongside the larger rivers supplemented these foods with fish, while those of the mountains hunted for wild pigs, phalangers, bandicoots, snakes, flying foxes, and, in New Guinea, wallabies and cassowaries.

Native life revolved around the gardens. The people spent half their working time there and preferred to adorn the borders of the plots rather than the fronts of their houses with flowers and brightly coloured shrubs. In many places the men spoke not of 'owning' ground but instead said that they 'watched over' or 'looked after' this or that allotment. Several of the languages, too, used the word that literally meant 'to cultivate' for the general expression 'to work'. A person wishing to deride the members of another settlement singled out differences of diet and spoke of them as 'those filthy sweet-potato chewers', for instance, or perhaps sneered at them for pounding their taro into a mixture of coconut cream. The pagan religion was inevitably bound up with cultivation. Many of the ceremonies were carried out for the explicit purpose of securing bountiful harvests, and in those regions where the principal crop was seasonal the people offered the first fruits to the spirits before consuming anything themselves. Such groups also regulated their activities by the agricultural year. Dance festivals, visits to friends, and attacks on enemies were confined to periods when the gardens did not need attention.

Despite the general uniformity, the natural resources of the districts varied, and a limited amount of trade took place, usually on the basis of gift exchanges between individuals. In some areas clays suitable for moulding into pots were found solely in the vicinity of one or two settlements. The inhabitants made all the cooking-vessels, which they offered to their neighbours in return for extra supplies of vegetables and such other goods as mats, nets, carved bowls, bamboo musical instruments, cosmetics, shell ornaments, and feathers. Each object was as a rule equated with certain others, and a pot of a particular size, for instance, was worth so many baskets of taro or so many nets. A number of areas had a form of ceremonial currency consisting of shell discs, cowrie shells, mother-of-pearl shell, or dogs' teeth. This could sometimes be substituted for a few of the larger items.

From time to time trade took place in religious rituals and dances. The exchange was not now between individuals, but between settlements. The buyers through their leader presented the leader of the sellers with large quantities of pigs and ceremonial currency, and in return were taught what to do.[1]

Men and women were allotted separate work, but specialization was rare, and everyone was a Jack of nearly all the trades. The only experts were the priests, magicians, and certain craftsmen, such as the wood-carvers and the supervisors in house-

[1] At times ritual forms were traded and then used for the worship of spirits already being honoured, and at times the spirit was passed on with the ceremonies. In Guadalcanal, for example, if the local division of a clan had been markedly successful in war the members allowed friendly units in other villages to buy the privilege of taking over the ancestral being judged to have been responsible. Several groups held sacred the spirit of a woman named Kulanikama, who derived her fame from the fact that she had sprung to her husband's rescue during an attack and killed his assailant with a pudding spoon.

building and canoe construction, and even these practised their speciality solely as a spare-time occupation. Thus the community priest and wood-carvers spent most of their days gardening, fishing, or hunting like everyone else. A person who engaged an expert generally rewarded him with a gift of food, but for a lengthy job he might have to organize a feast in the man's honour.

Some tasks could be carried out by the members of the family acting alone, but for others further help was necessary. A householder in need of such outside assistance turned to his relatives, whom he numbered by the score or even by the hundred. All the residents of his own settlement were included, as well as several persons from other places round about. The ties were maintained by frequent gifts of food and attendance at the various family ceremonies.

Structural arrangements were built up on kinship, and this large body of kindred was divided into smaller units, which were often named. The significant factor in most areas was descent in one line. Here the persons who traced themselves from the same ancestor either through males exclusively or through females exclusively considered that they were specially close to one another. If they claimed to be aware of the connecting links, even though the information might not have been strictly accurate, we speak of the group as a patrilineage or matrilineage; if, on the other hand, the forbear was some mythological character from the far-distant past and the precise nature of the links was not considered to be of sufficient importance to be memorized, we speak of it as a clan. Less common were the communities in which all lines of descent were stressed equally. A man's closest ties were then with the persons having one or other of the same grandfathers or great-grandfathers as himself. This type of organization is referred to as cognatic.[1]

The details of kinship behaviour showed considerable

---

[1] For a general classification of the social structures of Melanesia see H. I. Hogbin and C. H. Wedgwood, 'Local Grouping in Melanesia', *Oceania*, Vol. XXIII, pp. 241–76, and Vol. XXIV, pp. 58–76.

variety. In some areas a man exercised control over his sons and transmitted his wealth to them, whereas in others he had the rôle of disciplinarian in the households of his sisters, whose sons eventually became his heirs. Yet the general rule remains true that all relatives, including those united by marriage, were expected to be mutually helpful. The householder accordingly satisfied his needs by working with some or all of his kinsmen, depending on the magnitude of the job in hand. For routine tasks like gardening and fishing he was content with the co-operation of a few men from his lineage, clan, or cognatic group; but such activities as house-building and canoe construction demanded forty or fifty; and if disaster threatened he called upon everyone.

The senior men of each kin group directed the affairs of the rest by virtue of their age and status. These were the elders of the community, looked up to by everybody. Technically one or other of the elders was also the owner of the items for whose fashioning a large number of persons had collaborated. The object might not have been of any use to him by himself, but he enjoyed the prestige of being able to say that it was his. In return for this honour he was expected to shoulder the responsibility of maintaining it in good condition and deciding when and by whom it was to be used. Thus in Busama when a kin group needed a new seine one of its elders always made the appropriate arrangements. He enlisted the help of his juniors, who agreed after the task was completed that the net belonged to him. They let him give the word for it to be taken out and say where it was to go and which persons were to man the canoes and which the ropes, and afterwards they waited for him to distribute the catch. He also had to see that the seine was properly dried, mended if torn, and safely stored away.

The importance of the owner was demonstrated by an incident that occurred in Busama in 1945, just after the Pacific war ended. The seines had all been destroyed a year or two before when the village was bombed by Allied planes under the mistaken notion that Japanese soldiers were lurking there, but now at last I secured one as a partial replacement from an army fisheries unit. I intended offering it as a gift to the people at large until several of them warned me that a presentation on such terms was the height of folly and an invitation to dis-harmony and waste. They asked me how did I imagine that quarrels would be composed and repairs effected. Each person would say to himself that the net was not his and that he had no need to take any trouble over it. Give it to one man, they told me. Acting on this advice, I handed it to a close friend. He has looked after it so well that it is still in constant service.

The elders in Melanesian communities also had a great deal to say about the choice of marriage partners. As in Africa, they argued that working capacity, good temper, and willingness to co-operate were prime considerations, and that, because they were disinterested, their judgement was better than that of the young people. The match was a means of creating new connec-tions or reaffirming those already in existence, and the seniors were keen to ensure that the greatest advantages should accrue from it. Marriages were always exogamous, and the bride-groom and bride had to belong to separate lineages or clans. The contract was usually ratified by the transfer of bride price, the handing over of food and ceremonial currency donated by most of the man's kinsmen to the kinsmen of the woman.

Every settlement, in addition to the elders, had a headman, or, if it included more than about two hundred inhabitants, one for every component section. In the majority of the islands this office was open to all, and anyone could rise to the top if he displayed the appropriate qualities to an outstanding degree. He had to be a natural leader and organizer of men, to be even-tempered, tactful, and industrious, and it was advisable for him also to have shown resourcefulness and strength in battle. Often a reputation as a sorcerer helped. The procedure to secure advancement was to accumulate wealth, which consisted of food supplemented by ceremonial currency. He needed many assistants both within and without the household, and, partly with this aim in mind, he married a number of wives. Each woman looked after a separate garden and when the occasion arose could be relied upon to call for aid from her kinsmen. Supplies over and above the needs of the family were used for the benefit and entertainment of the rest of the people. The person fired by ambition contributed to the bride price of the young men of the settlement, fed visitors who came to his dwelling, and made himself responsible for the great feasts with which every event of outstanding importance was celebrated, including the performance of the major pagan religious ceremonies, the building of the club-houses where the men spent their evenings, the inauguration of trading voyages, and the successful conclusion of an attack on an enemy settlement. The members of the community were thus in a permanent state of debt to him and felt obliged to acknowledge him as their superior.

There were a few places, however, where the members of certain families were alone eligible for the post of headman. The Trobriand Islands and Wogeo are examples. The man ultimately selected owed the distinction to the fact that, by virtue of his birth, he had inherited from his predecessors special magic of general benefit. He was thought to be able to control the weather, promote the growth of crops, annihilate enemies by means of specially deadly sorcery, and ensure victory in war. These powers enabled him to demand either the services of his fellows in the gardens or else contributions of foodstuffs for his storehouses. Like the leaders elsewhere, he was therefore rich and in a position to make the usual distributions and feasts.

The headman was in constant consultation with the elders, and although his word carried the greatest weight, he could do little without their support. He was in a sense their spokesman when he announced the decision to hold a ceremony, organize a trading voyage, or carry out an attack against a neighbouring village. A headman who ignored the wishes of the community and tried to act arbitrarily was quickly removed. Revolt was easy when he had no personal bodyguard and everyone could handle a spear.

As has been mentioned, the small local community possessed a system for the maintenance of order. Breaches of the peace were infrequent. The residents depended upon one another's help and regularly combined to carry out their daily work; moreover, they considered that, as kinsmen, they were under a moral obligation to live in amity. Each person was accordingly careful to do his best to avoid injuring his fellows. Further, if by chance he was himself injured, he normally refrained from showing resentment. He knew that if he picked a quarrel he was likely to lose the co-operation of his opponent for some time afterwards. Yet on the rare occasions when some serious wrong was actually committed regular procedures existed for securing redress. The man who had suffered assembled his lineage mates, his fellow clansmen, or the members of his cognatic group, and they all set off together to have the matter out with the offender. They were unwilling to injure him severely, for this would have meant a loss to the community as a whole, and unless he was a consistent defaulter, and thus a general embarrassment, they were as a rule content with perhaps reproaching him for his conduct or giving him a beating. A wordy argument frequently developed, but the elders closely related to both parties used their influence to restore harmony. An injured person who was still dissatisfied could as a last resort appeal to the headman. The latter, if he considered a case must be answered, summoned the elders to a more or less formal gathering at which the rights and wrongs of the matter were fully investigated. He then pronounced judgement in the light of their deliberations. Usually the culprit had to apologize and hand over food and ceremonial currency as compensation. Civil disputes were settled in similar fashion. If rival claims were put forward for a strip of land, or a disagreement occurred over the value of foodstuffs destroyed by a village pig, or bridal payments were outstanding, the headman and elders discussed the question until they reached a definite conclusion about what ought to be done.

Those beyond the kinship range, in contrast with those inside it, were treated as strangers whose goodwill and animosity were alike of no consequence. The householder did not require their aid and could thus afford to disregard their feelings. Such persons ran the risk of being killed on sight. Travellers generally took the precaution of restricting their journeys to settlements where they had a kinsman living and on arrival at once placed themselves under his protection. The headman, too, when seeking allies in warfare went only to places where he and some of the principal elders were relatives. Again, if he wished to arrange a trading voyage he collected a fleet of canoes in case the expedition was driven off course by a gale and those taking part had to defend themselves from attack.

The result was that no judicial body existed with authority to deal with offences committed by a man of one settlement against a man from another. Yet if relations between the two places had for a long period been friendly, and a good deal of intermarriage had taken place, the headmen sometimes called a joint conference of the respective elders to offer advice. Their verdict was not binding, but the parties usually accepted it in the interests of continuing harmony. They listened and obeyed because they were anxious to secure a settlement. But when the groups were not closely associated or already enemies the aggrieved person tried to persuade his kinsmen to join him in taking vengeance. If they agreed, they went fully armed and endeavoured to kill the accused or, failing him, a member of his family, possibly a brother or a son. More often than not, however, they declined through fear lest the dead man's relatives might regard the slaying as a reason for declaring war. The wronged man then fell back on one of the lethal forms of sorcery. He either performed the rites himself or else requested the headman to do so on his behalf. He was now prepared to believe that the victim would meet a just punishment even while unaware of the precise direction whence it had come.

Desire for revenge was the most frequent cause of war. Almost all deaths, apart from those brought about by violence, were attributed to black magic, and if the deceased was an important personage the members of his settlement were anxious to make an onslaught against the alleged sorcerer and his fellows. Conflicts also arose over insults to headmen; the abduction of women, especially if they were betrothed or already married; theft of produce; and, in a few areas only, the killing of someone to provide a human victim for ritual purposes, perhaps to complete the ceremony connected with the launching of a large canoe or the opening of a new club-house. Warfare to extend territorial boundaries, except in the highlands of New Guinea, where land is short, was on the whole exceptional. The communities on the coast mostly had as much ground as they needed. Attack led to retaliation, and the hostilities then went on till one side was utterly defeated. In such circumstances the victors carried away the movables as booty and burned the houses. The survivors fled to places where they had relatives living and, unless at a later date they felt strong enough to reorganize themselves and take over the old site, were there gradually absorbed into the surrounding community. The successful warriors acquired great prestige and were allowed to wear a special ornament, such as the beak of a hornbill, to represent each kill. Often the shedding of blood in combat was regarded as the essential proof of manhood, and marriage was delayed until such time as the bridegroom had slain an enemy.

The religion was based on the worship of various spirits. Only fully initiated males were aware of the secrets of the system, and women and children depended on a guardian for their well-being. The natives honoured the spirit beings with ceremonies and sacrifices and hoped to be granted in return the blessings of good health and material prosperity. They believed, too, that certain offences angered the spirits, who then punished the wrongdoer. The penalties, however, like the rewards, were supposed to be meted out in this life and not postponed to the existence hereafter. The ancestors especially, as elders translated to a sphere where they enjoyed even greater authority, were thought to take a keen interest in the proper fulfilment of kinship obligations, and the people considered that a person who failed to help his relatives or otherwise ignored their legitimate claims, stole their property, or entered into unlawful sexual relations with one of them was sure to be overtaken by a judgement. He could expect a severe illness or some other misfortune. As expiation he had to admit his fault and beg for forgiveness.

Magic served to secure further non-human aid. Spells and other magical paraphernalia formed a valuable part of an inheritance, and the older men faithfully transmitted them to each oncoming generation. There were magical rites to ensure good crops and fine hauls of fish, to achieve victory in war, to cure illnesses, and so forth; and also magical rites to blight the cultivations of enemies, to frighten the fish away from their canoes, to undermine their strength, to inflict them with disease, and, if they had done some serious harm, to cause their death. Certain of the rites were performed by one man alone on behalf of the whole community, while others were an individual matter. Thus in those regions where the rainfall is seasonal a specialist carried out the gardening magic. The different rituals fixed the time when the successive tasks had to begin, and it was left to him to organize clearing, burning off, fencing, planting, weeding, and harvesting. Similarly, a war magician led the warriors when they set out on a campaign, and a weather magician took charge of the fleet of trading canoes.

Like all pre-industrial peoples, the natives were dominated by religious and magical thought. They had a fund of practical information about the things that were vital to them and never denied the importance of skill and hard work; but they were given neither to philosophical speculation nor to experiment, except perhaps very occasionally in the pursuit of some specific objective. Further, they were inclined to attribute success mainly to the favour of the spirits or to beneficent magic and failure mainly to the wrath of the spirits or to black magic. A

satisfactory crop or a victory in war was to them an indication
of divine goodwill or magical power, a poor harvest or a defeat
an indication of divine anger or the machinations of an evil
magician. Disease and death, as has been explained, were accounted for in similar terms. Responsibility was thus projected
on to extraneous forces, and a ready explanation could be
offered for inadequacy and inefficiency.

In their primitive state the Melanesians would have found
our Western notion of progress meaningless. I have mentioned
that they placed the golden age in the past and believed that the
culture heroes and ancestors laid down the correct modes of
behaviour at the beginning of time. Goodness consisted essentially in following precedents, and departure from immemorial
custom was considered to be in some sense sacrilege.

Religious beliefs and practices reflected the social structure
and emphasized the isolation of the different communities. The
fundamental patterns were similar, but each small group was
concerned with its own spirits to the exclusion of the rest.
Rituals, and the spirits themselves, may have been traded over
considerable distances, but when this happened, though each
new set of people remembered the origin of the cult, they always gave the rites and associated mythology a local twist.
Morals, too, operated over a narrow span. A person was loyal
to the members of his own small society and to his other relatives living nearby but had no compunction about harming
anyone else. The ancestors were thought to be swift in their
punishment of an offending descendant, but a descendant attempting to secure redress from a man of another group often
sought their help.

European Contact

The islands, although they had been discovered long before by
early Spanish, Portuguese, Dutch, and English navigators, remained practically unknown till the third and fourth decades
of the nineteenth century, when traders and whalers began
making calls there, the former for sandalwood and turtle-shell,

the latter for fresh water, food, and firewood. The people, less hospitable than the friendly Polynesians of the central Pacific, killed a number of these first visitors. It appears that the earliest permanent white residents were a few missionaries in the period shortly before and after 1850. Then in 1865 slavers started kidnapping the natives for work on the sugar and cotton plantations of Fiji and, later, Queensland. The traffic in human beings caused grave concern in Europe, and numbers of Her Majesty's ships of war were posted to the western Pacific in an endeavour to ensure that the islanders should not be taken away against their will. The efforts met with little success, and in 1894 the British Government took over the Solomon Islands as a Protectorate for the express purpose of regulating the expatriation of labour, which ceased shortly afterwards. Before this date the Australian States, fearful of the colonial ambitions of the foreign powers, had made representations to Great Britain that eastern New Guinea be annexed. The south-eastern portion, together with the outlying islands, did in fact become a British colony in 1884, and later in the same year Germany claimed the north-eastern section and the Bismarck Archipelago. The Australian States federated in 1900, and six years afterwards Britain handed over British New Guinea to the Australian Commonwealth. The territory now received the name of Papua. Australian troops captured German New Guinea and the Bismarcks in 1914, and since that time this area also has been administered by the Commonwealth, first under a Mandate of the League of Nations, subsequently as a Trust Territory of the United Nations.

Japanese forces overran many of the islands during World War II, and some parts were still in enemy hands at the cessation of hostilities. Bitter fighting went on with the Japanese on the one hand and the Australians and Americans on the other, and the natives suffered great hardship. Yet the effects of this sudden major catastrophe were less remarkable than the steady erosion that had been going on for so long.

Melanesia has never proved attractive to European settlers,

and the total white population is still only a few thousands, consisting largely of government officials, missionaries, traders, planters, gold-miners, and geologists and technicians engaged in the search for oil. The chief agencies of contact are therefore the several administrations, which have suppressed native warfare, imposed a new system of law, introduced health services, subsidized education, and here and there set out to teach the people how to grow crops for sale; the missions, which have converted the natives to Christianity and given them elementary schooling; and the commercial concerns, which have engaged the men as labourers on the coconut, rubber, coffee, and cocoa estates, in the gold-mines, and on the oil surveys, paid them a money wage, and brought in Western goods for sale.

The process of Westernization has gone farthest in the vicinity of the larger European towns, some of which were founded more than three-quarters of a century ago. They include Port Moresby, the old capital of Papua and at present the centre from which the combined New Guinea territories are governed; Samarai, also in Papua; Madang and Lae in the New Guinea Trust Territory; and Rabaul in New Britain, the largest of the Bismarck Islands. The schools here are of higher standard than elsewhere, and in most cases there are also agricultural and technical training establishments. Many of the people in consequence speak and write English and have abandoned a large number of their old ways. Some have even adopted a full money economy and European living standards. The natives of the coast and foothills elsewhere have been affected by the West but not to the same extent. If they come from the Trust Territory of New Guinea or the Solomons they all speak Melanesian pidgin-English (sometimes referred to as neo-Melanesian), and if from Papua police-Motuan, a simplified version of the language of the residents of Hanuabada in Port Moresby. Each of these is a *lingua franca*, and a European who is familiar with them can easily make himself understood anywhere. On the coast and in the foothills, too, raiding has ceased, most of the people have been baptized, the young men accept employment as normal routine, and a good many imported goods have found their way into the villages. The folk from the interior of the bigger islands, such as New Guinea and New Britain, form a third category. Some of these have not yet seen a white man, and they are in consequence still completely primitive. But patrol officers penetrate more deeply each year, and missionaries and labour recruiters are always close behind them.

The main factors in the present situation are the new legal system, wage labour, new equipment, cash crops, and Christianity. I shall deal with each one in turn.

The New Legal System

Sir William Fitzgerald, a former chief justice in the colonial service, recently deplored what he referred to as 'the dumping' of English legal machinery on African territories. Present-day political forms display great diversity, he pointed out, but the judicial processes exhibit a monotonous sameness. 'We have a High Court fashioned on the High Court of Edward I, and we have judges who set themselves the very difficult task of applying the legal principles born in Norman England to conditions that have arisen in a totally different atmosphere.' These officers find that they are often obliged to settle native disputes about the ownership of a maize patch on lines laid down by 'a dissertation of Lord Coke to a young farmer from the manor of Warminster in the county of Wiltshire many hundreds of years ago'.[1]

This statement applies with equal force to the western Pacific. The codes are all based on those of the metropolitan power, and customary rules have received scant recognition. The natives may perhaps be permitted as a legal concession to keep their several wives but are denied the traditional right of personal retaliation against those who injure them. Even when the law has been modified, as has occasionally happened, the result

[1] W. Fitzgerald, 'Dangerous Rigidity of the Colonial Judiciary', *South Africa and Rhodesia*, December, 1950 (reprinted in *South Pacific*, Vol. V, p. 28).

seldom gives full satisfaction. Adultery, for example, is treated
as a crime, and both the lover and the erring spouse are liable
to imprisonment.[1] The members of groups that formerly
allowed the offended partner to demand compensation complain just as much as those from communities that permitted
him to spear the interloper. Except in the Solomons, too, where
village courts were established a few years ago, judicial authority is exercised nowadays solely by alien tribunals presided
over by a European magistrate or judge.

Yet the number of white officials has always been small, and
from the first natives were appointed to act as representatives
of the government. The earliest administrative procedure was
to confirm the principal headman of a settlement in office by
bestowing a special title upon him. He was then expected to
maintain order or, if this proved in particular cases to be impossible, to report the offenders to the nearest district station
so that they could be arrested and brought to trial. The task
was easy so long as he had risen to the top by the usual means
and on that account already enjoyed prestige. His followers
went on obeying his orders as they had done before the irrelevant honour was conferred upon him. After a generation of
extensive contact, however, the old offices disappear, and, as
we shall see, almost no true headmen now exist. The administrations go on appointing representatives, but these men are
necessarily leaders of a new type. They do not possess the
qualifications of their predecessors, and any influence that they
exert is dependent solely on government backing.

Administrative officers on the spot have during the last decade become increasingly sensitive to the criticism that the
natives play such a small part in the judicial processes. The
Australian Government in Canberra has so far proved unsym-
pathetic and made no changes in New Guinea. The British
Government, on the other hand, has taken the necessary steps
to permit the setting up of village courts in certain parts of the

---

[1] Adultery among natives is treated as a crime in Papua, the Trust Territory of New
Guinea, and the Solomons. I have not been able to discover the reason.

M

Solomon Islands. The local group elects a small body of justices who are empowered to deal with petty crimes and most of the civil disputes. They commit offenders to the ordinary gaols or order them to carry out public work, such as road or bridge repairs. The passing of sentences by natives on natives is having a marked effect on the growth of responsibility.

The New Guinea administration, prevented from taking action in this direction, is concentrating on political development. With this object in view it has set up village councils in some of the more economically advanced areas. Each set of councils is under the care of a native authorities officer, whose job is, in effect, to make his services ultimately unnecessary. These officials are at present engaged in giving guidance in recognized democratic procedures, including the conduct of meetings, voting, recording decisions, and keeping accounts. The biggest hindrance so far has been illiteracy, and at almost every sitting the officer may be seen drawing attention to elementary arithmetic to make the councillors realize that the allocation of funds for educational and other projects should remain within the limits of the money available.

The first lessons must begin at the settlement level, but no real progress can be made until the units become larger. The population of the average community is only a couple of hundreds, and not many of the families could afford to contribute more than a few pounds annually in direct taxation. A revenue of £100 or so is too small to provide much experience in spending but can hardly be increased until the representatives of several villages are prepared to come together as a district council. Such an organization, although it has no precedent, is in one or two instances being built up by the natives themselves.

Wage Labour

Once the menfolk remained in or near the settlement where they had spent their earlier years for the whole of their lives: nowadays the vast majority go away to work for Europeans.

The only areas in which wage labour is not important are those in the vicinity of some of the towns, where money can be acquired by other means, and those not yet fully opened up. Throughout the rest of the islands the youths leave home at the age of sixteen or seventeen and spend an average of six years as paid workers. Most of them go to the plantations, though some are absorbed by the oil surveys and the gold mines.

European commercial agriculture, and the mines also, are concentrated in a few places, and the bulk of the labour has to be brought long distances. In the Solomons, for instance, the larger plantations are all located in the sparsely populated Russell or Cape Marsh Islands, but the principal reservoir for labour is Malaita; and in the Trust Territory of New Guinea the chief development has been in the eastern Bismarcks—in New Ireland and on the Gazelle Peninsula of north-eastern New Britain—whereas the native employees come mainly from the central highlands and the Sepik River district of the mainland of New Guinea. Travel is costly, and the labourers must serve for a couple of years before they are eligible for repatriation at the employer's expense. Those who stay for the usual period thus see their homes only once or twice until they finally go back and marry.

The youths dislike the thought of being considered provincial and are eager to see something of the world. Village life also offers fewer attractions for young people than in the old days, when exciting festivals and dances took place. 'Back here there's only toil and church', one returned labourer told me in boredom and disgust. 'In the labour compounds we had dances after knocking-off time. We painted our faces, put on ornaments, played the hand-drum, and enjoyed ourselves.' The Christian sexual code, too, with its strong emphasis on chastity before marriage, though it is in line with the customs of some communities, is the direct opposite of those of many others. In the Trobriands and Wogeo, to quote two instances, promiscuity was the rule. Again, going away to work is often an easy way of escaping from unpleasant consequences when a man has committed an offence. He signs up with a labour recruiter in the hope that the person he has wronged will have forgiven him by the time he returns.

But the principal reason for entering employment is undoubtedly poverty. The natives, though formerly self-supporting, ceased to be independent from the moment when they first accepted steel. They quickly forgot the techniques for fashioning stone implements and would today starve if deprived of Western tools. The sale of labour is usually the sole available means of earning money to buy such goods, and only where the people can grow a cash crop is the percentage of absentee labourers small.

Wants soon expand, and even in comparatively isolated areas clothing, nails, razors, looking glasses, and tobacco are now regarded as necessities. The inhabitants of Busama, although by no means as Westernized as the householders living on the outskirts of Port Moresby or Rabaul, are typical of the peoples who have had fairly prolonged contact with Europeans. The district came under government control in 1900, and the flourishing town of Lae, originally developed in 1930 as an air base for servicing the gold fields of the interior, is within easy reach by canoe. (Salamaua, another settlement dating from a slightly earlier period, was even nearer, but this was obliterated by aerial bombardment in 1943 and has never been rebuilt.) When these natives set out their claims for damage done during the Pacific war twenty-five per cent of the sum asked for, £540 out of a total of £2,200, was for Western goods or money. The items, in addition to those just enumerated, included a dozen bicycles, several sewing-machines, three full sets of carpenter's tools, sundry saws, planes and hammers, two or three gramophones, books, household furniture, bedding, lamps, crockery, saucepans and other cooking utensils, enamel dishes, benzine irons, clocks, and watches. A small native-owned shop in the village today stocks tea, coffee, cocoa, lemonade, sugar, tinned meat, bread, butter, rice, flour, kero-

sene, soap, talcum powder, toothpaste, brushes, shaving out-
fits, towels, calico, sewing cotton, needles, fishlines and hooks,
tobacco, cigarettes, axes, knives, table cutlery, and crockery.

The jobs that the average labourer is called upon to do seldom require any special skill, and earnings are in consequence
low. Rations are supplied, but the average wage is about thirty
shillings per month. A few tasks, such as rubber tapping and
some of the work connected with mining, demand elementary
instruction but have little relation to the man's future at home.
Knowledge of how to tap a rubber tree, for instance, is useless
unless he also learns how to establish and care for a rubber
plantation and market the produce.

Yet the number of men who have been taught English and
the practice of the simpler crafts, though still small, is growing,
and today a few hundreds are able to hold positions as clerks,
carpenters, motor-drivers, telephonists, and mechanics. In this
class the natives in the senior non-commissioned ranks of the
police force and in the medical services must also be included.
Such workers command considerably higher pay than the
general labourers. The largest proportion come from Hanuabada, where the country is too dry for intensive agriculture,
and the people have to become wage-earners if they want cash.
As they live close to Port Moresby they are readily absorbed
locally and go home each afternoon. But there are also skilled
workers from the remoter areas. A few may have been chosen
for training because of their early promise, but the majority
probably owed their good fortune to luck. Such men are unwilling to surrender their advantages by returning to the village
at the end of the usual six years. They either bring a wife to
their place of employment or else marry a woman from near at
hand. They may continue to correspond with their relatives
and spend holidays in their place of birth, but many of them in
course of time gradually lose touch.

Life in the labour compounds is squalid. The workers, all
of them youths or young men, are detached from village influences and inevitably throw off moral restraints. The allied

armies faced a similar problem during the last War and found a solution in educational and amenities units, which were instrumental in maintaining standards of citizenship and, in some cases, of promoting intellectual growth. The island administrations and missions have so far ignored the example, and welfare institutions and night schools for native labourers do not exist anywhere. Apart from dancing and a little cricket and football, the chief pastime for the hours of leisure is gambling. The police make frequent raids but are powerless to stop the play. They are also unable to curb male prostitution.[1]

The absence of so many of the young men does not as a rule cause material hardship in the villages. The use of steel tools has meant that the daily tasks are easier, and they can also be carried out in a fraction of the time. Clearing a patch of ground for a new garden when implements were made of stone must have been extremely arduous, but today the felling of a tree, instead of occupying a gang of men for perhaps a whole day, is finished by two or three persons in a few minutes or hours. The same is true also of house-building and canoe construction. The governments recognize that the safety limit can be exceeded, and officials are empowered to forbid recruiters entering areas that appear to be in danger of losing too many workers. At the same time, a good deal of latitude is permitted in the interpretation of the regulations, and it occasionally happens that, while the proportion of absentees from the district as a whole is reasonable, individual kinship groups are handicapped. The houses cannot then be repaired or rebuilt, the gardens shrink in size, and the old folk, women, and children may be inadequately provided for. But even in the most-favoured villages the living standards are low, and there is some doubt whether these can ever be raised while the fittest males are obliged to spend such long periods away. Effective education, for which the natives are already clamouring, will

---

[1] Alcohol is not a serious problem. The labourers steal spirits if they have a chance, and they occasionally make brews of their own, but fermented drinks have never played a part in Melanesian cultures.

take up more time and the cultivation of some of the cash crops demand extra workers.

The social effects of wage labour are more significant. It has undoubtedly contributed to a moral decline. The young men are away from home for so long that they forget the precepts inculcated in childhood; moreover, they learn no others during their absence with which these might have been replaced. Their sense of obligation to their fellows is in consequence dulled, and petty crimes such as thieving become more common.

New Equipment

I have enumerated the European objects found in the villages. Although there is considerable variety, the vast bulk of them are simple consumer goods. Native purchases are still restricted by poverty, inexperience, and lack of education.

The only capital goods commonly met with are sewing-machines and carpenter's kits. The owners of the sewing-machines, most of them men, fashion their own garments and, for a small fee, make up material supplied by their neighbours. Trained carpenters who have decided to return home in middle life also accept engagements, again for a fee, to direct the construction of a house and build the flight of steps to the doorway. These sempsters and builders resemble the old-time specialists in that they carry out jobs for others in their spare time. But whereas the magicians and canoe-makers were given food, the surplus of which they distributed among their kinsmen, the new experts receive cash and may spend it on themselves.

The native qualified for nothing but general labouring can by dint of careful forethought save enough money for a sewing-machine. Except in special circumstances, this is his limit. His earning capacity is so low that the more expensive items are beyond his reach. But even if he were able to afford the price of elaborate equipment he would seldom have the knowledge required for using and maintaining it. Further, unless he lived close to a town, he could neither take a bulky object to

his home nor bring out the products for sale. Ships and aeroplanes ply between the commercial centres, but the islands have
few roads, and the villages are mostly reached by the roughest
of trails. Packages too heavy to be carried on the back therefore cannot possibly be transported. The result is that nowhere
is there a native-owned power-plant, sawmill, or anything of
the kind.

Conditions are different around the towns, and here the
people have wider opportunities. Better education is one factor.
As was pointed out, the schools are superior to those in the distant settlements, and the willing student can acquire a technical
background. He is then eligible for employment at a higher
wage than the unskilled labourer. But those with little schooling may also do well. The network of roads extends outwards
for several miles, and if the climate and soil permit it is possible
not only to grow but to sell commercial crops. In the villages
near Port Moresby, Rabaul, Lae, and one or two other places a
new moneyed class is growing up. In the Rabaul and Lae settlements numbers of men, some barely literate, have even managed to save enough cash to purchase trucks and set themselves
up as carriers. They charge a set tariff for delivering loads and
are also prepared to hire the vehicles out, with themselves as
drivers, to building contractors, storekeepers, and others. Their
working day is thus fully occupied, and they have no time left
for the traditional occupations of gardening and fishing. Earnings are sufficient, nevertheless, to allow a margin for buying
food from the town shops. A regular sum can also be set aside
for depreciation and paying the bills for major repairs demanding the appliances of a fully equipped garage. So far none of
these men has become completely Westernized. Nobody
thinks of moving out of the native circle and building a real
European house or of sending his sons to be educated in Australia. Some members of this wealthy class, indeed, use their
money as they would have done the old-style valuables and
hold feasts for the entertainment of their relatives.

The economic development of the communities of the

hinterland must obviously await the construction of highways, but near the coast, where schooners and launches can be employed, the co-operative movement offers some hope. In New Guinea the administrations and some of the missions are giving this every encouragement. Groups of persons form a society and then pool their resources to buy capital equipment. A recent report told of one such body ordering three small power-driven vessels from an Australian shipyard. The schemes have not been examined by anthropologists, and I am unable to say whether the people have taken the logical course of organizing the societies along kinship lines. If this is so the foundations will be deeply embedded in the past. The chief difficulty to be overcome will probably be that of allocating responsibility for property owned jointly.[1]

New Crops

The bulk of the commercial development of the islands has hitherto been carried out by the plantation method. This implies substantial concentration of capital and relatively advanced managerial capacity, both at present beyond the reach of most Melanesians. The estates are accordingly in the hands of individual Europeans or large companies. Modern techniques are applied, and the products are of high quality. Yet labour is a constant problem. Land is available only in areas of low population, and the workers must thus be obtained from far afield on long-term contracts. The natives, too, have always been inefficient in performance and barely adequate in numbers. The low level of work output is correlated with the fact already mentioned, that as the people gain experience or find other ways of making money they cease offering themselves as

[1] The report of the registrar of co-operatives issued in Port Moresby in July 1957 is not optimistic. Co-operatives were established in sixteen districts. 'There appears to be an element of dishonesty in many communities and this has contributed to society regression.' There were such irregularities as gifts to members (theoretically this was credit, but in practice the obligation to pay was contingent on detection), perquisites of office (free trips with pocket money), and directors' honoraria (marks of respect and appreciation unconnected with efficiency and attention to duty). In one district two major thefts had resulted in successful prosecutions.

unskilled employees. The supply has in the past been maintained solely by the recruitment of men from each new district
as it was opened up. A crisis must develop when at length the
islands have run out of such areas.

The plantation system is also vulnerable in another way.
The cost of salaries, wages, replacements, and rations for the
labourers is not only high in itself, but it is rigid in that the
same expenditure is called for throughout good times and bad.
In trade depressions many of the ventures fail.

Plantations, if they are an important element in the colonial
economy, have a bearing on general policy. They are the
stronghold of racial discrimination, an attitude that tends to
spread to all European residents. The planter believes that his
survival depends on keeping up the quantity of poorly paid
unskilled unorganized workers and is convinced that any welfare scheme that would take the people beyond the most menial
tasks is futile and dangerous. When in other territories political
ambitions have crystallized, the planters as a group have generally been the target of hostility. Any service they may have
rendered to the economy is overlooked because they are the
symbol of the master-servant relationship from which the
people wish to escape.[1]

The island administrations, now aware of these facts, have
committed themselves to introducing native cash crops. The
Melanesians, as keen horticulturists, are certainly more promis-
ing material to work on than hunting or pastoral tribesmen;
yet the cultivation methods for the traditional root vegetables
are quite different from those required for producing the
tropical crops that are in demand in world markets. Rice is a
grain, tea a leaf, coffee a berry, cocoa a fruit, kenaf a fibre,
rubber a sap, and cotton the downy substance inside a seed-
pod. If the natives are to grow these they must obviously
receive prolonged instruction.

One method of procedure would appear to be the establish-

[1] J. P. McAuley, 'Problems of Agricultural Organization', *South Pacific*, Vol. IX,
pp. 330–6.

ment of collective farms. Individuals would then own and manage the enterprise on which they were working. Further, if the acreage was extensive mechanical cultivation would be easy to apply. The main difficulty is to find adequate motivation to make certain that the natives will work hard, take initiative, and accept responsibility. In other parts of the world collectives have rarely survived over a long period without some special incentive, which has generally been religious in origin. In the few instances where island communities have taken to collective agriculture they have regarded it as a special undertaking, akin to hunting or trading expeditions. There is some doubt whether they would continue to favour it once it had ceased to be marginal to their economy.

Development by means of the small-holding probably offers more advantages. This would tap the full labour force, including the women and the aged, who are not sought after as plantation employees; costs would be low; and the farmer would to some extent be secure against economic adversity in that he could still feed himself if prices fell. The direct common interest in production would also continue to act as a binding force on the family and other small groups of kindred. Finally, the chances of political disorder occurring would be at a minimum if the majority of the people were securely rooted in small properties.

But many problems will have to be overcome. Yields from native small-holdings are generally poor; the quality of the produce is uneven; sprays and insecticides cannot be used effectively in the scattered plots, and pests and plant diseases in consequence remain uncontrolled; and bad farming methods are common and result in the destruction of soil and forest reserves. Then the price of machinery is so high that the farmer has either to do without or run into debt to money-lenders. Often the appliances cannot be employed economically without reorganizing the land-tenure system to create areas large enough for mechanical cultivation. Processing, transport, and selling techniques also tend to be unsatisfactory. Again, although the smaller kinship units persist, the larger groups lose their importance as community spirit and discipline give way to greater individualism. The traditional land law fails to solve the difficulties thrown up by commercialization, and friction occurs over titles, rights, and boundaries.[1]

Christianity

Each of the world religions as it spread from its first home to other countries lost some of its original elements and adopted others. Islam provides many examples. The 'Five Pillars' are faith in the one god Allah and acknowledgement of Mohammed as his prophet, prayers and the condition of ritual purity indispensable thereto, religious taxation, fasting, and the pilgrimage to Mecca. Yet many Muslim communities pay less attention to these than to the precepts that Mohammed laid down as desirable but not requisite. The Achehnese of Sumatra practically ignore the rules concerning religious taxation but regard circumcision as essential to salvation. They have also introduced touches that are entirely their own, including a prohibition on wearing trousers. Further, despite the fact that the Koran expressly forbids the performance of rain magic, which was a regular practice among the herdsmen of Arabia, the Achehnese in times of drought return to ancient rites dating from the era before their conversion.[2]

Christianity met a similar fate. The Romans began the pro-

[1] J. P. McAuley, 'Problems of Agricultural Organization', *South Pacific*, Vol. IX, pp. 330–6.

[2] C. Snouk Hurgronje, *The Achehnese*, London, 1906, Vol. II, pp. 272 ff.

Yet all Muslim peoples have accepted the religious calendar, often at great inconvenience. This is based not on the solar year but on a lunar year of twelve months, a period nearly eleven days shorter. The various festivals fixed by it therefore gradually come earlier and earlier and in course of time change from one season to another. The work of the Arab pastoralists was much the same in summer and winter, but converts who are agriculturalists often have to interrupt urgent tasks to attend ceremonies. The month of fasting, when between the hours of sunrise and sunset swallowing even the saliva is forbidden, is a still greater difficulty, for it sometimes coincides with the time for planting or for harvesting, activities calling for maximum physical effort. The explanation for the adoption of the calendar possibly lies in the fact that the observance of a clearly defined taboo, unpleasant though it may be, is easier than basing all conduct on the commands of the prophet.

cess by transforming it to suit the needs of the empire, and throughout the ages other peoples, without being aware of what they were doing, have followed a similar course.[1] In the Pacific the Bible story itself is fitted into the kind of setting with which the natives are familiar. The overthrow of Satan has become a struggle between rival headmen, the Jews are conceived as primitive horticulturists and fishermen, Pontius Pilate appears as a district commissioner, and Roman soldiers masquerade as policemen.

For a generation or so after conversion the Melanesians always continue to draw on the pagan past. The natives of Malaita were ancestor worshippers, as was indicated earlier. They believed that the dead possessed supernatural power to be used in the interests of their descendants. A person fortified with this power was assured, it was thought, both of adequate protection from sorcerers and of material good fortune. The elders of each kin group accordingly offered sacrifices through the intermediary of a priest at frequent intervals to the members now deceased. But the spirits also demanded proper behaviour, notably the fulfilment of kinship obligations and the maintenance of social distinctions between the sexes. Wrong

[1] Cf. W. R. Inge, 'Religion', *The Legacy of Greece* (ed. G. Murray), Oxford, 1937, pp. 30–1: 'The Christian Church was the last great creative achievement of classical culture. It is neither Asiatic nor mediaeval in its essential character. It is not Asiatic; Christianity is the least Oriental of all the great religions. The Semites either shook it off and reverted to Judaism purged of its Hellenic elements, or enrolled themselves with fervour under the banner of Islam, which Wescott called a "petrified Judaism". Christian missions have had no success in any Asiatic country. Nor is there anything specifically mediaeval about Catholicism. It preserved the idea of Roman imperialism, after the secular empire of the West had disappeared, and even kept the tradition of the secular empire alive. It modelled all its machinery on the Roman Empire, and consecrated the Roman claim to universal dominion, with the Roman law of *maiestas* against all who disputed its authority. Even its favourite penalty of the 'avenging flames' is borrowed from the later Roman codes. It maintained the official language of antiquity, and the imperial title of the autocrat who reigned on the Seven Hills. Nor were the early Christians so anxious as is so often supposed to disclaim this continuity. ... The second century apologists appeal for toleration on the ground that the best Greek philosophers taught very much the same as what Christians believe.'

The missionaries who converted the peoples of northern Europe took over many local customs that they were unable to stamp out. Thus the Feast of All Souls is simply a pagan celebration in honour of the dead with a new name (J. G. Frazer, *The Golden Bough*, Pt. IV, London, 1907, pp. 309–18).

conduct angered them, and they then withdrew their protection and left the offender bereft of support. He lost his shield against sorcery and was thus open to the effects of any rite directed against him by his enemies. A person who had suffered a serious misfortune first took steps to defend himself with counter magic and then made amends for his past evil deeds. He also begged the elders to arrange for a priest to offer a sacrifice and pray at an ancestral shrine for his forgiveness.

Many of the Malaita converts still accept the concept of supernatural power but regard it as an attribute of God. He uses it, they say, to aid those who regularly go to church services, which they consider to be ceremonies in His honour and hence in a way similar to the sacrifices. Such attendances, nevertheless, are insufficient: the worshippers, to retain His favour, must, in addition, obey the Commandments and certain other rules. The significance attached to the latter depends to a considerable extent on older ideas of right and wrong. Thus the small local group is still held to be more important than humanity at large. Mission teachings that conflict with tradition, too, tend to be neglected. These natives, as it happens, have always disapproved of sexual relations before marriage and are consequently prepared to agree that youthful affairs are sinful: on the other hand, many of them see no real reason why marriage should be monogamous. Disease and death, now as formerly, are believed to be the result of loss of supernatural protection. A person who falls ill hastens with all speed to make his peace with God. He confesses either in private or in public, depending on the practice of the sect to which he belongs, and promises to do better in future. An improvement in his condition is again looked upon as a sign of supernatural favour regained; and if he dies his relatives, after the manner of their forefathers, say that he has paid the penalty for his misdeeds.[1]

The pagan religions of New Guinea were not focused so exclusively on the ancestors, and various departmental deities

---

[1] H. I. Hogbin, *Experiments in Civilization*, London, 1939, Chaps. IV, VIII.

were also of importance. Around the Huon Gulf the natives gave offerings to the dead for supernatural help in pig-raising and agriculture and held, too, that these beings punished any person who ignored his kinship responsibilities, generally by destroying his animals and spoiling his crops. A second class of spirits had to be propitiated to secure protection from storms. These were believed to guard the land boundaries and punish trespassers. Then there was a male cult involving still a third class of beings. Men secured their favour not by giving sacrifices but by becoming initiated and learning the ritual of blood-letting, performed specifically to eliminate the contamination derived from association with females. A man who became ill therefore took the precaution of bleeding himself in the hope that he would now recover. If, notwithstanding, he later died the relatives attached no blame either to him or to the spirits. They concluded that a sorcerer was wholly responsible. Parties engaged in major undertakings, like warfare and trading voyages, also carried out the operation. They were confident that, once purified, they would be able to carry the enterprise to a successful conclusion.

The less sophisticated of the Huon Gulf Christians preserve their belief in the need for a periodical spring cleaning but adopt a new method of achieving it. A sinner, they say, cuts himself off from God and must expect divine vengeance in the form of economic loss, illness, or death. The only means of avoiding disaster is to seek absolution by confession. Stories are told of secret sins being discovered afterwards when a person who had apparently led a blameless life was struck down suddenly by the bite of a poisonous snake, by lightning, or a falling tree. Men about to embark on undertakings of which the outcome is doubtful also like to go to confession.[1]

These early Christians of both the Solomons and New Guinea thus resemble their pagan ancestors in dwelling to a great extent on the rewards and punishments of this life. Almost the only occasions on which hellfire comes up for

[1] H. I. Hogbin, *Transformation Scene*, London, 1951, Chaps. XI, XII.

discussion is when a notorious sinner, after a specially heinous offence, continues to enjoy good health.

Increasing contact leads to one or other of two things. As the link with the past grows weaker, so the values of Western society may be strengthened. This situation is most likely to be reached when the people advance economically and they and their missionaries enjoy mutual sympathy. If, on the contrary, the natives fail to progress they are likely to become disgruntled and lose their faith in Christianity. They may then return almost completely to the values of a previous age.

Although pagan beliefs linger beneath the surface for so long, one great change follows immediately on conversion. The religion of any primitive people inevitably reflects the social structure of the community in which it develops. Thus each of the various kin groups, and sometimes the other groups as well, has its own set of spirits with which the members are identified. Christianity reflects another type of social system in which genealogical relationship is not so significant. Every Church asserts its universality, and those who belong to it offer the same kind of prayers to the one Deity. A mission native may continue to believe for many years that his chief obligations are to the members of his own society, but a basis is now provided for broadening the concept of brotherhood until it embraces not only the inhabitants of neighbouring settlements but also strangers. In many parts of Melanesia the new faith has helped to break down barriers and hostilities. On the other hand, there are also places where it has served rather to emphasize them. Where two missions are at work within the one district, rival villages, and sometimes rival factions within the same village, deliberately join separate sects. In New Georgia in the Solomons two groups between which a traditional enmity existed chose respectively the Methodists and the Seventh-Day Adventists. Instead of raiding for heads, they until recently burned down one another's churches.

Christianity has also introduced a new kind of leadership. Like the governments, the missions find themselves obliged to secure local assistants, and church affairs within the village are entrusted to a native teacher or catechist. The appointment of these men has no precedent. Some of their duties run parallel to those of the pagan priest, but they are not subject, as he was, to the council consisting of the headman and elders. Further, they have the right to suspend a sinner from church membership, thus denying him access to God and bringing him into public disgrace. Many of them accordingly exert a great deal of authority not only in religious matters but also in the everyday concerns of the people.

We can now proceed to the changing institutions themselves. That of kinship will be the most suitable for a beginning.

CHAPTER VII

Changing Melanesian Institutions

KINSHIP still provides the essential basis for the native social structures; indeed, it has proved to be the most conservative element in Melanesian society. The reason is clear. At the purely subsistence level the life of the bulk of the population has not been greatly altered. Despite all the changes, the people continue to cultivate the same food crops by the same methods as in times gone by, raise pigs, take part in hunting or fishing expeditions, and fashion the old-style canoes, weave the old-style nets, and build the old-style houses. Sheet iron may be preferred to sago-leaf thatch, but it cannot be used unless the village is easily accessible, and the majority of the householders are obliged to go on seeking their materials in the forest. Co-operative effort is just as necessary now as ever it was, and the lineages, clans, and cognatic groups persist because they supply the framework for joint endeavour. For the average native the closer genealogical and affinal ties thus retain all their former significance.[1]

The Busama villagers, to quote an example already familiar, are divided into two sets of groupings. Each group of one set has a few members, each group of the other set rather more. Everyone belongs first of all to a matrilineage, from which he receives his land rights. Lineage mates hold their ground in

[1] Cf. R. Firth, 'Notes on the Social Structure of Some New Guinea Communities', *Man*, Vol. LII, Nos. 99, 123: 'The old thesis put forward by Rivers, that in a situation of culture change the material culture and technological system are first affected, then the social structure and finally the religious system, does not hold in modern conditions. The religious system in its gross structural forms may be radically altered, and the basic aspects of the social structure such as kinship remain.'

common and also unite for clearing and fencing when new gardens have to be prepared. They may invite other relatives to come along, but such persons, if rewarded with a plot for their trouble, have no permanent claim to it. After harvesting it reverts back to the matrilineage. The second unit is derived from the club houses scattered through the village and is referred to by the same native term, *lum*. A man spends most of his evenings in the club nearest his dwelling and regards himself as one with those whom he habitually meets there. A fairly free choice of residence is permitted, but he is most likely to be living near his mother's brothers. The majority of his fellow clubmen are thus in most instances his matrilineal kinsfolk, though a sprinkling of patrilateral relatives and even an affine or two may be included. These persons form a nucleus for the team that undertakes such tasks as constructing canoes, weaving seines, and building houses.

A Busama native of today, then, can no more satisfy his basic need for food and shelter alone than one of his primitive forbears could. He still depends on his relatives, and, equally, they still depend on him. As in times gone by, the offer of assistance is a moral imperative. The pagan spirits are largely forgotten, but God is thought to have taken over many of their functions. The carry through from the past goes further. The practice of maintaining the bonds by constant gifts of food continues.

Disagreements between close kinsmen occur from time to time but are almost always speedily resolved. One morning I found the two brothers Awasa and Nga'sele' working together amicably although the night before they had been quarrelling. Awasa, when I inquired was the trouble settled, replied that it had been a trivial matter and that I ought not to have taken any notice. A neighbour later made the following comment: 'If Awasa wants help he goes to Nga'sele', who can't refuse him, and if Nga'sele' wants help he goes to Awasa. Well, that sort of thing becomes irritating, and you feel tied all the time. So every so often they become angry and abuse each other.

But before long they realize they're doing wrong. You see, they are of one blood, and when they remember that they feel ashamed.[1] They go away in silence and next day are asking for help again as usual.'

Groupings like those of the Busama are present from one end of Melanesia to the other. In Wogeo, another New Guinea example, work is similarly organized, except that here different sets of relatives combine. The smaller group, concerned with tasks demanding up to about a dozen individuals, is the patrilineage; the larger, carrying out those requiring about twenty, the pair of patrilineages that together occupy a hamlet. If more men are wanted, as in house-building, the residents of several neighbouring hamlets are called in.

Distant kinship ties have not in general withstood the recent pressures so well. The explanation is to be sought in the fact that remote cousins no longer interact regularly. Better tools have reduced the size of the working gangs, and many of the bigger undertakings, once held to be so vital, have either been abandoned or are carried out in perfunctory fashion. Initiation ceremonies ceased with the arrival of the early missionaries; club-houses are beginning to disappear, and, when they are still built, their dimensions have shrunk and the elaborate carvings are omitted; and, because travel is now safe, the trading expeditions are conducted by small parties. The banning of personal retaliation for offences also means that a man who has been injured is not obliged to enlist the help of the widest possible circle. Today he goes along to the court accompanied by one or two witnesses. With warfare outlawed, too, neighbouring communities never have occasion for entering into offensive and defensive alliances. The new marriage customs adopted by some groups have reduced the need for collaboration on a big scale. Thus the kin are involved neither in those places where the bridal payments have been stopped nor in those where money has taken the place of the food and cere-

[1] Persons who have a grandparent in common are said to be 'of one blood' (*datigeng*).

monial currency. In these latter the bridegroom, as the wage-earner, is expected to provide the greater portion himself.

The contraction of the area within which kinship ties operate is readily apparent when a man distributes his wages. The uses to which the traditional valuables could be put were so restricted that the owner had little temptation to keep them. Instead, he preferred to acquire prestige by giving them away to all those whom he regarded as relatives. Money is different: it can be turned into a wide variety of Western goods at a moment's notice. The home-coming labourer and the man with a sewing-machine or a carpenter's kit would probably always like to retain their cash for personal spending. They need the daily assistance of their immediate kin, however, and dare not offend them. After some slight delay they therefore give these persons a few shillings each. But distant kinsfolk are in a different category. Their aid is no longer necessary, and ignoring them is not likely to be directly harmful.

Yet the sense of moral obligation to distant relatives is not entirely dead, and many labourers, especially in the remoter areas, are bothered by a troubled conscience. This has brought the fear of sorcery within a narrower range. In earlier days a man would not normally have attributed any serious misfortune to a kinsman: now if he becomes ill he may suspect that a kinsman he has neglected, perhaps for excellent practical reasons, may be taking vengeance on him by black magic. Numbers of settlements are accordingly breaking up. Groups of brothers and their families splinter off and found a hamlet apart from the original village.

Friction between the generations is a feature of all societies undergoing rapid changes. Melanesia is no exception, but here again the overt expressions of resentment are mainly confined to distant kin. In the stable conditions of primitive times the knowledge and experience of the elders entitled them to deference. They knew how problems had been solved previously and were thus in a position to deal with difficulties as these arose. In the world of today past experience is of lesser worth, and the young people are often better equipped to meet the new needs. Elementary though their formal schooling may have been, it was usually an advance on that available during the first years of contact; and they alone have had recent acquaintance with outsiders during their years of employment. The introduction of money is another complication. Formerly the seniors owned nearly all the valuables, and other people left economic undertakings to them: now in most areas cash comes in through the efforts of the labourers. Christianity also has a bearing on the problem. The older men are no longer responsible for the spiritual well-being of their families, and anyone can approach the supernatural powers. Many a youngster on returning to the village imagines that he is more thoroughly knowledgeable about civilization than is actually the case. He then not only rejects the tradition of respect but shows superiority on his own account. But eventually, when he has taken up the daily round and married, he comes to realize that the sensible course is to conceal his irritation with his immediate elders. He at last appreciates that every communal task must have its leader and that chaos would result if nobody obeyed orders. At the same time, he rarely sees any good cause for curbing his feelings towards elders in general. Codrington, writing as long ago as 1891, said that the old men of Florida, in the Solomons, frequently wept at their loss of power and privilege.[1] The same thing still happens in the other islands.

Various forces are operating in a contrary direction, nevertheless, and here and there the remoter ties are gradually being strengthened once more. The missions, where they have avoided rivalry within a particular district, are reaffirming the old solidarities, and the recently established councils may help if they succeed in finding objectives that are of interest to all sections of the community. The provision of good schools and perhaps hospitals would be an example. But the chief impetus is coming from the new religious cults, which contain the germs

[1] R. H. Codrington, *The Melanesians*, Oxford, 1891, p. 99.

of a nationalist movement. These will be dealt with in the next chapter.

The foregoing account applies to all communities no matter how long the period of contact has been. In the villages that are more economically advanced, however, a few natives stand somewhat apart. They are in a sort of no-man's-land between the kinship society of their fellows and the impersonal society of the West. These men are forerunners. 'It can be stated as a theorem, valid in a high percentage of cases, that the greater the opportunity for profit in any social-cultural situation, the weaker the ties of extended kinship will become', says Linton. The industrialization of primitive societies, with the un-exampled chances offering to persons of intelligence and initiative, cannot fail to weaken and eventually destroy lineage and clan structures.[1]

The primitive social systems of Melanesia were egalitarian, as we have seen, and everyone did similar work, ate similar food, and enjoyed a similar standard of living. A person could differentiate himself from the ruck in one way only, by acquiring prestige as a headman or as a famous warrior, craftsman, or magician. Money has opened up other possibilities. A typical example of someone moving outside an older world and failing to enter a new is the Busama storekeeper, a native named Yakob. He is unsuccessful alike as a member of the encircling kinship society and as a Europeanized business man. The people disapprove of him so strongly that they always scolded me for talking to him. They were never indignant if I spent an hour or two associating with criminals, but they used to criticize me severely when I bought a tin of cigarettes from him. 'He's a black man who wants to behave as though he were white, and you oughtn't to encourage him', they used to tell me.

Yakob went away as a labourer like everyone else in early

---

[1] R. Linton, 'Cultural and Personality Factors Affecting Economic Growth', *The Progress of the Underdeveloped Areas* (ed. B. F. Hoselitz), University of Chicago, 1952, p. 84.

manhood and had the good fortune to be trained as a skilled carpenter. He earned high wages and saved a considerable sum of money. On returning home in 1947 he also received the compensation due to him for the war damage done to his property. He was married, but his brother and sister were dead, and apart from his wife and children no immediate relatives depended on him for support. He accordingly determined to invest his cash in a shop, the first establishment of the kind in the village. He obtained material from an old army camp and almost unaided built himself a house with an extra room. Then he set to work purchasing the stock. Limited capital forced him to confine himself to the cheaper goods for which there would be a ready sale, but, as he is close at hand, he charges higher prices than those current at Lae, the nearest town. The customers complain that he robs them, yet convenience outweighs their desire to economize, and they patronize him for most of their casual needs.

No more than 1,300 persons live within a radius of five miles, and Yakob's profits are insufficient to support him fully. He and his family consume a good deal of rice and tinned food—perhaps thereby rendering themselves liable to attack by disease arising from vitamin deficiency—but he also cultivates a few small areas of taro. His relatives refuse to help him with the fencing and clearing, and he finds himself obliged to do all the work alone. 'My kinsmen forget that we are of one blood and leave me to garden and repair the house by myself', he grumbles. 'Kinsfolk ought to stand together, but I have to do without mine. They leave me out of their feasts and won't help me to bring down a log from the forest so that I can hollow out a canoe. What happens? I have to pay for the hire of a vessel when I want to bring more things for them from Lae. They envy me and make me waste my money.'

The villagers reply that Yakob is himself to blame. 'He never comes near us', one of his cousins pointed out. 'We cut the forest without him, repair our houses without him, and drag our canoe logs down to the sea without him. Why, he hasn't given me a single tin of meat or a single pipe of tobacco. What a way to carry on! Relatives ought to be always giving one another food. He must think we're his unpaid workboys. You know, we're all wondering what will happen when his house-posts decay. There are no old army camps now, and he won't be able to put up a new dwelling alone. If he expects us to do the job we'll want wages—£20 or £30, something like that.'

No one else in Busama has attempted to enter the field of commerce, and for parallel examples we have to go to the truck owners of Butibam, 'the native quarter' of Lae. These men are more fortunate than Yakob in that they can earn enough money to pay for all their food, but housing is still a problem. In the tropics an unpainted timber-dwelling, as most of them are, lasts seven or eight years. After this period it is unsafe and must be rebuilt. The job presents no serious difficulties for the ordinary villager. He regularly assists his neighbours and can rely on their help in return. But a truck-owner, busy every day as a carrier, finds that his relatives make excuses or else demand payment for their services. He resents giving out money for such work and complains, often with truth, that although he may not have been able to supply the kinsmen with labour, he has driven them about without asking for fares and also allowed them to share his meals when they were short of taro or wished to have a change of diet. One man whom I knew well was so in-censed when two of his cousins asked for ten shillings each for carrying out repairs to the roof of his house that he instructed his wife to close the door on them. He relented later and ex-plained to me that being mean with food made him feel un-comfortable. 'They forgot the blood tie and asked for wages,' he said, 'but if I didn't feed them when they were hungry I'd feel ashamed.'

Various truck-owners also tell of their unhappiness at being debarred by their occupation from sharing in the communal activities of the village. They cannot refuse hirings and in con-sequence are seldom present at any of the gatherings, such as those that accompany a wedding. The rest of the people still occasionally organize small trading expeditions to the southern areas for clay pots, but, here again, these men never take part. They often say that they miss the excitement and pleasure of seeing their friends. Several lament, too, that they are so tired after driving throughout the day that they are obliged to forgo fishing excursions during the night.

In most of the villages near the other towns a few natives are similarly withdrawing themselves from the meshes of kinship. Hanuabada is an exception in that here the individualist has scarcely made his appearance. The inhabitants, as we know already, are prevented by the climate from engaging in commercial agriculture and have become skilled workers or clerks. A few of them bought second-hand trucks from the army after the War but found that the investment brought in a lower return than their old employment, to which they soon returned. Yet the men who earn the highest wages are still too inexperienced to spend their money as a European might do; or perhaps they have become disillusioned at the repeated failure of their hopes to achieve rapid progress. (In this connection it should be noted that they speak with greater pride than most of the Melanesians of the differences between themselves and the whites and are also beginning to adopt a distinctive native dress.) The wealthier natives make their houses a little more comfortable and perhaps eat a little better food, but instead of saving for the purchase of capital equipment they prefer to spend the bulk of their cash in the accustomed way by holding feasts. Weddings and holidays provide the excuse, and the only departure from age-old practice is that rice, meat, biscuits, and lemonade have replaced the traditional foods.[1]

Marriage

No Christian may have more than one wife, and in all villages where a mission operates the people have abandoned polygamy. Opposition occurs during the early stages after conversion, but in time the majority accept the rule almost without

[1] C. S. Belshaw, *The Great Village*, London, 1957.

question, possibly from a realization that even under the old order most persons would of necessity have been monogamous. By the second generation the only complaints come from the men who are childless. They do not know that a male may be sterile and invariably blame the women. But although the husband may yearn to raise a family, he usually hesitates to take an extra spouse lest he should be suspended from the church. The sole non-conformer of my acquaintance was a native of Malaita who in other respects was regarded as an admirable member of his congregation. His first wife after their marriage had become such an invalid that the birth of a child seemed unlikely, and he at length decided that God would assuredly excuse him if he brought another woman into the household to produce an heir and also help with the nursing. His fellow Christians sympathized but declined to let him take any daughter of theirs, and eventually he was obliged to go looking among the pagans. After the marriage the mission teacher expelled him, much to his annoyance. So confident was he of the purity of his motives that, instead of slipping back into ancestor-worship, he conducted prayers in his own house. Some years later, when I revisited the Solomons, I found him still without an offspring. He was sure the teacher was responsible and insisted that the man must have expressed his resentment at the loss of one of his flock by begging God to withhold the blessing of fruitfulness.

In earlier times the marriages were more often than not arranged by the elders: today the missionaries are always willing to try to convince the parents that a boy and girl who are romantically drawn to each other ought to be allowed to have their way no matter how unsuitable from the native point of view the match might be. Government officers if appealed to will also intervene and prevent forced unions with an uncongenial partner. The result is a growing tendency for the young people to exercise personal preferences in which great stress is laid on physical attractiveness. The rule of lineage and clan exogamy is still widely respected, but more and more breaches occur. If the number of irregularities goes on mounting, as seems probable, the kinship structure will necessarily change.

In many areas, including the Rabaul villages, bride price continues to be paid in ceremonial currency and food. Here the elders are still able to discipline a youngster and ensure that, at least until he marries, he does an honest day's work. But in some places money is now offered instead. The African material suggests that the substitution ultimately leads to higher and higher demands by the girl's relatives and thus to long delays. This state of affairs has already been reached in Hanuabada and one or two other places,[1] but elsewhere, for the moment, the amount seems to be stationary. If cash is given, whether or not the sum has increased, the elders expect the bridegroom to provide the biggest share. He is therefore in a strong position to insist that he alone should pick his wife. There are also places under the influence of missions whose policy has been to discourage any sort of payment. In these the seniors have usually lost the right to interfere.

Most husbands and wives work side by side for the support of the family and direct their attention towards achieving the same objectives, irrespective of whether they cultivate crops for home consumption or for sale. But in Hanuabada and in individual cases in Lae and Rabaul the man supports the household by his earnings from employment or business. His major activities are accordingly carried on apart, and he may not be able to discuss his problems at home or seek his wife's advice.

The emphasis on monogamy, the increasing appeal of personal appearance, the partial abandonment of the traditional bridal payments, and, in some areas, the loss of companionship between the married pair might reasonably be expected to have undermined the stability of the marriage relationship. Statistics are lacking, but I have the impression that this is not so and

---

[1] C. S. Belshaw, *The Great Village*, London, 1957, pp. 118, 125.

Mr M. J. Meggitt informs me that at Minj, in the New Guinea highlands, the price had risen so sharply and so many young men were being prevented from marrying that the district commissioner recently fixed an upper limit.

that divorce is actually less common than in the past. The new legal systems recognize the right of married couples to separate according to established native usage, yet it is a fact that several of the primitive communities of Melanesia failed to make any provision for unions being broken up, especially after the birth of the first child. Divorce was unknown in Busama and Wogeo, for instance, and rare in Malaita and Guadalcanal. If native custom does not allow for divorce the wronged party is permitted to initiate proceedings in the civil courts, but the threat of expulsion from church membership has then to be faced. Most of the missions accept the doctrine that husbands and wives at marriage enter into a binding contract with God. Thus Roman Catholics, Anglicans, and Lutherans all refuse to entertain the notion that Christian spouses may be parted by anything but death. A man from Florida in the Solomons who obtained his decree and subsequently remarried was held by the Anglican mission teacher to have automatically severed his connection with the rest of the congregation.

It is possible, however, that the number of unstable domestic units, as distinct from marriages, may be growing. Again no figures are obtainable, but I have frequently found dissatisfied husbands who had left a wife in the care of kinsfolk and taken another term of European employment. The lover of such a woman is under no obligation to support her, and he also has no right to the children.

Leadership

Headmen have disappeared from those communities, the vast majority, where social distinction depended on giving away food. The pagan festivals, which provided the principal opportunities for lavish generosity, are not kept up; warfare, also involving feasts, has ceased; and the trading expeditions, once demanding the construction of a fleet of canoes and the distribution of supplies to the workers, if organized at all, are now the concern of the small household groups. Saints' days and other church holidays might have made suitable occasions for feasting and display, but, as polygyny is forbidden, converts are deprived of the chance of gaining extra workers. At present the villagers have enough to spare for weddings, funerals, and the celebrations connected with the completion of a house or canoe, but even the residents of Hanuabada who earn high wages could not possibly finance the huge entertainments of the past. The ban on sorcery and raiding is also relevant here. A headman who rose to the top by his own efforts was usually required to have a reputation for black magic and fighting. Nobody in New Guinea, at least, would nowadays dare run the risk of imprisonment by asserting that he was familiar with the ritual to cause death, and without wars there can be no warriors.

The sole remaining persons holding the title of headman are those who have acquired it by right of birth, and even these exercise little influence. The administrations have deprived them of their ancient right of tribute and services from their followers, they are no longer in control of any scarce resources, and they would be gaoled if they threatened to carry out sorcery and cast out of the church if they performed magic for good weather or abundant crops.

A recent study of the decline of hereditary leadership in the Kiriwina community of the Trobriand Islands is instructive.[1] (Malinowski referred to the 'chief', the word I shall use here, though the expression 'headman' would have been more appropriate.) The chief owed his position in earlier days to the magical powers that had come down to him through his ancestors from the culture heroes, reputedly the founders of all Trobriand customs. The natives believed that he could carry out rites to command the sun, rain, and insect pests and that if angered he would ruin the harvest by causing drought, flood, or plagues of caterpillars. It is important to note that his abilities were phrased in negative terms—an unusual feature. The future was thought to be secure so long as he abstained from interfering.

The chief was set apart from the people by his magic, and

[1] I am indebted to Mr H. A. Powell for permission to quote the information, which he has not yet published.

everyone stood in such awe of him that the different kin groups
sought to win his favour by each sending him one of their girls
as a wife. Descent in the Trobriands is traced in the female line,
and a man is expected to fulfil certain obligations to his sister,
her husband, and their children. The chief, with his many
wives, thus had a host of brothers-in-law working for him.
They tended his gardens and stocked his storehouses with
yams, labour which he repaid by providing them with feasts
and organizing all the important enterprises, including the great
kula trading expeditions.

Today the natives are no longer afraid. They know that the
chief cannot use his magical power, and they feel confident that
should a famine occur the government officers would issue
rations. They also prefer to keep their food for themselves.
Europeans pay good prices for native produce, which they then
export to the mainland of Papua to feed plantation labourers.
To'uluwa, the chief of Malinowski's day, in 1917 had about
eighty wives; Mitakata, his successor, the present chief, has
less than twenty; and the man who will follow him is unlikely
to have more than one.

Yet the government still looks upon Mitakata as the head of
the community and expects him to settle the people's disputes.
If both parties are unrelated to him they pay little attention to
his remarks and ignore his decisions; if one party is unrelated
and the other a kinsman, and hence a valued helper, the verdict
is invariably in favour of the latter.

The disappearance of the headmen, or, where they still exist,
the whittling down of their authority, has led to the emergence
of a new kind of leader, the native representative of the government. He has little or no legal power but can afford to be indifferent to public opinion. The rare individual who is devoted
to the welfare of his people and of outstanding character, wisdom, and integrity often succeeds in preserving harmony
within the settlement by the judicious use of persuasion.
Trouble arises, however, if the person chosen is a nonentity,
when the villagers disregard his advice, or if he becomes

ambitious. European officers are constantly moved from station to station and so have few opportunities for learning any of the vernaculars or acquiring knowledge of the intimate details of village life. They find that they are forced to rely to a considerable extent on information supplied by the native representative, who is thus placed in the situation where he can use his office for private gain. He may make a practice of supporting his close kinsfolk against others, or he may be open to bribery. The people are free to complain but are likely to discover that the European official of the moment, whose ear and sympathy the man already possesses, is impatient with them. Generally, indeed, they find that their charges are dismissed on the score of malice. They have no land rights elsewhere and so cannot run away. The despotism that results would have been impossible in earlier days when presumptuous headmen were superseded or killed.

A well-known government representative in Busama, from his appointment in 1926 until his dismissal after a magisterial enquiry in 1944, hoodwinked a succession of district officers so cleverly that none of them even guessed that the villagers were being subjected to the grossest forms of exploitation. Every plea for his removal failed, and in the end the people had almost given up hope. He set out to enrich himself in all sorts of ways at their expense, and if they disobeyed his orders he beat them —one woman he permanently blinded—forced them to carry heavy weights, or compelled them to sit for hours with their hands in a latrine. He also conducted a series of intrigues with various young women, one of them his niece, and fathered a number of illegitimate children. During the War, when gardening became dangerous and supplies were so depleted that the army authorities supplied rations, he took the greater part of the food himself for sale to the natives in other settlements. This case is but an extreme example of what has happened again and again.[1]

The native missionary or teacher is another new kind of

---

[1] H. I. Hogbin, *Transformation Scene*, London, 1951, Chap. VIII.

leader. His authority to suspend members of his congregation is almost as powerful a weapon as that of the administration to pass sentences of imprisonment. He can exert a healthy influence if he acts with tolerance and discretion, though usually his narrow views on moral questions have an adverse effect on his judgement. In particular cases, too, he is prone to despise the government representative, who is seldom as well educated as himself. A rift may then develop, with different sections of the community supporting each one. Such quarrels have sometimes resulted in the establishment of breakaway settlements.[1]

Economic Institutions

The governments are trying out a variety of experiments in the villages with such cash crops as coconuts, cocoa, coffee, and rice, but the only one to be studied by outside observers is that of the Mekeo of Papua. This began as an attempt to start collective rice farms but was then switched over to small holdings.[2]

Missionaries and agricultural officers of the pre-War administration had proved that the Mekeo country was ideal for growing rice. Much of it is flat and subject to minor flooding, but the weather in the months before the harvest is hot and sunny. The first scheme was the outcome of a visit by the director of agriculture in 1948. The people asked him to arrange for them to be taught how to grow rice on a big scale and to request the government to provide financial assistance so that they might improve their living standards. Further discussions led to the formation of a Rural Progress Society in each of the villages. The members contributed sums of money to form a capital fund for the purchase of hullers, and the agricultural department promised to obtain tractors and other

[1] Cf. P. Lawrence, 'Lutheran Mission Influences on Madang Societies', *Oceania*, Vol. XXVII, pp. 73–89.

[2] See C. S. Belshaw, 'Recent History of Mekeo Society', *Oceania*, Vol. XXII, pp. 1–23; J. P. McAuley, 'Mechanization, Collectives, and Native Agriculture', *South Pacific*, Vol. VI, pp. 276–81; and J. P. McAuley, 'Economic Development among the Mekeo', *South Pacific*, Vol. VIII, pp. 217–20.

machinery, to give the essential training, and to teach the natives to take responsibility.

In 1951 each village had its own Society, which was controlled by an elected committee. Two tractor pools were then established under the care of European officers at places situated within easy reach. In that year the Societies together placed 192 acres under mechanical cultivation. They were free to dispose of the rice to any buyer, though the government took most of it at a price agreed upon beforehand. This was paid over after the bills for the service of the machines and for fuel and sacks had been deducted. The village of Jesubaibua, which was specially studied, received a total of £165 after settling an account for £225. The number of members in the local Progress Society is not given, and I am unable to say how much each one received.

These results were considered to be unsatisfactory. According to one writer, what was really happening was that the administration was growing rice at a loss. The dividend allotted to each person depended on the number of days he had turned out to watch the officials and a few native assistants make money for him. Only to the extent that mechanization was still imperfect were the people called upon to make a significant contribution. The tasks amounted to very little and were apparently meant to decrease. The men also continued to enter the migrant labour market instead of staying at home, as the authorities had hoped they might. European employment maintained its attraction because the amount of cash that could be earned was greater than that received from growing rice. Thus during 1951 the twenty-seven paid workers from Jesubaibua collected £300 in wages. Mechanization, too, cut down the number of young men needed in the villages, and more rather than less were available as labourers. A further difficulty was the cost of the tractors, at that time £12,600. It was doubtful whether the eventual return would ever justify such an expenditure. Then the Mekeo land-tenure system, which was based on the rights of individual persons to small blocks, presented serious obstacles. Various men had lent the areas they controlled to the Progress Society to make up a large tract for the rice farm. So far they had not asked for rent, but it was felt that they might soon do so. Such payments, if made, would reduce the total profit and cause friction within the community. The householders who were unlucky in that their plots were located elsewhere would almost certainly have resented seeing their neighbours benefit without having to do a corresponding amount of work.

By 1953 confidence had declined, the people had begun to lose interest, and their relations with the government officers had become unsatisfactory.

It was therefore decided to inaugurate a new scheme for the purpose not only of increasing rice supplies but of improving general native administration. The officers felt that the Mekeo must be convinced that the plan was of genuine advantage to them and not an official manœuvre to get cheap grain. They also hoped to be able to provide incentives to continual effort and, to this end, were determined to adopt a more realistic attitude towards the groups that were to be the units of production.

The scheme as eventually worked out by the end of the year abandoned the collective approach. No attempt was made to dictate in advance which bodies were to undertake production, and the people chose for themselves. The Rural Progress Societies were wound up and new co-operatives established under the Economic Development Ordinance. These groups were not concerned with cultivation but solely with buying, processing, and marketing. The Treasury lent funds for the first period of their operation to enable them to make spot-cash payments on the delivery of the grain, a necessary measure to restore goodwill. The administration provided any mechanical assistance asked for in cultivation, though not in harvesting, under a contract setting out dates and payments due.

Distrust had to be overcome, and the agricultural officers made no effort to push the unwilling into participation. The acreage cultivated, eighty-one mechanically and ninety-six by hand, was larger, nevertheless, than had been expected. The units of production varied from individual families to combinations of two or three clans, though the larger groups always divided the ground, after preparation and sowing, into family blocks for weeding and interplanting with vegetables. The growers brought the harvest in to a centre, where it was threshed at the rate of 1s. per hour charged against the Co-operative Society. The Society then bought the grain at a fixed price of 3¾d. per pound for treatment at its own expense, generally in mills purchased from the old Rural Progress Societies. The rice was subsequently sold at 9¾d. per pound. The profit, after the deduction of the costs of processing and transport, was 1½d. per pound. A total of 1,500 persons took part in the production, eighty tons of milled rice were sold and eight tons retained for home consumption and local trading. The Jesubaibua growers received the sum of £266.

It is as yet too soon to forecast the ultimate effect of the scheme, but rice supplies have increased, and relations with the administration are said to be better.

The decline of native trade must also be mentioned here. The people no longer have need to make exchanges with their neighbours since goods of superior quality are readily obtainable at the stores. A few objects still circulate, but the regular voyages, made by a dozen or more large canoes, have almost everywhere ceased, and several of the villages where particular crafts were carried on are in process of being abandoned. Such settlements were in many cases established close to the source of scarce raw materials without regard to the potentialities of the soil nearby for agricultural production. The inhabitants concentrated on their special skills and depended on relatives and trading partners outside for much of their food. There were also places where the gardening areas, though excellent in quality, were so limited in extent that the residents were forced to take up some speciality in order to have items to give in return for the additional supplies that they imported. If trade languishes these groups must either migrate or face semi-starvation.

In the Huon Gulf region of New Guinea the settlement of Lutu was founded in the vicinity of the one spot where stone suitable for adze blades could be quarried, and the settlements of Laukanu, Lababia, and Buso similarly grew up near the only deposit of pottery clay. All four villages stood on a narrow shelf of beach at the base of steep mountain slopes that were almost impossible to cultivate. The gardens of the Tami Islanders at the other side of the Gulf were also insufficient, but for another reason—the place was so tiny. The Tami natives found themselves obliged to specialize in carving wooden bowls, which they disposed of for taro and sago. Now that the stone is not in demand the bulk of the Lutu villagers have already moved to another site. Occupation of Laukanu, Lababia, Buso, and Tami continues but is becoming precarious as the other Gulf peoples take more and more to aluminium and iron saucepans and enamel dishes. The families from these places are beginning to discuss whether they ought to seek refuge with kinsmen living elsewhere. If they decide to move, the absorption of some of them may prove difficult. The Melanesian islands are nowhere closely settled, but the land around many villages is adequate only for a slight increase of population, and, unless production methods are radically changed, a great influx of migrants would imperil the already low living standards.

Reactions to the Present Legal Institutions

The Melanesians of earlier days had no institutions specifically designed to deal solely with legal matters, and the courts of to-day are wholly new. I do not intend to speak further about the actual administration of the law, but present views on the subject are worthy of comment.

Natives who so far have had little to do with civilization frequently discuss the divorce of the present system from their daily lives. A generation ago, when I was working in Malaita with a group that was then still primitive, I recorded some of the remarks. 'You white men give us orders;' the people used to say to me, 'we no longer give orders to ourselves.' 'You are familiar with the law', a man once told me. 'It belongs to you: it comes from the place where you were born. For us the law is different. In olden days we behaved as our fathers did before us. When you have asked me, in our conversations together, why did I do that, have I not replied, "It is the custom: our fathers did it of old"? Today that is changed. The white man has come and tells us that we must behave like his father. Our fathers? We must forget them.' 'In olden days we did this thing, we did that thing. We did not say to ourselves first, "This thing I want to do, is it right?" ' another man went on. 'No, we always knew. Now we have to say, "This thing I want to do, will the white man say that it is wrong and punish me?" '

Views of this kind may still be heard in the remoter areas. The chief causes of irritation seem to be the formal atmosphere and unfamiliar procedures of the courts, the prohibition on taking direct action against the members of other settlements, especially when one of them is suspected of having carried out sorcery, and the enforcement of the regulations designed to safeguard public health. I have explained already that native ideas about disease are unscientific, and that the people do not understand that they will reap a direct benefit from constructing latrines, burying the dead in cemeteries, and keeping the domestic pigs outside the dwellings.

Prolonged contact brings about a change of attitude. Many persons at last come to realize the hampering effect of a code that applies only within the settlement. They begin to appreciate their safety and the fact that they need not fear attack by warriors from other places; and they also see the advantages of being able to secure arbitration and possibly justice without having to go to war. At the same time, they still resent having no say in the framing of ordinances or, in New Guinea, the judging of cases. They continue to be irritated, too, by the way in which sorcery is handled.

Morals

One of the characteristics of an integrated society is the acceptance by the members of the established institutions with the accompanying rights and responsibilities. The people regulate their conduct according to the prevailing scheme of values, fully convinced that this is the proper way to behave. Melanesian communities in bygone days were no doubt subject from time to time to minor changes, but the evidence seems to indicate that they were at this period for the most part relatively well integrated. European contact has introduced a second set of values, thereby creating the confusion of a double standard of morals. Each of the two systems is able to offer satisfaction by itself, but they cannot operate together without friction. The fact that the natives are no longer sure in any situation which line of action they ought to follow and sometimes choose one and sometimes the other is in itself proof that the old social structure is in process of disintegration.

The Wilsons drew attention to this problem when they spoke of radical opposition and quoted the instance of the Nyakyusa native who wants to be both hospitable and a good Christian (see above, pp. 31, 32). If he is to have beer to offer guests he needs the help of several wives, but the missions forbid polygyny. Firth also has described how the New Zealand Maori is divided against himself if he tries simultaneously to be a good tribesman and make a modern farm pay. Achievement of the first objective demands that he should lay aside his work, no matter how pressing the job may be, in order to attend various gatherings and also be prepared to dispense hospitality to relatives for as long as they care to stay with him: achievement of the second that he should spend regular hours tilling the soil, tending the stock, and maintaining the fences and buildings and, in addition, carefully balance his expenditure against his cash returns.[1]

In the Melanesia of today a storekeeper like Yakob is in a

[1] R. Firth, *Elements of Social Organization*, London, 1951, pp. 118–19.

similar dilemma. He is torn between his desire to have the approval of his neighbours and the drive to better himself financially. But he is not alone in his predicament. The ordinary villager daily faces conflicts that differ from his only in degree. Some of these were listed earlier (pp. 38, 39). Should he stay at home to perform his kinship duties or enter employment, should he share his wages or keep the money, should he follow the sexual code of his ancestors and be promiscuous before marriage or abide by the Christian ideal of chastity? For these and similar questions there is no clear-cut right or wrong answer. Whatever he decides is from one point of view correct and from the other improper. New religious movements offer a partial solution to this and other difficulties. I shall devote the next chapter to an account of such manifestations.

CHAPTER VIII

Native Efforts in Melanesia to Achieve Further Changes

T HE *Annual Report on British New Guinea* (the old name for Papua) for the year ending June 30, 1894, on page 71 includes the following paragraph:

'One man named Tokerua, a native of Gaba-Gabuna (Milne Bay), made a great stir among the natives. He gave out that he had seen a spirit in a large tree that told him to tell all the villagers to kill their pigs, burn their houses, and take to the highest peaks of the ranges, as a large wave was coming and would swamp the place for two or three months, and after that they could come down from the hills and they would live in comfort. Tokerua was to form a new government and have a steamer of his own after the style of the [Governor's yacht] only larger. The people quite believed him, and built their houses in the bush and killed 300 or 400 of their pigs.' [1]

This is the first record of a type of incident that since then has occurred at some time in most islands. [2]

Mair remarks, for instance, that one of the most noticeable reactions of the peoples of New Guinea to White rule has been the repeated outbreak of—

[1] Cf. C. W. Abel, *Savage Life in New Guinea*, London, undated, pp. 104-14.
[2] The fact that official records are silent about such incidents in a given area is not to be accepted as proof that they have never occurred. Similarly, the absence of any mention of characteristic features in an account may only mean that these escaped observation.

'. . . a manifestation which used to be known as "Vailala Madness", but is now commonly described as the "cargo cult".[1] The first time this attracted the attention of the Australian authorities was in 1919, on the Vailala River in the Gulf Division of Papua.

'As this was described by the officer who investigated events at the time, reports spread among the natives that their ancestors were about to return in the guise of white men, by steamer, or, according to one version, by aeroplane, and would bring with them a large cargo of European goods of every kind. These goods, it was said, were actually the property of the natives, but were being withheld from them by the whites. The latter, however, would soon be driven out of the country. The leaders of the movement, who claimed to have received messages to this effect from the spirits, ordered the people to suspend all work and prepare feasts of welcome. Platforms were built and loaded with presents of food. The leaders, and some of their followers, imitated European manners in various ways, some ludicrous or pathetic. The leaders drilled their own "police boys". At a certain time each day they would sit, dressed in their best clothes at the tables, decorated, European fashion, with flowers in bottles, which had been set up to entertain the returning spirits. . . .

'A feature of the Vailala movement was a violent reaction against the native religion. The leaders ordered their followers to abandon all traditional ceremonies and destroy the ritual objects associated with them, and they met with an enthusiastic response.'[2]

The anthropologist on the Papuan government staff referred to the mass hysteria with which the movement was accompanied.

'Great numbers were affected by a kind of giddiness; they

---

[1] 'Cargo' (in the usual orthography of pidgin 'kago' or 'kako') is in this context the collective term in pidgin-English for the various Western goods that arrive in the islands as cargo in ships and aeroplanes.

[2] L. P. Mair, *Australia in New Guinea*, London, 1948, pp. 64–5.

lost or abandoned control of their limbs and reeled about the villages, one man following another until almost the whole population of a village might be affected at the same moment. While they indulged in their antics the leaders frequently poured forth utterances in "Djaman", or "German", a language composed mostly of nonsense syllables and pidgin-English which was almost wholly unintelligible.' [1]

'By now the cargo cult has appeared in every administrative district of [Papua and New Guinea], and even in the highlands, which have only known the white man for fifteen years . . . [Mair goes on]. The common characteristic is the insistence on the cargo of European goods to be sent by the ancestors, and the disappearance of the white man and his rule. Underlying the cargo myth is the idea that all trade goods have been manufactured in the spirit world by the ancestors as gifts for their descendants, and are misappropriated by white men. . . . In every case, the leaders order economic activities to be suspended. No gardens need be made, since the ancestors will provide all the food required—but only to those who have shown their faith by not growing any for themselves. The people spend their time preparing to welcome the ancestors; sometimes this involves special songs and dances. In the highlands, where it would be unrealistic and beyond the scope of the people's imagination to expect a ship, they make airstrips and decorate the borders. . . . On Karkar Island the root conception of the natives' entry into the kingdom from which the whites have debarred them was expressed in the belief that the whole island would be turned upside down, and those who survived would have white skins.

'Usually there was some attempt to set up a rival "government". The leader of the movement would often be a village official, but if he was not he would disregard . . . authority. He drilled his own "police boys", sometimes with dummy rifles

[1] F. E. Williams, 'The Vailala Madness in Retrospect', *Essays Presented to C. G. Seligman* (ed. E. E. Evans-Pritchard, etc.), London, 1934, pp. 369–70.

made of wood, and on some occasions set up an "office", where he sat in imitation of the government official, surrounded by the paraphernalia of writing.'[1]

Since the publication of Mair's account a cargo cult, or something resembling it, has even been reported from an isolated 'portion of the New Guinea highlands beyond the reach of government patrols. Steel tools and cloth had come into the area by ordinary trading channels, together with tales of the mysterious white beings, believed to be spirits of the dead, from whom the goods had been obtained. The purpose of the movement, at least in its early stages, was to secure increased supplies. The social life of the natives, unlike that of the other communities, had not as yet been disturbed, and they were able to fit the new practices into the old framework.

'During almost the whole history of the situation . . . the various manifestations, although instigated by external stimuli, were expressed within the indigenous context. The manner in which the people coped with these conditions was their own, drawn from their own range of experience. To do this they found it necessary to interrupt their normal routine activity; but unsettlement of this sort, internally implemented, was less severe than it would have been had they been subjected to direct, instead of indirect, alien contact. . . . There was no emergence of a prophet . . . no appearance of a messianic movement.'

[1] *Op. cit.*, pp. 65-6. See also I. Leeson, *Bibliography of Cargo Cults and other Nativistic Movements in the South Pacific*, South Pacific Commission Technical Paper No. 30, Sydney, 1952. Note especially *Annual Reports of Papua* for 1912-13, 1914-15, 1919-20, 1920-21, 1924-25, 1937-38, 1939-40, 1940-41; *Annual Reports for the Territory of New Guinea* for 1928-29, 1930-31, 1933-34, 1935-36, 1937-38, 1939-40, 1940-41, 1950-51; F. E. Williams, *The Vailala Madness*, Port Moresby, 1924; E. W. P. Chinnery and A. C. Haddon, 'Five New Religious Cults in British New Guinea', *Hibbert Journal*, Vol. XV, pp. 448-63; and P. Lawrence, 'Cargo Cults and Religious Beliefs among the Garia', *International Archives of Ethnography*, Vol. XLVII, pp. 1-20. P. Worsley, *The Trumpet Shall Sound*, London, 1957, a full study of cargo cults, based on Marxian theory, did not appear until after the despatch of the MS. of this book to the publisher.

Later on several men who were not at the time accepted as headmen began organizing little cults of their own.[1]

The true cults have all been strongly authoritarian, and the leader has insisted on implicit obedience on pain of severe punishment by his 'police boys' or other assistants. Sometimes he has promulgated various rules of conduct allegedly inspired by a communication from the other world. These have cut clean through the doubts and hesitations arising from the conflicting sets of values and once more established a single standard. Information on the point is inadequate, but it seems that most of the codes have been largely based on one or other of the two systems and that few serious attempts at compromise have occurred.

The administrative officials, when at length aware of what was taking place, have generally brought charges against the leaders and sent them to gaol or into exile for a period. The overt manifestations of the cult in that particular area have then ceased, though the underlying beliefs continue. The people often say afterwards, apparently with conviction, that a portion of the cargo actually arrived and that the rest would have followed had the government not stepped in to protect the Europeans. I quote the following passages from a native account of a cult that had been at its height among the Mekeo of Papua more than a decade before:

'The three villages were asked to build an altar . . . late in the afternoon all the altars were brought to Inawaia; they were all decorated with beautiful bird feathers and bird-of-paradise feathers. At about nine o'clock they all gathered to pray so that the stuff and cargo would fall from heaven early. They believe that some of the things really happened, such as tobacco, money, books, handkerchief, knives, permit for a truck, a gun, and several other things. . . . The people knew that it would really happen; only the government stopped them by putting

[1] R. M. Berndt, 'A Cargo Movement in the East Central Highlands of New Guinea', *Oceania*, Vol. XXIII, pp. 144–5.

them to gaol, and they say that people would never do this again for fear that they were short of food and things. The people now say that it really happened because the things actually happened . . . They say all they asked for they received.' [1]

The leaders after their liberation, although careful to take no further steps to organize the people, as a rule retain all their prestige and are often revered as martyrs.

The earliest of the Solomon Islands cults apparently arose in part as a result of a missionary suggesting that the natives should agitate for representation on the advisory council of the administration. He told them to hold meetings but stressed the need for a chairman and rules of procedure. A number of primitive villagers took up the proposal but misinterpreted the advice, and before long they were treating an ordinary chair and a foot-rule as objects of ritual importance. These people wanted higher wages, and in the end the government felt obliged to ask the missionary to leave the country.[2]

Mention may also be made of the New Hebrides, another Melanesian group, where conditions resemble those of New Guinea and the Solomons. The most persistent of a long series of cults is that known as John Frum.[3] The first signs were noted early in 1941, when the Tanna islanders suddenly withdrew their children from the mission schools and refused to attend church services. Soon afterwards they abandoned their villages, which they had built a generation or two before under mission encouragement, and returned to living in isolated homesteads. They also seemed to be determined to rid themselves of their money, and although some of them spent lavishly in the stores, others threw their cash into the sea. The district agent became anxious and conducted an enquiry, which

---

[1] The statement is given in full by C. S. Belshaw, 'Recent History of Mekeo Society', *Oceania*, Vol. XXII, pp. 5–7.

[2] C. S. Belshaw, 'Significance of Modern Cults for Melanesian Development', *Australian Outlook*, Vol. IV, pp. 116–25.

[3] See J. Guiart, 'Forerunners of Melanesian Nationalism', *Oceania*, Vol. XXII, pp. 81–90; and 'The John Frum Movement in Tanna', *Oceania*, Vol. XXII, 165–77.

revealed that the leader was a man named Manihevi from the west coast. He asserted that he was the spokesman of the pagan spirit Karaperamun, whose name was corrupted to 'John Frum'. He had told the people that this John Frum would shortly land in Tanna, bringing all the material goods that the whites had hitherto denied them. Work would no longer be necessary—there would be John Frum money for all, John Frum stores, John Frum schools, John Frum iron houses, and John Frum ships, aeroplanes, and cars. John Frum would drive out the Europeans, level off the ground, and offer the natives renewed youth and better health. The agent arrested Manihevi and his principal supporters, who were known as 'the ropes of John Frum', and committed them for trial. The court found them guilty of disturbing the peace and sentenced them to imprisonment.

The churches still remained empty, and a year later the movement broke out again, this time on the east coast of Tanna. Certain men from this locality announced that they also had had revelations from John Frum. The process was repeated here, and again the leaders were gaoled.

By this time an American base had been established in the New Hebrides, and the people were becoming familiar with the might of a modern army and the excitements that it provided. Yet the cult still flourished underground, and in 1943 a native called Neloiag proclaimed himself as John Frum in person, king of the United States and Tanna. He surrounded himself with an armed police force and, helped by labour from the surrounding villages, cleared the jungle for an airfield where the Americans could land. The district agent arrested Neloiag, who had come to see him in his office, and then found himself surrounded by a large body of the man's followers. After some argument they permitted the agent to telegraph administrative headquarters on the understanding that he would request a ship to take him away. He in fact asked for assistance to quell the riot, and a military detachment arrived shortly afterwards. Neloiag was later pronounced insane and confined in a mental hospital. The people returned home, and calm was once more restored, though not for long. A further outbreak occurred in 1947, when the leaders said that their messages were coming not from John Frum but from his sons. The usual imprisonments followed, and since that date nothing of note has occurred on Tanna itself. But these natives trade with the neighbouring islands of Ambrym and Malekula, and the movement has now spread there. The different prophets aptly compare themselves with the recently introduced sweet potato. 'At first there were only a few,' they say, 'but soon the island is covered with them.'

Interpretation of the Cults

Characteristics common to all the cults, that of the New Guinea highlands included, are the belief in the coming of the cargo, special ceremonies, the killing of the pigs and feasting, and the carrying out of constructional works. Some communities have built a wharf or a large storehouse, some have cleared the jungle for an aerodrome, and others, such as the Mekeo, raised up elaborate altars. The highland cult is in a sense unique in that, at the start, it was grafted on to the indigenous social structure, which had not then been altered by pressures from outside. If for the moment this is ignored, then we can also say that in each case a new leader, or sometimes a set of new leaders, has emerged as the supreme authority and law-giver of the movement. He is usually the prophet to whom the revelations were made, though at times this person remains a comparatively lay figure. Thus the Mekeo movement originated in the dreams of a seventeen-year-old girl. She received the title of Queen and was given a retinue, but the real heads were two or three of her relatives, cousins of her father's, one of whom declared himself to be a god, too holy to be touched by ordinary mortals. A hierarchy of officials, who are generally called by special names—'police boys', 'custom chiefs', 'ropes of John Frum', and so forth—act as the leader's executive assistants.

In other respects the cults show certain differences, especially in the emphasis laid on the elements stemming from the past. Some communities have looked to the ancestors or a pagan deity for the cargo, some to God or one of the apostles. If the ancestors are involved there is often a return to the rituals associated with the worship of the dead, and the graves and cemeteries are carefully tended. If the emphasis is on God or an apostle, however, the ceremonies are inspired by Christian teaching. A prophet from the Watut River in New Guinea in 1944 persuaded his followers to prostrate themselves regularly before a crucifix stolen from a bombed church, and on Sundays he administered a form of Communion. He distributed pieces of sweet potato dipped in 'holy water' drawn from a spring which Saint Peter had indicated to him in a dream.[1]

Further differences are the presence or absence of mass hysteria and trance-like shaking fits, of destructive features such as those that marked the Vailala cult, and of explicit hostility towards Europeans.

In seeking an explanation we must look first to the universals—the belief in the cargo, the ceremonies, the feasting, the constructional work, and the emergence of the leaders with their codes of correct behaviour.

The natives who fall victims to the movements are all dissatisfied with their economic conditions. They enter employment for low wages to earn the money to buy a few simple tools and sundry paltry garments and then return home to a life of unending toil to support their families. They must continually build houses, construct canoes, clear and plant gardens, catch fish, hunt, and tend pigs; moreover, they are always beset by fears of drought, flood, famine, pestilence, and sorcery. In olden days this was the only world they knew, but now they are surrounded by all the wealth of the West—and are unable to come by any of it. Their resentment is perhaps augmented indirectly by the work of the missionaries. Christianity, which

---

[1] Busama natives who had visited the Watut country gave me an account of the cult, which escaped official notice.

P

they know to be the religion of the Europeans, proclaims the spiritual equality of men; but colonial settlers are rarely willing to practise the ethical implications of the doctrine. Such hypocrisy has repelled dependent peoples everywhere.

A person from one of the outlying villages, despite a few years of simple schooling and a term of service as a wage labourer, is still not emancipated from his magical beliefs and so is unaware of the scientific relation between cause and effect. He is also ignorant of what goes on in any country but his own. He has learned nothing of our system of economy or manufacturing techniques, and he does not understand the steps that have to be taken to make Western goods, pay for them, and bring them to the islands. All he knows is that cargoes arrived in some mysterious fashion from beyond the horizon and are then seized by white men, who apparently offer nothing in return. Further, these white men seem to do little work, that is work in the native sense. Their hands are seldom soiled, and yet they live in superior houses and possess quantities of money and unlimited supplies of food and clothing. They never feel the pangs of hunger and can afford to laugh at the forces of Nature and at disease.[1]

Here is an example of the incompatibility of wants and the means of satisfying them. The natives can take no practical steps to redress the balance. They lack the resources, training, and opportunity for making the desired goods themselves or for acquiring them from outside. Dominated as they are still by magical thought, they take refuge in fantasy. The pagan religions concentrated on the fulfilment of material ends, and the people continue to follow the pattern. They dwell on the hope of change, perform rites to improve their lot, and pray for the

---

[1] A native member of the party that had represented New Guinea at the coronation of Queen Elizabeth II is reported to have made the following remark when interviewed in Sydney on his way home: 'I will tell my people to forget the cargo cult. I will tell my people that white men work harder in their own country than the Papuan natives. We are dependent on the white man working. While the white man works we can expect a good life. As natives we are unable to control our own affairs. If the white man does not work that's the end of us.' (*Sydney Morning Herald*, June 22, 1953.)

intervention of the ancestors or, if they are Christians, for some sign from God. The ground is ready prepared, and when the prophet arises everyone listens to what he has to say. If he is a respected member of the community, or if he is backed up by a relative with suitable qualifications, the cult has already begun. The leader is there, and the rest gather around him.[1]

The believers are prepared to make a gigantic effort to achieve their aims. The labour is from our point of view mis-applied, but to them this is irrelevant. They justify their desires by the endeavour and find a substitute satisfaction in perform-ing the ceremonies, celebrating the feasts, and building the storehouse or wharf or clearing the bush for the aeroplanes to land. They hope thereby to prove that the ends are morally right and will be of benefit to the group as a whole. The attempt to convince themselves is so successful that they gladly sacrifice their pigs, throw away their money, and neglect their gardens.

Europe has seen such manifestations of faith from the time of the Crusades onwards. I quote an extract from a letter written in the twelfth century by Archbishop Hugo of Rouen to Bishop Thierry of Amiens:

'The inhabitants of Chartres have combined to aid in the construction of their church by transporting the materials; our Lord has rewarded their humble zeal by miracles which have roused the Normans to imitate the piety of their neighbours. Since then the faithful of our diocese and of other neighbouring regions have formed associations for the same object; they ad-mit no one to their company unless he has been to confession, has renounced enmities and revenges, and has reconciled him-self with his enemies. That done, they elect a chief, under whose direction they conduct their wagons in silence and with humil-ity. Who has ever seen!—Who has ever heard tell, in times past, that powerful princes of the world, that men brought up

---

[1] Firth has given an account of the underlying cargo beliefs in Tikopia, where the society is for the present still so well integrated that the appearance of a prophet is un-likely (R. Firth, 'The Theory of Cargo Cults', *Man*, Vol. LV, No. 142).

in honour and in wealth, that nobles, men and women, have bent their proud and haughty necks to the harness of carts, and that, like beasts of burden, they have dragged to the abode of Christ these wagons, loaded with wines, grains, oil, stone, wood, and all that is necessary for the wants of life, or for the construction of the church? But while they draw these burdens, there is one thing admirable to observe; it is that often when a thousand persons and more are attached to the chariots—so great is the difficulty—yet they march in such silence that not a murmur is heard, and truly if one did not see the thing with one's own eyes, one might believe that among such a multitude there was hardly a person present. When they halt on the road, nothing is heard but the confession of sins, and pure and suppliant prayer to God to obtain pardon. At the voice of the priests who exhort their hearts to peace, they forget all hatred, discord is thrown far aside, debts are remitted, and unity of hearts is established. But if one is so far advanced in evil as to be unwilling to pardon an offender, or if he rejects the counsel of the priest who has piously advised him, his offering is instantly thrown off the wagon as impure, and he himself ignominiously and shamefully excluded from the society of the holy. There one sees the priests who preside over each chariot exhort everyone to penitence, to confession of faults, to the resolution of better life! There one sees old people, young people, little children, calling on the Lord with a suppliant voice, and uttering to Him, from the depths of the heart, sobs and sighs with words of glory and praise! After the people, warned by the sound of trumpets and the sight of banners, have resumed their road, the march is made with such ease that no obstacle can retard it. When they have reached the church they arrange the wagons about it like a spiritual camp, and during the whole night they celebrate the watch by hymns and canticles. On each wagon they light tapers and lamps; they place there the infirm and sick, and bring them the precious relics of the saints for their relief. Afterwards the priests and clerics close the ceremony with processions which the people follow with devout heart, imploring the clemency of the Lord and of His Blessed Mother for the recovery of the sick.'[1]

From this distance we can well argue that the citizens of Rouen were also misapplying their energies. But 800 years ago Europeans were in many respects as ignorant as the primitive natives of today. Only knowledge recently acquired enables us to say that disease is more effectively prevented by improving housing, water supply, and drainage than by holding processions and building cathedrals.

The prophets who appear today had their predecessors. The natives have always regarded their dreams as significant, and spirit mediums frequently gave guidance on the treatment of illness, the identification of sorcerers, and the conduct of wars, trading expeditions, and harvest festivals.[2]

The majority of the visionaries, now as formerly, are doubtless genuine and truly believe that they have been inspired. Belshaw suggests that their second sight and political striving may in individual cases be an aggressive outlet for feelings of guilt. He calls attention to two cult leaders, known to him personally, who were about to contract marriages within the clan, unions that the rest of the people held to be incestuous.[3] It is possible that investigation might reveal further examples traceable to emotional strain.

Other prophets deliberately exploit the credulity of their fellows for personal ends. This applies also to the men who become leaders without themselves experiencing the revelations. Such individuals might once have bent their talents towards becoming headmen, but now that the office has lapsed the cargo motive supplies an alternative means of achieving social

[1] Quoted by H. Adams, *Mont-Saint-Michel and Chartres*, Boston and New York, 1913, pp. 104-5.

[2] Cf. K. O. L. Burridge, 'Social Implications of Some Tangu Myths', *Southwestern Journal of Anthropology*, Vol. XII, pp. 425-6 (the Tangu live in the Madang district of New Guinea): 'The dream ... is a normal Tangu technique for solving a problem or finding a way out of a dilemma ... A man faced with a problem retires for the night with the hope that a dream will shed light on the matter and present him with a directive.'

[3] C. S. Belshaw, 'Recent History of Mekeo Society', *Oceania*, Vol. XXII, p. 8.

distinction. They probably feel that the power they enjoy is worth the risk of arrest and imprisonment. It is perhaps no accident that the absence of a new leader in the outbreak in the New Guinea highlands should be without recorded parallel. If the old social structure remains untouched anyone who wishes to advance can readily do so by adopting the time-honoured methods of his forbears.

The hierarchy of assistants required to maintain the cult provides further openings for men of ability who would otherwise be condemned to obscurity. Some of them have subsequently become leaders in their own right.

The leader strengthens his position by his authoritarian attitude. The people are the more ready to hear and obey because he offers a way out of the psychological morass into which they have been plunged by the introduction of a second set of moral standards.[1] Instead of being obliged to make up their own minds they can now take a ready-made solution for their problems. At last they are able to cling to a system that clearly distinguishes between right and wrong lines of action.[2] The cults may thus be regarded as a spontaneous effort to reach social integration.

Whether the cults are purely native, without any admixture of alien features, or a syncretism of the native and the alien, or made up entirely of Christian theological and ritual elements depends largely on the history of the society concerned. If

[1] Appropriate investigations have not been carried out in Melanesia, but the anxiety engendered by having to solve problems alone has probably been responsible here, as elsewhere, for an increase in emotional instability. Cf. A. Joseph and V. F. Murray, *Chamorros and Carolinians of Saipan*, Harvard, 1951. These authors do not claim to have measured anything with their tests, but they maintain that their results suggest that the Saipan natives, who are being subjected to great changes, are in a confusional state manifested by 'perplexity which is the correlate of inadequate comprehension of the environment, with the additional symptom of dissatisfaction with the inadequacy' (p. 142). The people seem to be functioning also on a precarious level of adjustment. 'Their anxiety tolerance is low,' and 'their propinquity to concrete dysphoric associations goes beyond the reasonably expected preoccupation with such matters' (p. 198).

[2] The Roman Catholic Church and the Communist Party are authoritarian institutions, and each gives a final answer to many moral problems. The conversion of some Europeans in recent years to one or the other may have been inspired by motives comparable to those of the natives in joining cargo cults.

missions have not been active for long, the people remember
their earlier practices and go back to them; if, as in other places,
the population was converted years and years before, at a time
when no one now living had as yet been born, the customs that
were once observed are generally gone beyond recall. A recent
letter from one of my native friends in Malaita is of interest in
this connection. He requested me to send him another copy
of the book *Experiments in Civilization*, which, with the
help of himself and others, I had written after my visit there in
1933. The first copy that I had given him, he said, had been
lent so often that it was worn out. Everyone was still interested
in learning about the ancestors, and this volume was felt to be
the only trustworthy source of information.

The differing attitudes to Europeans are to be explained
along similar lines. Communities that have had little to do with
white men and found them friendly do not as a rule wish to
banish them from their territory. But more often than not the
relations between the two races are unpleasant. The majority of
the settlers are strongly imbued with colour prejudice and
sensitive about what they refer to as 'White prestige'. They
consider that they are entitled to respect by virtue of their pale
skin and argue that dignity and authority are best maintained
by discourtesy and even brutality.[1] The natives resent such
treatment and project their animosity, which they are ordinarily
forced to conceal, into the fantasy world of the cults.

Magico-Rational Movements

Cargo cults do not occur nowadays in the villages around Lae
and Rabaul. The people tell of outbreaks in the early days of
European contact, but at present they are too experienced to

[1] See H. I. Hogbin, *Transformation Scene*, Chap. XIII. Cf. Keesing's statement:
'The factor of European race consciousness and superiority might perhaps be brought
out more fully as driving the native back upon himself and limiting opportunity. A
dual education task exists, one facet native education, the other education of Europeans to realize the seriousness of the by-products of their attitudes.' (Quoted by J.
Guiart, 'Forerunners of Melanesian Nationalism', *Oceania*, Vol. XXII, p. 90.)

P 3

succumb. They are familiar with a money economy and live at such close quarters with the white man that they appreciate the basis of his technical advantages. They are constantly asking the government to provide better educational facilities and, as far as lies in their power, take positive steps to raise their standard of living. They undertake courses of training as clerks and mechanics to fit themselves for skilled employment at good wages, where possible cultivate coconut and cocoa plantations and maintain a high level of production, and save in order to buy motor-trucks and other capital equipment.

Thus at one extreme there are the raw bushmen retreating into dreams and frenzies, and at the other the sophisticated townsmen whose behaviour is for the most part rational. Many groups stand half way between. Such peoples were perhaps brought under full administrative control forty or fifty years ago, and for decades they have been Christians and gone away to work on plantations. They are sufficiently well-informed to be dimly aware that they cannot alter their conditions without intelligent effort but have little idea how to begin. Their reactions are in consequence compounded partly of common sense and partly of unreason.

The current Masinga (or Marching) Rule movement of the Solomons is of this type. The islanders were already reasonably familiar with Europeans, but most of them did not come into close touch with whites until the outbreak of the Pacific war, when huge American establishments were set up in Guadalcanal and Florida. Many natives were employed in the labour corps, and to these and to the few villagers who were living near the camps the soldiers gave money, cigarettes, food supplies, and surplus equipment. In one settlement in Guadalcanal during 1943 I found all the men engaged in laundry work, for which they were receiving sixty dollars per week each, plus rations for themselves and their families. The district officer, on learning what was taking place, ordered two-thirds of the population to go back to their neglected gardens. The American officer in charge of the army unit camped nearby thereupon ran out a mile of power line to the village and installed two washing-machines.[1]

Within a year or two the natives had started Masinga Rule, which rapidly spread to most of the eastern islands, particularly Malaita, where half the population of the Protectorate is concentrated. Europeans imagined that the name was derived from 'marching' or 'Marxian', but it in fact came from a word meaning 'brotherhood' in one of the dialects. The objectives were at first avowedly political. The people wanted a few strong leaders and their own native law courts. The Malaitamen divided their island into nine districts, each under a 'head chief'. Six of these men were mission teachers, and all were powerful. They ran their affairs independently, but from time to time met together to discuss general policy. The hierarchy under the 'head chiefs' consisted of 'full chiefs', 'leader chiefs', and 'line chiefs', all of them assisted by clerks who were responsible for the despatch of instructions, listing the members, and codifying the customs that were to be adopted. A bodyguard of young men armed with truncheons also supported the senior chiefs. These 'duties', as they were called, when not engaged in official Masinga Rule tasks, were drilled by 'strife chiefs', who functioned as non-commissioned officers.

After some months the natives began building 'towns'. Groups that had for countless generations lived scattered through the jungle uprooted themselves and came down to the coast to form large settlements laid out with streets crossing at right angles after the manner of an army camp. The people cultivated communal gardens under the direction of 'farmer chiefs', who later divided the produce among the individual families. They also built enormous meeting-houses where high officials of the Masinga Rule could be entertained, custom and policy debated, and cases tried.

Finally the myth of the cargo arrived, though in altered

[1] Australian soldiers in New Guinea during the War were also lavish with gifts, and the people still contrast their behaviour with the meanness of the permanent European settlers (see H. I. Hogbin, *Transformation Scene*, p. 287; and K. E. Read, 'Effects of the Pacific War in the Markham Valley', *Oceania*, Vol. XVIII, pp. 106–11).

form. It may have been a spontaneous growth among the people at large, owing nothing to the leaders, who were probably too sensible to believe it themselves. The generous Americans were distinguished from the stingy British, and it was said that on a given day, known only to the chiefs, the former would return to the Solomons with their landing-craft and Liberty ships. These would anchor near the beaches and unload cases full of cigarettes, tobacco, candy, tinned foods, axes, knives, fish-hooks and lines, calico, and all the other items that had been stocked by the wartime canteens. Fired with enthusiasm, the natives erected huge sheds to be ready for the goods. They argued that anyone who refused to believe the story would be deprived of his land and forced to retire into the mountains.

In the beginning the adherents of the movement quietly declined to obey administrative orders or to enter employment on the plantations, which were now being reopened. Then, in mid 1946, the leaders felt that they were strong enough to make demands. They organized a series of gatherings of thousands of natives and issued threats not only against those who refused to join them but against Europeans in general. The administration was at first conciliatory and tried to enlist the people's co-operation. The attempt failed, and the leaders were then arrested and, as usual, sent to gaol. They have now been released, but whether their attitude has changed remains to be seen.[1]

The same ingredients are found in a movement in the Admiralty Islands of the Territory of New Guinea. About 5,000 natives, one third of the total, belonging to three language groups, are affected. The founder is a man named Paliau. He had been a sergeant in the police force before the war and was in Rabaul during the Japanese occupation, when he became a trusted official but still managed to give information to Australian intelligence officers. He is literate in pidgin English, and even his enemies admit that he possesses great

---

[1] C. S. Belshaw, *Island Administration in the South-West Pacific*, London, 1950; and C. H. Allan, 'Marching Rule', *Corona*, March, 1951 (reprinted in *South Pacific*, Vol. V, pp. 79–85).

energy, organizing ability, and a remarkable gift of oratory.

Paliau returned to the Admiralties to find the people much disturbed by two years of Japanese rule and two more during which the United States and Royal Navies had used one of the harbours as a base. Those from his own and neighbouring communities accepted his advice to carry on a campaign of non-co-operation with Europeans. They avoided the officers of the administration, would only agree to accept employment at a wage that no planter could afford to pay, and demanded a greater say in the running of the affairs of the local Roman Catholic mission, to which most of them belonged. The missionaries pleaded with their congregations but eventually withdrew when Paliau started a sect of his own. He asserted that he was in direct communication with Jesus, but his doctrines were mainly derived from the teachings of the Catholic fathers. He laid great stress on confession and taught that the Garden of Eden would return when men forsook evil ways.[1]

Paliau now appointed a cadre of lieutenants, known as 'boss men', and with their help has endeavoured to transform native life into what he and the people imagine that of Europeans to be. First he persuaded the different groups to come together into large villages. The biggest, Lipan-Mouk, is described as being made up of 'raised huts impeccably lined and spaced a dozen feet apart. They are identical in design, with separate kitchens, and surround three sides of a central square. The fourth is occupied by an exceptionally well-built native-material church.' Each house has the inevitable accompaniment of progress in New Guinea, its own latrine. The most surprising feature is that more than half of the inhabitants originally belonged elsewhere. Before the War they lived on an islet nearby, which was so rocky that agriculture was impossible, and supported themselves by trading. Paliau induced the owners of the village site to invite these folk to join them. All

---

[1] Confession played an important part in the old pagan religion (see R. F. Fortune, 'Manus Religion', *Oceania*, Vol. II, pp. 74–116). Paliau recently revived divination and seances as a means of discovering the secret sins that are still believed to be responsible for illnesses.

gardening is now done collectively, and land-dwellers and traders live side by side in amity. He also advocated the adoption of European clothing and discouraged most of the customary usages, including funeral feasting and bride-price payments. He has set up Paliau schools for the children, too, with the former mission teachers in charge, Paliau hospitals for the sick, and even Paliau customs houses. Finally, he required his supporters to pool their money. They handed it to him and the lieutenants for safe keeping.

At length, towards the end of 1946, talk of the coming of the cargo began to circulate. The government, suspecting that Paliau had spread the story, brought him and several other men to Port Moresby. Here 'the plans of the administration for the economic, social, and political development of the native people, and how they could assist, was explained to them'. Investigations carried out simultaneously proved that the cargo cult was a separate movement and that Paliau had remonstrated with those of his adherents who were mixed up with it.

Paliau returned and began setting up village councils. The legislation authorizing them had not at this time been approved, and they were necessarily informal bodies. Government officers therefore kept them under close surveillance to see that the members did not exceed their powers. One council, inspired by Paliau's advocacy of the new system of values, passed the following set of resolutions:

'Rule belong all things we clear out from our village.
'All ornaments belonging to ancient times because the customs no good that
  1. Kill us dead all the time,
  2. We no more get angry with other men,
  3. We cannot think badly about their wives,
  4. Wives cannot think badly about their husbands,
  5. No more decorating women with women's work [local beadwork, belts, anklets, etc.],
  6. No more making feasts for a man just dead cannot be done,

7. No more anger about intercourse between young men and young women,

8. No more deceiving no lying,

9. No more custom of child marriage,

10. No more customs from ancient times,

11. No more arranged marriages the wishes of the man and the woman,

12. No more women's initiation,

13. No more anger,

14. No more fighting,

15. No more stealing.'

This village must in many respects have resembled medieval Rouen.

Reports mention that here and there a lieutenant was becoming increasingly important and probably using Paliau's name for his own personal advancement. By the end of 1949 government officers feared that some of the men were attempting to usurp magisterial powers and subjecting the people to fines and forced labour on the roads. These rumours were never substantiated. Then early in the next year Paliau was himself found guilty of having promised to allow a lieutenant to make appointments to a court replacing that of the European magistrate. He was sentenced to six months' imprisonment.

The Native Councils Ordinance had in the meantime been approved, and three months later an officer arrived to establish properly constituted councils. He also investigated the village finances and found that the large sums collected, totalling about £8,300, were stored in Paliau's house. The book-keeping methods were chaotic, but it was clear that neither Paliau nor the lieutenants had contributed. Most of the money was later placed in banking accounts in the names of the councils of the various villages.

On Paliau's release from prison, the director of native affairs again took him to headquarters for instruction, this time on how to set up co-operatives. He was subsequently elected to the council of his own village and is now doing his best to encourage the people to send their children to the government school. He has said that he realizes that literacy is a necessary preliminary to further native progress.[1]

A comparable movement has occurred in the Purari Delta of Papua. The leader, Tomu Kabu, although barely able to read and write, was the only Papuan native to join the Royal Australian Navy during the war. Under his influence the people of his own and neighbouring communities destroyed their old villages, rebuilt them according to an ordered plan, and then collected several thousands of pounds in shillings and pence to set up their own version of a sago-producers' co-operative. Failure of the business venture would have been inevitable had the government not stepped in with advice and supervision.

Masinga Rule and the Paliau and Tomu Kabu movements, unlike the cargo cults proper, have united masses of natives whose mother tongues are mutually unintelligible. The people have sunk their differences and come together, using pidgin-English or some other *lingua franca* for communication. The leaders, too, have shown powers of organization in handling thousands of followers and effectively preserving public order. Fifteen years ago no one would have deemed such an achievement possible. The local circumstances have differed, and a single method would hardly have sufficed for dealing with all the manifestations. The administration of New Guinea is handling the Paliau movement along local-government lines, that of Tomu Kabu on the basis of economics.

The movements have been described as the forerunners of Melanesian nationalism, and observers have noted that Paliau's followers know all about Masinga Rule. If in the future leaders

---

[1] Information on the Paliau movement is derived from the *Annual Report on the Territory of New Guinea*, 1950–1, pp. 26–30; from Mr G. C. O'Donnell, Assistant District Officer, Admiralty Islands, 1947–8; and from Mr D. M. Fienberg, senior Native Authorities Officer. An account differing in details is given by M. Mead, *New Lives for Old*, New York, 1956. A MS. by T. Schwartz, 'The Paliau Movement in the Admiralty Islands,' which I did not see till after my own was in the publisher's hands, will shortly be published by the American Museum of Natural History, New York.

with a sound educational background arise, machinery may well be available for a mass protest against the foreigner.

Comparison with Similar Movements

Outbreaks such as those described have been noted among colonial peoples the world over. Thus in 1863 a prophet in New Zealand established the Hauhau cult, named after the dog-like barking used as a pass sign by the members. Under the spell of this man's ideology, which combined Christianity with a military vocabulary, the Maori revived cannibalism and reck-lessly attacked the whites. Other New Zealand cults since then have included the Te Whiti, which postulated that the Maori were the lost tribes of Israel, the Uplifted Hand, and the Ratana Church. The Hawaiians, to take another example, in 1886 sud-denly reverted to paganism, with the old-time priests and some of the old-time rituals, under the active encouragement of their then king, Kalakaua, and at a later date they adopted a local form of Christian Science (the Hoomana Naauo or Wisdom Religion and its offshoot Ke Akua Ola or Church of the Living God). In Fiji also there were the cults of the Water Babies and of Immortality, and in the Gilbert and Ellice Islands in 1930 a prophet pronounced himself to be the Father of God and sur-rounded himself with a body of women, called 'The Sheep', and an army of young men dressed in scarlet, 'The Swords of Gabriel'. These last attacked the Roman Catholic minority and had murdered two of them before the authorities could inter-pose. Again, in North America in 1869 a Paiute of Nevada named Wodzibob preached the end of the world, the destruc-tion of Europeans, and the return of the dead. Widespread knowledge of the English language enabled this 'First Ghost Dance', as it came to be known, to cover a great area, and within two years the natives of California were in a ferment. The cult then broke into three movements, one of which required the adherents to live in underground houses. A 'Second Ghost Dance' followed among the Paiute under the leadership of the son of Wodzibob's foremost convert. He told his followers that the whites would be overwhelmed by landslides and whirl-winds and that the Indians would then be rulers of the country and own herds of buffalo sent by the ancestors.[1]

The behaviour is best seen in perspective by an examination of a classification proposed by Linton.[2] He calls 'any conscious organized attempt on the part of a society's members to revive or perpetuate selected aspects of their culture' a nativistic movement. Such a manifestation always concerns itself with elements, never with culture as a whole. Attempts to revive a previous phase in its entirety are immediately blocked by the recognition that past and present conditions are in certain respects incompatible; and even the current phase includes a multitude of features that seem too trivial for deliberate perpetuation. Revivalist nativism is illustrated by the Irish emphasizing the Celtic tradition and resuscitating a moribund language, perpetuative nativism by the Indians of the Rio Grande developing techniques to preserve their culture in its present form in order to avoid assimilation. Magical nativism must also be distinguished from rational nativism, though in fact the latter is never entirely free from magic. Magical nativism always leans heavily on the supernatural and embodies apocalyptic and millennial elements; rational nativism either accentuates cultural items dating from when the society was 'free', and thus helps to maintain the self-respect of the members (rational revivalist nativism) or else stresses cultural items that symbolize the existence of the society as a separate entity (rational perpetuative nativism).

---

[1] The literature is so vast that only a few references can be given here. See, for example, S. B. Babbage, *Hauhauism*, Wellington, 1937; F. M. Keesing, *The Changing Maori*, New Plymouth, 1928; I. L. G. Sutherland, *The Maori People of Today*, Wellington, 1940; *Territorial Papers of the United States*, Washington, 1934; F. M. Keesing, *Hawaiian Homesteading on Molokai*, Honolulu, 1936; A. B. Brewster, *Hill Tribes of Fiji*, London, 1922, pp. 222–9; A. C. Cato, 'New Religious Cult in Fiji', *Oceania*, Vol. XVIII, pp. 188–204; J. V. de Bruyn, 'Mansren Cult of Biak', *South Pacific*, Vol. V, pp. 1–10; B. G. M. Sundkler, *Bantu Prophets in South Africa*, London, 1948; and A. Lommel, 'Modern Culture Influences on the Aborigines', *Oceania*, Vol. XXI, pp. 14–24.

[2] R. Linton, 'Nativistic Movements', *American Anthropologist*, Vol. XLV, pp. 230–40.

Linton goes on to deal with the situations in which the movements occur. The common denominator is the inequality of the societies in contact, an inequality that may or may not involve political subjection. Each group may consider itself to be superior, or one may consider itself to be uniformly superior and the other consider itself to be uniformly inferior, or they may both consider themselves to be superior in some ways and inferior in others. This last condition is favourable to cultural exchange and does not produce nativistic movements.

The Mexicans and Indians of the south-west in the United States provide an example of two communities each convinced of its own superiority. Dominance is ruled out by the presence of the Anglo-Americans, who are in political control. The two groups are neighbours, but each feels that assimilation would be followed by loss of prestige. They have similar per-petuative rational movements, are conscious of their own culture, and endeavour to keep it distinct. The differences do not produce envy or frustration, and friction is almost unknown.

The state of affairs in which one society holds itself to be superior and the other acquiesces is more common. If actual dominance is not involved, as with the Japanese and the West in the later nineteenth century, magical movements probably do not usually occur. The superior group is so sure of itself that it hands over its cultural elements freely, and the inferior group takes them in expectation of being treated as an equal when the differences have been obliterated. Occasionally, how-ever, the superior group inaugurates a perpetuative rational movement designed to restore the *status quo*, and the inferior group retaliates with a revivalist rational movement.

When one group dominates another politically the members of each may feel themselves to be either superior or inferior. Nativistic movements can occur in dominant as well as in dominated communities. Until recently technical equipment gave colonial Europeans assurance, but they still practised an unconscious nativism. They retained the habits of the home country, sent their children away to school, and eventually themselves returned to a suburban villa. In the empires of the pre-machine age the perpetuative rational movements were more deliberate. The various nomadic conquerors of China all attempted to preserve their distinctive culture by repressive measures not only against the Chinese but also against those of their number who adopted Chinese customs. The whites in South Africa face a similar threat and react in the same kind of way.

Dominant groups seldom see themselves as culturally inferior. The Goths who invaded Italy provide one of the rare instances, but we know nothing of their reactions.

A dominated group that feels superior develops a revivalist movement from the moment of defeat. The magical element consists in the belief that if the people will only stand firm and keep their individuality they will ultimately again become independent.

Dominated groups that consider themselves inferior often fall back on magical revivalist nativism as soon as they suffer hardship or frustration. The threshold of suffering at which the movements occur varies from society to society and is influenced not only by the degree of hardship but also by the pattern of reliance on the supernatural. Thus a devout community turns to nativism before a sceptical community.[1] If the hardship is not extreme the inferior group generally tries to devalue its own culture and assume that of the superior body. The nativistic movement arises when the subject community feels that the transfer is being opposed and that no real improvement is possible. The revolt can be avoided if the higher group is willing to adopt a realistic policy of assimilation.

Yet it must be emphasized that most of the Melanesian cargo cults, together with the Masinga Rule, Paliau, and Tomu Kabu

[1] The different societies of Melanesia vary in their reliance on religion and magic. The traders of the Admiralties, for instance, undoubtedly the most skilful and intrepid voyagers in the western Pacific, never invoked the aid of supernatural powers for protection on the sea; the 'argonauts' of the Trobriand Islands, whose journeys were by comparison fiddling affairs, carried out magic on every conceivable occasion.

movements, are revivalist only in an intangible sense.[1] The
adherents wish to throw out the Europeans so that they will
again be masters of their fate; and they also want to recapture
unity and common endeavour and to re-establish the dignity of
their group. But the ideal they envisage is not a return to the
past: it is a new world in which natives will live after the style
of white men. The Vailala people wiped out their pagan religion, and Paliau, with nothing specifically associated with the
old rites left to destroy, ordered the abandonment of all the remaining secular practices. The administrative authorities have
never been anxious about his aims, which are in line with their
expressed policy: they are concerned about his failure to seek
advice, his haste in carrying out the transformation, and his
determination to retain power in his own hands.

Revivalist nativistic movements, whether magical or
rational, readily turn to aggression.

'Since the dominated society has been frustrated in its earlier
desire to become assimilated and to achieve social equality, it
can frustrate the dominant society in turn by refusing to accept
even those elements which the dominant group is eager to
share with it [Linton warns]. Dominated societies which have
acquired these attitudes and developed conscious techniques
for preventing further [changes] present one of the most difficult problems for administrators.'

The governments of Melanesia may in the future find themselves confronted with a Mau-Mau cult or, if a Gandhi and a
Nehru appear, with a serious attempt to obtain political independence.

---

[1] It is possible, of course, that Paliau's successors, like the Hawaiians, may ultimately try to restore the old customs.

CHAPTER IX

Forecasting the Future

THE chemist, because he can arrange his apparatus so that each of the variables in a chain of causation is in turn held constant, is able to say with confidence that, given identical conditions, a reaction once observed will always be repeated. In anthropology the material studied is not amenable to this sort of manipulation, and it follows that prediction, in the strict sense that the word is used in the physical sciences, is impossible. An anthropologist asked to outline precisely what is going to happen to a particular society within a fixed period of time, or to tell beforehand which parts of a native culture will respectively resist and yield to outside influence,[1] would be in a similar predicament to that of meteorological officers called upon to make a forecast for a year hence. Like the weather men, he has to contend with forces beyond his control. Government policies may be altered, as they were in New Guinea between

[1] These have been distinguished as the 'hard' and 'soft' parts. See F. C. Bartlett, 'Psychological Methods for the Study of "Hard" and "Soft" Features of a Culture', *Africa*, Vol. XVI, pp. 145-55. Bartlett quotes the following extract from a letter of the Reverend Edwin Smith (pp. 145-6): 'When I look back at the Ba-Ila as I knew them first over forty years ago I can see that their culture had its "hard" and "soft" points. I can perhaps recognize them now if I say that changes took place in the "soft" while they did not take place in the "hard": but how was I to know at the start which would change and which would not? In personal appearance the Ila men were distinguished by three features; their nakedness; their peculiar ... headdress; the absence of front teeth. Time proved each of these to be "soft": the nakedness ... went first; ten years after our arrival the headdress was almost extinct; and the boys were beginning to rebel against having their teeth knocked out ... [But the] Ba-Ila were so strongly attached to their cattle that they would not dream of training oxen to draw a plough or wagon: this was a "hard" point; but how were we to know until time had shown these attitudes to be so strong? ... In this matter of using oxen, the Basuto ... very readily took to the plough and wagon: why the one tribe and not the other?'

1939 and 1945. Before the War the territories were expected to pay their way out of taxes, and the welfare programme was geared to the amount of revenue that could be raised locally: nowadays the Australian Commonwealth, largely for strategic reasons, is offering subsidies worth millions of pounds annually. Colonial dependencies, too, have on occasion unexpectedly become battlefields for the warring armies of great nations. Nobody could have known early in 1914 that Australian soldiers would soon be throwing the Germans out of north-eastern New Guinea, or early in 1939 that within a few years Japan would control Malaya, Indonesia, and a large part of Melanesia. The discovery of oil or precious metals can be equally productive of sudden unforeseen changes. If the search for oil now being carried out in a remote district of western Papua is successful the native population, which till recently had seen Europeans only during rare administrative patrols, will be in close touch with a great industry. Again, disaster overtaking one or other of the kinship groups in a community has often brought about abrupt cultural readjustments. Fishing-nets are in some parts of Melanesia made exclusively by one lineage or clan, the members of which alone know the appropriate magical ritual. If all these persons are wiped out by an epidemic or some other catastrophe, and the rest of the people have no other source of supply, they must thenceforward do without. Some such explanation probably accounts for the absence of the canoe from the Torres Islands at the time of their discovery. In several of the New Hebrides Islands, too, potsherds are found in the ground, but no pots have been fashioned there during the historical period.[1]

Yet both the meteorologist and the anthropologist are competent to give forecasts of limited range. The former says whether tomorrow is likely to be wet or fine on the assumption that the pressure systems will continue to travel at the usual

[1] W. H. R. Rivers, 'The Disappearance of Useful Arts', *Festskrift tillägnad Edvard Westermarck*, Helsingfors, 1912, pp. 109–30; and B. Deacon, *Malekula*, London, 1934, pp. 713–14.

rate along their accustomed paths; and the latter isolates single
institutions and speaks of the probable sequence of changes. In
the earlier pages of this book I have stated, for instance, that if
money replaces the traditional valuables in bride-price payments the amount demanded may rise so sharply that the young
men must postpone marriage; that if a cash income can be obtained by domestic production the custom of polygyny will
often persist; that if individuals are given the chance of earning
large sums by their own efforts they tend to ignore the claims
of their lineage mates and fellow clansmen; and that if a community dominated by foreigners is denied the opportunity for
economic and political advancement a nativistic movement
may develop.

Such generalizations as these are based on the examination of
the interdependence, or co-variation, of social phenomena, according to Nadel the one method of explanation open to anthropology.[1] He advocated a more precise use of the technique
and offered an analysis of the relation between differing witchcraft beliefs and social structure as an illustration.[2]

To reduce the number of variables Nadel selected societies
that closely resembled one another except in a few significant
characteristics. First he took the Nupe and the Gware of
Nigeria. These peoples live in a similar environment, speak
allied languages, have identical forms of political organization
and religion, and base their kinship structure on patrilineal descent, patrilineal inheritance, and patrilocal residence. Both
peoples believe in witchcraft, but whereas the Nupe hold that
witches are always female, the Gware say that they may be
either male or female. The main collective weapon against
Nupe witches is the activity of a secret society made up of
men, who, by threats and torture, periodically cleanse the villages one by one; the Gware protect themselves by divination
and the annual performance of a special ritual to cleanse the

---

[1] S. F. Nadel, *Foundations of Anthropology*, London, 1951, p. 101.
[2] S. F. Nadel, 'Witchcraft in Four African Societies', *American Anthropologist*, Vol.
LIV, pp. 18–29.

whole community. Hand in hand with the fear of female witches goes sex antagonism. Nupe women engage in trade and nowadays are better off economically than the men. The husband is usually in debt to the wife and allows her to assume responsibilities that he feels he ought to be discharging himself. Thus he allows her to pay for the children's education, provide bride price for the sons, and bear the expenses for the family feasts. He resents this reversal of the institutional rôles but is powerless to redress the situation.

The Korongo and the Mesakin of the central Sudan are another pair of societies sharing a common environment, economy, political organization, and religion. Both of them base their kinship structure on matrilineal descent, matrilineal inheritance, and residence of married couples with the man's matrilineal kinsmen. The Korongo, however, have no belief in witchcraft at all, while the Mesakin are obsessed by it and maintain that they are always in danger of being bewitched by the mother's brother. This difference is related to the regulations that fix the time when the heirs receive their maternal uncle's wealth. The Korongo rule allows him to retain control of it till old age, when, with powers now failing, he hands over to them gracefully without bearing any grudge. The Mesakin rule forces him to give it up immediately they reach maturity. He is at that time barely middle-aged and resents their claims upon him.

The conclusion is that witchcraft beliefs reflect the anxieties and stresses inherent in the social system. Marriage relations among the Nupe give rise to friction, and the men in consequence suspect the women; the relations between the mother's brother and the sisters' sons among the Mesakin also cause friction, and here the nephews suspect their uncle. Accusations of witchcraft deflect tensions and aggressive impulses away from maladjusted institutions and hence permit their continuance. The witchcraft beliefs enable a society to go on functioning in a given manner, fraught with conflicts and contradictions that the society is powerless to resolve, said Nadel. They thus absolve the society from radical readjustment, a task that is apparently too difficult.

Nadel agreed that the interdependence of social phenomena is most clearly visible in the contact situation but did not himself apply the method to the study of a changing society. Various anthropologists have employed it in a general way and divided their time in the field between the areas that have been exposed to Western influences for shorter and for longer periods. Variation in one aspect of an institution is then revealed as provoking concomitant variations in others. Yet the investigations have not been undertaken systematically. The selection of a series of peoples with similar institutions where the degree or kind of contact has been different—or the converse, a series of peoples with dissimilar institutions where the degree or kind of contact has been more or less the same—might well lead to the discovery of some of the reasons, at present obscure, why particular changes have taken place.

In Melanesia the possible divergencies in the effects of the teachings and practices of the several missions could be a starting-point. Two or more sects are frequently to be found in close proximity within the same culture area—Church of England, Roman Catholic, and South Seas Evangelical Mission in most of the eastern Solomon Islands, for example; Roman Catholic, Methodist, and Seventh-Day Adventist in most of the western Solomons; and Roman Catholic and Lutheran around Madang in New Guinea. The first task would be the selection of paired societies, each belonging to a separate Church, representing all the many forms of social structure—a set of pairs with villages consisting of a single localized patrilineal clan and another with villages consisting of a single localized matrilineal clan, a set of pairs with villages made up of several patrilineal clans and another made up of several matrilineal clans, and so on. An examination of a single pair of each type would suggest certain conclusions, but much checking would be necessary. It is always easy to prejudge and thereby confuse the significant and the chance factors. The personality of an individual missionary could perhaps have a bearing on the problem, or special circumstances could be relevant, as in Hawaii. The ultimate result might prove to be that all missions produce either the same effects everywhere or else one set of effects on patrilineal institutions and another set on matrilineal institutions; or each might have effects peculiar to itself regardless of the native social structures; or the sects that emphasize ritual might have a different impact from those that do not.

The educational policies of the missions also merit study. Some of them focus attention on the smaller schools and try to build up a feeling of responsibility within the village community: others, while they do not neglect the villages entirely, lay greater stress on training a native intellectual *élite* within the European mission station. Again, different methods have to be followed when the people live in fairly large settlements and when they occupy tiny homesteads. If the local organization is of the latter kind the pupils may have to be brought in to boarding schools.

The respective effects of Christianity and wage labour might be similarly examined were it not for the fact that nowadays the missionary and labour-recruiter usually tread upon each other's heels. Very few places remain where primitive natives who have been converted do not go away to work, or, alternatively, where natives who have been missed out by the missions regularly leave home to enter employment. New Hanover, in the Bismarck Archipelago, is a rare example from the former category, the mountain areas of central Malaita one from the latter. Leprosy has gained a firm hold on the peoples of New Hanover, and the government, in an endeavour to prevent the spread of the disease, many years ago imposed a ban on their travelling; and in central Malaita, although the people want money to buy tools and other goods, they are hostile to all strangers, including missionaries. Two of the communities in which I have lived also present the appropriate contrast. The Ontong Javanese at the time of my stay among them in 1927 and 1928 had been Christian for about twenty years but were not being recruited as labourers; and the Wogeo, when I visited them first in 1934, had been entering employment for twenty years but were still without a missionary. The social structures of the societies were different, but both were intact despite the disappearance in Ontong Java of all the great ceremonials.

Other matters for analysis include the effects of introduced cash crops and of co-operative marketing.

Long-Term Changes

While the course that any given society will take during the next few decades must remain somewhat obscure, we can still be reasonably certain that all groups everywhere are becoming Westernized and that the gaps between native societies and our own are gradually closing up. The nomadic hunters of the Australian continent have farther to go than the agriculturalists of the Pacific islands; but, on the other hand, the nine million white inhabitants of Australia are having a greater impact on the few thousands of aborigines than the handful of whites on the natives of Melanesia, who themselves number nearly two millions.

Yet even in Europe, where travel since the end of the Dark Ages has presented comparatively few difficulties, absolute uniformity has not been achieved and probably never will be. The southern English dialect prevailed over most of the British Isles, but the Welsh speak another tongue, and the Irish are now reviving their ancient language. Further, just as southern English later developed a number of local forms in North America and another in Australia, so Americans and Australians are now modifying several of the practices of the Old World. Western Europe, America, and Australia at present have one culture that can be divided into many sub-types, English, French, Italian, Spanish, and the rest; and of each of these in turn there are several variants. We may safely assume that this is the microcosm of the future world.

Redfield has analysed the process of Westernization in Yucatan, Central America.[1] The region has been subject to influence by Europeans from the Spanish conquest onwards, and the people have assimilated so much that it would be a perplexing task to sort out the elements into those that are Indian in origin and those that are importations. Redfield concludes, nevertheless, that a century or so ago the cultures everywhere were an approximation of that which he found as an integrated and unified mode of life in some of the forest villages. Customs that are kept up in the villages are remembered in the towns as having been usual there also, and practices now current in the towns are similarly remembered in the capital. Thus in the capital today the young man selects a girl for himself and asks her father's permission to take her in wedlock, but many persons recall that the parents once made the request on the boy's behalf; in the towns this latter procedure is general, but the members of the older generation lament that the parents do not now arrange the match entirely; and in the villages the selection of partners is always parentally controlled, and the boy and girl have no say in the matter. Redfield and his associates made surveys simultaneously of a typical village, a typical town, and the capital itself. The description can be interpreted in either of two ways, as an account of the general response of Yucatecan cultures to contact or, alternatively, as the culture history of the capital.

The communities become less homogeneous as one passes from village to town to capital. In the village the people are all agriculturalists, work is organized on kinship lines, land is handed on to the heirs intact, the magicians are the only experts, and the mental outlook of each person is like that of his fellows. In the capital, however, the division of labour is complex; men work for pay, and their rewards, instead of being traditional as with the village magicians, are dependent on the fluctuations of free economic competition; persons wishing for

[1] R. Redfield, 'Culture Change in Yucatan', *American Anthropologist*, Vol. XXXVI, pp. 57–69; and *Folk Culture of Yucatan*, Chicago, 1941.

extra help are obliged to hire labour; and land is freely bought and sold. These differences are correlated with modifications in the social structure. In the villages women are subordinate to men, the young defer to the elders, and everyone has various obligations to his remote kinsfolk: in the capital the women are free, the young go their own way, and ties with the nearer kin are alone significant. The emphasis on religion also alters. In the villages the men take the leading part in ritual, which is concerned equally with the pagan harvest gods, the local patron saint, and the Christian deity; in the towns the men are not so conspicuous, the ceremonies for the pagan gods and the patron saint are performed without much care, and the chief place is taken by the family saints and the Christian deity; and in the capital, although some persons are good Catholics, others are Protestants, and many ignore the Churches. The only un-Western characteristic of the capital is the fear of black magic, which is stronger here than in the villages. The explanation seems to be that the city-dwellers, who are still almost illiterate, feel insecure. Their kinship ties are broken, the neighbours are strangers, the authority of established belief is removed, and nobody is certain that he will always have enough to eat.

A second study of this kind was conducted by Eggan among several related tribes in northern Luzon in the Philippines.[1] They included the Ifugao in the interior, the Bontoc and Tinguian, who are the next peoples on the seaward side, and the Ilocano on the coast. Spanish influence, which was considerable from the late eighteenth century onwards in the districts near the sea, decreased farther inland and barely reached the Ifugao. An account of the Ilocano written in about 1800 has survived, and from this it may be gathered that their culture was then like that of the Ifugao today.

Eggan's results in many respects parallel those of Redfield. In proceeding from the interior towards the coast, from Ifugao to Ilocano, he found that the social structure was based less and less on kinship and that the political organization became more and more complex. The Ifugao live in small villages within which kinship is practically the sole social bond, and control outside the group is regulated by a number of specific rules; Bontoc villages are large, but the effective political unit is the village section or ward; Tinguian villages are larger still and have a single headman; and Ilocano villages are not only large but are combined into groups of two or three under a supreme authority. The number of relatives recognized also diminishes. The Ifugao have a terminology of Hawaiian type, which stresses generation level rather than lines of descent. All first, second, and third cousins call one another by the words for 'brother' and 'sister' and together form a closely knit body firmly bound together by reciprocal obligations. The Bontoc and Tinguian systems approximate more to the European type, and the effective range is narrower; and that of the Ilocano does not go beyond first cousins. In religion there are great differences. The Ifugao worship a hierarchy of deities and the souls of the dead; the Tinguian pay more attention to non-human spirits; and the Ilocano are mainly Christians. Each community is divided into social classes, but these are more clearly differentiated on the coast than in the interior. The key to social status is the amount of rice land that a person owns, and the Ilocano have the most rich men and the Ifugao the fewest. These differences in wealth determine the marriage customs. The bulk of the Ifugao and Bontoc young people choose their own spouses, and the parents only step in to insist that the parties must not be related. Even here, however, the principal families arrange the matches of their children. They do this, so they say, to conserve the property. Among the Tinguian and the Ilocano, on the contrary, the parents always take full charge, and then husband and wife are generally cousins. Such alliances keep the groups united and hold the rice lands together.

Eggan attributes the changes mainly to European influences, even the strengthening of the class structure, with the consequent parental intervention in the marriage arrangements. The

Q

Spanish considered themselves to be the topmost stratum and thus hardened the layers below. The Americans after 1900 attempted to break the system down, but the period of forty years that elapsed before Eggan carried out his researches was too short for much progress to have been achieved.

A statement by Hoernlé and Hellmann on what is happening in South Africa is also instructive. They put forward an analysis of present trends as a criticism of the *Report of the Commission on Native Education in South Africa, 1949–51*, in which the conclusions were based on the belief that the traditional Bantu cultures contained the seeds from which a new Bantu culture might grow. This view they regarded as untenable. 'The logical end of the process of contact and change which has been set in motion is the total assimilation of the kinship, techniques, standards, and values of Western culture by the Bantu', they said.[1]

They pointed out first that the traditional Bantu economic organization and magico-religious system were being replaced and that corresponding changes were occurring in social attitudes and values. They then showed that the traditional governmental and legal systems had been largely rendered superfluous by the institutions superimposed upon them and that the old family structure had been disrupted in consequence. The church, the school, and the hospital are already established features in African life. 'What remains, then, of Bantu culture?' the authors ask. 'The languages remain. But, apart from language, we are unable to find those institutions in traditional Bantu culture which contain in them seeds from which "a progressive, modern, and self-respecting Bantu order of life" will develop.'

The changes in native life, particularly among urban Africans, who show many indications of being the advance guard of the people as a whole, far outweigh the survivals from traditional Bantu cultures. The material basis of living has been

[1] A. W. Hoernlé and E. Hellmann, 'The Analysis of Social Change and its Bearing on Education', *Colonial Review*, Vol. VII, pp. 237–40.

revolutionized: clothing, housing, and furniture are completely Western. The limits on the adoption of the various forms of material goods are those imposed by poverty. Even diet, despite the fact that food habits are probably the most persistent, even more persistent than language, is altering. African leaders are conscious of the changes and, apart from the chiefs and other office-holders who have a vested interest in the preservation of the old order, seem fully prepared to accept the necessity for change, even if this should mean wiping out the traditional Bantu cultures. They realize the technical superiority of the West and want to obtain for their peoples the fullest opportunities to be trained in its skills and techniques; and they also desire the spirit of Western civilization. These African leaders understand far better than many Europeans that it is not possible to halt industrialization half way. Their determination to adopt the Western way of life in its fullest sense is a force that cannot be stopped.

But although Hoernlé and Hellmann believe that Bantu cultures must go under, they do not think that everything will disappear without leaving a trace. They insist that European culture in South Africa, itself a variety of Western culture, will be modified, at least for a time. Bantu music, songs, and dances have already had an influence on South African art, and the architecture of South Africa has often drawn on Bantu models for new ideas. Both official languages have also incorporated Bantu words into their vocabularies. Further, just as English-speaking and Afrikaans-speaking South Africans have developed their own sub-cultures, so the Bantu are bound to develop distinctive characteristics that will mark them off from other peoples. The basic structure made up of economic, political, legal, religious, and family institutions will be essentially alike, but there will be minor differences. The fact that a person plays jukskei rather than cricket and is addicted to boerewors rather than roast beef, however, is not indicative of his total cultural background; these things merely give a clue to his group affiliations. Whether the sub-cultures will continue to be recognizably distinct in the future or whether even the nuances will be submerged it is impossible to say. At the same time, it 'requires no bold venture into prophecy to be able to predict that while the different languages survive, so long will the sub-cultures exist. Whether the languages themselves will survive in perpetuity or not is utterly beyond the bounds of prediction. The pages of history record instances of the extinction of lan-guages, instances of the re-emergence of languages once thought to have died as spoken languages, and abundant evi-dence of the tenacious hold which language has on a people and a people on its language.'

The Death of Cultures

The last Tasmanian aboriginal, a woman named Truganini, died on May 8, 1876, and with her a way of life vanished. Her uncle had been shot, her sister stolen by sealers, her mother stabbed, and her husband mutilated. One by one her com-patriots had all gone, some shot, some brained by musket butts, some rotted with drink. They had been raped, emasculated, robbed, and starved; they had been driven from place to place, taken from their country to an unfamiliar island, and brought back to languish in a pest-ridden gaol. Nothing remains of them now but a few carefully preserved skeletons. William Lanney, the last male of the race, who had predeceased Truganini by five years, was dismembered before burial in an attempt to foil the body-snatchers, and her own final vain request to the sur-geon as she lay dying was, 'Don't let them cut me up. Bury me behind the mountains.' One or two writers made some notes on the people's customs, and collections of implements and other objects survive in museums, but not one word of the language enriches any living speech.[1]

Other populations have been killed off by murder, warfare, or epidemics, but the problem of cultural death is in general somewhat different. Would it be true to say, if a group of per-sons no longer behave in the manner of their ancestors, that the

[1] See C. Turnbull, *Black War*, Melbourne, 1948.

original culture is dead? The question might be asked of the residents of the capital of Yucatan, the Ilocano of the Philippines, and the Bantu of South Africa—or of the Egyptians, the Romans, the Greeks, and ourselves. What of the relation between our present culture and that of England at the time of Elizabeth I? Since her reign the New World has been fully explored and re-settled; the physical and biological sciences have made great advances; the social sciences have come into being as separate disciplines; our technology has changed; and we have revised our attitudes to the monarchy, social class, and religion. The language, of course, is altering continually. When Francis Bacon referred in his essays to particular men as 'indifferent', 'obnoxious', and 'officious' he was describing them as impartial, submissive, and ready to serve; when James II observed that the new Saint Paul's cathedral was 'amusing', 'awful', and 'artificial' he implied that Sir Christopher Wren's masterpiece was pleasing, awe-inspiring, and skilfully constructed; and when Dr Johnson said that Milton's *Lycidas* was 'easy', 'vulgar', and 'disgusting' he meant to convey that he thought it effortless, popular, and not in good taste.[1]

Standardized behaviour patterns can exist only by being practised by persons, and when the members of a group, the carriers of a culture, give up one pattern for another it ceases to be. Other patterns have to be modified accordingly, as we have seen, sometimes many of them, sometimes a few. The totality is therefore different, and to this extent the culture has come to an end. Today most societies are imperfectly integrated and hence subject to frequent changes. The argument, if pressed to its logical conclusion, would thus mean that cultures tend to die with each generation. I would myself prefer to say that cultural death occurs not with the substitution of each new pattern but when the greater part of the configuration has been lost. Roman culture, I suggest, endured until its basic patterns had gone out of existence, a date usually fixed as that of the emperor Romulus Augustulus. The fact that some of the

[1] S. Potter, *Our Language*, London, 1950, p. 116.

institutions survived, such as those relating to law and religion, and are now part of the matrix of Western civilization, does not affect the issue: Roman culture was dead.

The same is true of Egypt.

'There can be no question that the culture of ancient Egypt is dead [says Kroeber] though a more precise formulation would be that its specific pattern assemblage has long ceased to function or exist anywhere. . . . By A.D. 600 the old civilization had disappeared substantially as completely as now. No one worshipped Osiris or the hawk-headed Horus, no one could read hieroglyphs, no one mummified his dead, no one was Pharaoh . . . Egyptian culture as a unique nexus and entity thus went out of existence. But the society to which it was attached went on.[1] The Hellenized Egyptians of Cleopatra's time, the Hellenized Christian Egyptians of A.D. 500, the Mohammedan Egyptians of A.D. 1000, and those of today are no doubt mainly the bodily descendants of those Egyptians who first shaped their distinctive civilization around 3500–3000 B.C. . . . The stream of biological heredity rolled on through the millennia with only minor alterations; above it, civilizations grew, dissolved, entered, and replaced one another. [But] the components of the old Egyptian civilization did not perish equally. Here and there bits of it persist into the thoroughly different culture aggregate of present-day Egyptian culture: . . . If it is difficult to name such, that is only because the expansive phase of Egyptian culture productivity took place so long ago . . . that transmitted elements have reached us indirectly, at second and third hand, in much altered dress. Original Egyptian traits perhaps first became Asiatic, then Minoan, Greek, finally Roman . . . with reselection and remodelling all along the slow, devious route. But elements, ideas, or stimuli of probable Egyptian origin are recognizable

---

[1] Kroeber is not using the word 'society' as I have defined it, a totality of relationships. Egyptian society, in this sense, was as dead as Egyptian culture. Kroeber's meaning becomes clear if the term 'population' is substituted.

in our calendar, writing, religion . . . architecture, plant and animal husbandry.' [1]

The cultures of the primitive peoples of today are rushing towards the same doom, and while some of them will ultimately be effaced as completely as that of the Tasmanian aborigines, others may leave traces behind, possibly in the home territory alone, possibly, like Roman and Egyptian culture, in many places. Western industrial civilization, though of hardier growth, is just as mortal, and doubtless it too will die. A growing knowledge of the processes of social change should enable our successors to plan something better to take its place.

[1] A. L. Kroeber, *Anthropology*, London, 1948, pp. 383-4.

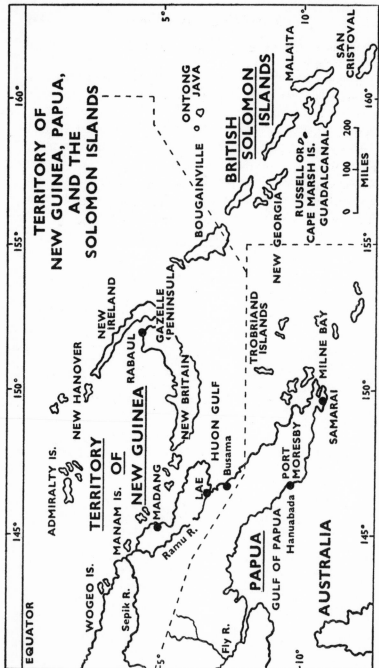

TERRITORY OF
NEW GUINEA, PAPUA,
AND THE
SOLOMON ISLANDS

INDEX

ABEL, C. W., 207 n

Aborigines. *See* Australian aborigines.

Achehnese, 178

Adams, H., 219 n.

Adjustment, social, 32, 35

Admiralty Is., 224–8, 232 n.

Africa, East, 76; South, 74, 75, 98, 232; West, 90, 93, 143

Age groups, 50, 94, 136, 187, 188

Agriculture. *See* Crops.

Alexander, W. D., 2 n.

Allan, C. H., 224 n.

American Indians, Californian, 229; Creek, 28 n.; Makah, 99–102, 104; Navaho, 111; New Mexican, 79–82; Paiute, 229, 230; Plains, 101, 102; South-western, 231

Ancestors. *See* Religion; Religious cults.

Animals, domestic, care of, 108, 109

Apodaca, A., 79 n.

Arapesh, 41

Arensberg, C. M., 5 n.

Aristocracy. *See* Class

Arnhem Land, 66–8, 86–8

Ashanti, 83, 84

Australian aborigines, 10, 15, 91, 92, 240; and counting, 61; women and change, 63 n.; pre-European changes, 86–8; and depopulation, 102, 103; and steel axe, 135–9; Indonesian influences on, 66–8, 86–8

Australian Government, 97, 103, 167, 235

Australians, white, 88, 91–3, 240

Babbage, S. B., 230 n.

Balandier, G., 52 n.

Bantu, 74, 75, 112, 234 n., 244–7

Barnett, H. G., 63, 64

Bartlett, F. C., 234 n.

Beals, R. L., 20 n., 69 n.

Bechuanaland, 98

Belshaw, C. S., 8 n., 192 n., 194 n., 199 n., 212 n., 219, 224 n.

Bemba, 31, 112, 149, 150

Berndt, C. H., 68 n., 87

Berndt, R. M., 68 n., 87, 211 n.

Birth control, 64, 82

Boas, F., 59 n.

Bontoc, 242–4

Bott, E., 48 n.

Brazil, 83

Brewster, A. B., 230 n.

Bride price, traditional in Africa, 141; traditional in Melanesia, 157, 159; money payments, 94, 142, 186, 187, 194, 237; prohibited, 98, 186, 187, 194

Bruyn, J. V. de, 230 n.

Buck, P. H., 6 n., 127 n.

Burridge, K. O. L., 219 n.

Busama, 41, 73, 74, 107, 116–18, 145, 156, 180, 181, 184–6, 189–91, 198

Calendar, 66, 178 n.

Cargo cults. *See* Religious cults.

Caribbean Is., 81

Cash. *See* Money.

Cash crops. *See* Crops.

Cato, A. C., 230 n.

Cattle, 79, 80, 89; and bride price, 141, 142; and social relationships, 93, 94

Ceremonial currency. *See* Currency.

Change, stimuli of, 3–9

Chief. *See* Headman.